DEMOCRACY for ALL

DEMOCRACY
for ALL

Restoring Immigrant
Voting Rights in the
United States

Ron Hayduk

Routledge
Taylor & Francis Group
New York   London

Published in 2006 by
Routledge
Taylor & Francis Group
270 Madison Avenue
New York, NY 10016

Published in Great Britain by
Routledge
Taylor & Francis Group
2 Park Square
Milton Park, Abingdon
Oxon OX14 4RN

© 2006 by Taylor & Francis Group, LLC
Routledge is an imprint of Taylor & Francis Group

Printed in the United States of America on acid-free paper
10 9 8 7 6 5 4 3 2 1

International Standard Book Number-10: 0-415-95072-4 (Hardcover) 0-415-95073-2 (Softcover)
International Standard Book Number-13: 978-0-415-95072-5 (Hardcover) 978-0-415-95073-2 (Softcover)
Library of Congress Card Number 2005015175

Library of Congress Cataloging-in-Publication Data

Hayduk, Ronald, 1958-
    Democracy for all : restoring immigrant voting rights in the United States / Ron Hayduk.
       p. cm.
    Includes bibliographical references and index.
    ISBN 0-415-95072-4 (hb : alk. paper) -- ISBN 0-415-95073-2 (pb : alk. paper)
     1. Immigrants--United States--Suffrage. 2. Voting--United States--History. 3. Immigrants--United States--Political activity. 4. Political participation--United States. I. Title.

JV6477.H39 2005 2006
324.6'2'0869120973--dc22
                                      2005015175

informa
Taylor & Francis Group
is the Academic Division of Informa plc.

Visit the Taylor & Francis Web site at
http://www.taylorandfrancis.com

and the Routledge Web site at
http://www.routledge-ny.com

To Susanna and Rita, our ancestors, and future generations

Contents

Acknowledgments

Although this book bears my name, it would not have been possible without the tireless work of many people: the countless immigrants, activists, scholars, and organizations that struggle on a daily basis for human rights and social justice.

I owe a great debt to several in particular: Jamin Raskin, whose landmark scholarship and personal encouragement inspired my work and also nourished activists across the country to launch campaigns for immigrant voting; J. Philip Thompson and the folks at the Aspen Institute Roundtable on Community Change, who fostered my interest in this research and the ongoing project of attacking racism and building community; Michele Wucker, whose collaborative work—particularly on the Immigrant Voting Project—helped put this subject on the virtual map; the many advocates that led campaigns for immigrant voting rights, including Kathy Coll, Mario Cristaldo, Joyce Hamilton, Bryan Pu-Folkes, and Tom Perez, which the Center for Voting and Democracy brought together a few years ago in Washington D.C. and gave a timely boost to their respective campaigns; Demos, which did the same thing the following year at the Graduate Center of the City University of New York (CUNY), which especially helped the campaign in New York City, ably led by Cheryl Wertz and the amazing individuals and member organizations that comprise the Coalition to Expand Voting Rights; David Chiu, Matt Gonzalez and all the people involved in the historic effort in San Francisco, which put immigrant voting back on the map in California and nationally; and to the many other advocates who have championed immigrant voting rights in dozens of cities and towns across the U.S. during the past twenty years. I also want to thank Andrea Batista Schlesinger, who believed that immigrant voting

ix

rights was a subject worthy of public discussion and debate; members of the CUNY Faculty Publications Program, skillfully led by Stephen Steinberg, that commented on earlier drafts of portions of what became better chapters of this book; Joaquin Avila, whose research, legal advocacy, and data collection immeasurably helped this project; John Mollenkopf's important scholarship and support; members of the New York University Law Students for Human Rights who helped uncover some of the lost history of immigrant voting in the United States; colleagues across the oceans, especially Jo Shaw and Felicita Medved who convened a conference, "Citizens, non-citizens and voting rights in Europe" (co-sponsored by the European Science Foundation, the Europa Institute and the Edinburgh School of Law, where it was held in 2005); and Fidele Mutwarasibo, Mark Kenny and the Immigrant Council of Ireland. Many thanks to the Drum Major Institute for Public Policy, and the Professional Staff Congress of the City University of New York (PSC-CUNY) for their financial and political support.

Finally, I am eternally indebted to my family and friends, particularly my parents and grandparents, who helped shape my view of immigrants and justice; and, most importantly, to the love of my life, Susanna Jones, whose steady encouragement and support provided needed editorial assistance, daily inspiration, and intellectual rigor to realize this project. Lastly, to our beloved daughter, Rita, who makes it all worthwhile. My thanks to you all.

CHAPTER 1

Introduction

The rule of citizens over noncitizens, of members over strangers,
is probably the most common form of tyranny in human history.

—Michael Walzer, *Spheres of Justice*[1]

Riayan Tejeda grew up in the Washington Heights section of New York
City and joined the Marines after graduating from George Washington
High School. After serving for eight years, Tejeda became a staff sergeant.
The oldest of three sons, Tejeda planned to work for the U.S. government
when he got out of the Marines. Tragically, however, Tejeda was killed
during a battle in Baghdad. Tejeda, one of the first American casualties of
the War in Iraq, was hailed as a local hero. When Mayor Michael
Bloomberg spoke at his funeral, he said, "We are proud he was a citizen of
New York." But Tejeda was born in the Dominican Republic and was not
yet a U.S. citizen. Why should Tejeda be prevented from voting on policies
like the one that resulted in the loss of his life?[2]

On the night of Riayan's funeral his father, Julio Tejeda, said, "Eight
years in the Marines and they never gave him citizenship. I wouldn't be
surprised if President Bush wanted to give it to him now after he's dead.
But it's too late. A piece of paper won't bring back my son."[3] At the time
of Tejeda's death, 37,000 noncitizens were serving in the U.S. military out
of about 71,000 foreign-born immigrants on active duty, about 5 percent
of all military personnel. In fact, ten of the first twenty casualties in Iraq
were immigrants. Shortly after the tenth immigrant died, Congress

passed a bill that reduced the time it takes for soldiers like Tejeda to become citizens from three years to one year and also granted citizenship posthumously. On July 3, 2002, an executive order was issued that eliminated the mandatory waiting period for military personnel, further reducing the time in which military personnel could become citizens.[4] Congressman Charles Rangel (D-NY), who represents the district where Tejeda grew up, subsequently introduced the Riayan Tejeda Memorial Act, which would expedite naturalization for those who serve in combat zones.[5] At the time of Tejeda's death, Rangel said, "Sargent Tejeda was a hero in every sense of the word, a man born in the Dominican Republic who made the ultimate sacrifice for the United States. He has been a role model to his family and his community. Now he is a model of heroism to our city, our nation and to the great land of his birth."[6] On the night he learned of his son's death, Tejeda's father expressed pride and love of his adopted country and his homeland, a common reality of families living in two worlds: "This is the night for America to appreciate what the Dominican Republic has done for us. We love this country, but we love Dominica, too."[7]

Their faces look the same, but they are without formal political voice. Today, more than 20 million people in every walk of life—are immigrants who are not U.S. citizens: teachers, students, firefighters, police officers, stock brokers, shopkeepers, nurses, doctors, sports players, movie stars, musicians, construction workers, gardeners, nannies, workers of every kind, and neighbors who live in every state, city, and suburb, and nearly every town in the United States. Like citizens, noncitizen immigrants work in every sector of the economy, own businesses, pay taxes, raise their families, make countless social and cultural contributions, are subject to all the laws (and then some), and participate in every aspect of daily social life—from sending their children to school to serving in the military. Although noncitizens behave in much the same ways as citizens, they possess fewer rights and benefits. For one, they cannot vote for representatives who make policy that affect their daily lives.

Moreover, immigrants are here to stay and their numbers will only increase, according to projections by the U.S. census. Contrary to popular belief, immigrants pay more in taxes than they receive in public expenditures. The National Research Council of the National Academy of Sciences reported that immigrants typically pay about $80,000 more in taxes over the course of their lifetimes than they receive in federal, state, and local benefits.[8] Immigrant households pay an estimated $133 billion in property, sales, and income taxes to federal, state, and local governments.[9] In New York, for example, immigrants pay 15.5 percent of all taxes collected by the state, although they comprise only 12 percent of the total population.[10] Most immigrants want to become U.S. citizens, but the average time it takes to naturalize is eight to ten years, largely due to bureaucratic red tape. In addition, not all immigrants are eligible to become U.S. citizens today, unlike earlier times when almost everyone who came to the U.S. was able to naturalize; it was a much easier and faster process. Today, in some jurisdictions anywhere from 10 to 50 percent of the adult population are barred from voting because they are noncitizens.[11] The political exclusion of noncitizens raises troubling questions about the nature of our democracy. Why shouldn't immigrants be able to vote?

To many, the idea of allowing noncitizens to vote may sound odd or outlandish. For most Americans, voting is the essence of citizenship. But it was not always so, nor need it be. Noncitizen immigrants enjoyed voting rights for most of America's history and in much of the country. From 1776 to 1926, as many as forty states and federal territories permitted noncitizens to vote in local, state, and even federal elections. Noncitizens even held public office, such as the position of alderman. The notion that noncitizens should have the vote is older, was practiced longer, and is more consistent with democratic ideals than the idea that they should not. Curiously, this 150-year history has been eviscerated from national memory.[12]

Benjamin Franklin framed the issue of voting rights pointedly: "They who have no voice nor vote in the electing of representatives do not enjoy liberty, but are absolutely enslaved to those who have votes." Many of the early colonies had already allowed noncitizen residents to vote, and the practice was continued when the new states formed their constitutions.[13] The emerging republicanism and liberalism in early American history made noncitizen voting a reasonable practice tied to inhabitants and difficult to challenge. America's diversity was increasingly evident at the time of the Revolution, and alien suffrage was a logical extension of the revolutionary cry "No taxation without representation!" Democratic notions, such as the belief that governments derive their "just powers from the consent of the governed," became increasingly "common sense." Thomas Paine declared he was a "citizen of the world."

Early Americans viewed alien suffrage as an effective method to encourage newcomers to make the U.S. their home. And it worked. Budding Americans learned civics by practice. Getting a taste for democracy furthered immigrants' understanding of our political system and nurtured attachments to their adopted communities.

For a good part of our country's history, voting rights were determined not by citizenship, but by whether or not one was a white, male property holder. Thus, women and post-emancipation blacks—who were considered citizens—could be denied voting rights. In fact, alien suffrage was compatible with the exclusion of other categories of residents (women, men without property, and blacks) and actually buttressed the privileging of propertied white, male Christians.[14]

Voting rights have always been linked to questions about who would wield political power. With the influx of different kinds and increasing numbers of immigrants, noncitizen voting rights began to be disputed, especially those of newcomers who held political views that challenged dominant groups. For example, the War of 1812 slowed and even reversed the spread of alien suffrage, in part by raising the specter of foreign "enemies." Leading up to the Civil War, the South opposed immigrant voting because many of the new immigrants opposed slavery. One of the first planks in the Confederate Constitution was to exclude voting to anyone who was not a U.S. citizen.[15] After the Civil War and during Reconstruction, nevertheless, alien suffrage spread in the South and West with the growing need for new labor. Many new states and territories used voting rights as an incentive to attract new immigrant settlers and as a pathway to citizenship, though not as a substitute.

But as the twentieth century approached, large numbers of Southern and Eastern European immigrants came to the U.S.—who were not universally seen as "white" at the time and who often held politically "suspect" views—and immigrant voting rights were increasingly challenged.[16] These newer immigrants, coupled with the rise of mass social movements and third political parties (e.g., Populist, Labor, Suffragette, and Socialist), posed a potential threat to the dominant political and social order, and noncitizen voting was gradually eliminated state by state. The anti-immigrant backlash at the turn of the twentieth century and wartime hysteria during World War I led to the elimination of this long-standing practice.

Importantly, noncitizen voting was abolished at the same time that other restrictive measures were also enacted by elites, including literacy tests, poll taxes, felony disenfranchisement laws, and restrictive residency and voter registration requirements—all of which combined to disenfranchise millions of voters. Voter participation dropped precipitously from highs of nearly 80 percent of the voting-age population in the mid- to late nineteenth century down to 49 percent in 1924. Additional legislation drastically reduced the flow of immigrants into the U.S. and limited the proportion of non–Western European immigrants. It is revealing—but not coincidental—that immigrant voting has been buried in the annals of American history.

This silence is striking for a second reason: noncitizen voting is being revived today. Nearly a dozen cities in the U.S. have recently won voting rights for immigrant residents, and another dozen are currently waging campaigns to re-enfranchise noncitizens from coast to coast. This growing movement to win universal suffrage is gaining momentum and national attention.[17]

Since 1970, immigrant voting rights have been restored in several municipalities in the U.S.: Chicago permits noncitizens to vote in school board elections (as did New York City from 1970 until 2003, when school boards were eliminated for unrelated reasons), and noncitizens currently vote in six municipalities in Maryland. Cambridge and Amherst, Massachusetts, have also extended the right for noncitizens to vote for local offices (but state action is needed to implement these local laws).

In addition, over a dozen other jurisdictions from coast to coast have considered or are currently moving toward enfranchising noncitizens in local elections, including San Francisco and several other cities in California (San Bernardino, San Diego, and Los Angeles); Washington D.C.; New York; Portland, Maine; Madison, Wisconsin; several towns in Massachusetts (e.g., Newton, Somerville, and Chelsea); Denver, Colorado; Connecticut; New Jersey; Minnesota; and Texas.

Globally, over forty countries on nearly every continent permit voting by resident immigrants. The Maastricht Treaty in 1993 granted all Europeans the right to vote in European Union countries other than their own, expanding what has been practiced for years in Ireland (1963), Sweden (1975), Ireland (1975), the Netherlands (1975), Denmark (1977), and Norway (1978). In the 1980s, the Netherlands, Venezuela, Ireland, Spain, and Iceland enacted legislation enfranchising resident aliens; several Swiss cantons (e.g., Neufchatel and Jura) have permitted noncitizen voting for over a century; Finland and Iceland allow Nordic citizens voting rights, while Estonia allows noncitizen voting at the local level. Belgium and Rome have more recently joined the fold as well. Noncitizens vote in countries in Latin America, the Caribbean, the Middle East, North America, and New Zealand.[18] Thus, the trend to expand the franchise is hardly unique to the United States.

Oddly enough, few have explored this controversial area of American politics. While some have examined the history and laws of alien suffrage, I will focus on the politics of noncitizen voting rights. This book provides historical background, which is crucial to understand current developments, but my main concern is with contemporary campaigns to establish—or restore—voting rights for members of communities, regardless of their citizenship status. We will examine debate about this contested terrain and make the case for noncitizen voting rights.

Different terms are used to describe noncitizen voting, including "immigrant voting," "local citizenship," "resident voting," "municipal voting," and "alien suffrage." Essentially, all these terms mean the same thing: enfranchising or re-enfranchising those who are excluded from the electorate, in this case immigrants who are not citizens of the United States. There is some variation, however, in which categories of noncitizens are included or excluded. Some cities and towns allow both so-called undocumented or illegal immigrants to vote, while other places grant suffrage only to documented or "legal" immigrants. Differences also exist between various jurisdictions regarding which elections noncitizens can vote in, such as in school board elections, municipal elections, or state races.[19]

Demographic Change and Globalization

The last three decades of mass migration have produced the largest immigrant population in the United States since the turn of the last century. Today, more than one in ten individuals in the U.S. is foreign born (11 percent, or 34 million, as of 2004), the highest level since 1910. Moreover, a large and growing proportion of immigrants remains noncitizens. In 2000, more than 18 million of the 31 million immigrants were noncitizens; in 2004, more than 21 million of the 34 million immigrants were noncitizens. Nearly one in ten families in the U.S. is a "mixed" family, having at least one parent who is a noncitizen and at least one child who is a citizen. In many states and localities, the proportion of adult noncitizen residents rivals that of their citizen neighbors.[20]

Most of the new arrivals come from Latin America, Asia, and the Caribbean, and are changing the ethnic and racial composition of the U.S. population. Several states and locales now have a "majority minority" population—such as California—led by Latinos, who have surpassed African Americans as the single largest "minority" group in the U.S. The Census Bureau projects that the U.S. will become a country of "minorities" in the next fifty years. Latino and Asian populations in particular will grow rapidly. Latinos are expected to reach 25 percent of the population by 2050, and Asians are expected to reach 10 percent of the population by 2050. African Americans are projected to grow slightly, to about 15 percent, largely due to the influx of black immigrants.

The triumph of globalization has helped propel both mass migration and ideas of "citizens without borders" or "global citizens." The extension of free trade across the globe and the wholesale removal of trade barriers, embodied in international agreements such as the North American Free Trade Agreement (NAFTA) and policies of the World Trade Organization (WTO), make products and people from remote parts of the world highly mobile and readily exchangeable.

These changes have prompted heated debate about the status and impact of these newcomers and our national immigration policy. Controversy swirls about the impact of immigrants on everything from labor markets and wages, crime and public morals, electoral outcomes, and public spending to awareness about race, ethnic, and national identity and basic questions about what is America and who is an American. Nativistic responses range from Samuel Huntington's book *Who Are We?* to action by "minutemen," and have led to proposals that restrict immigration and foster sharp debate about where to draw lines between "aliens" and "citizens" across a broad range of social policies, such as who should hold drivers' licenses and be eligible for health care, education, and other public services.

Consequently, conflict over U.S. immigration and immigrant policy has intensified, heightening tensions between contending social and political groups. Emerging patterns of immigration are again reshaping group relations, creating new political fault lines with the potential to alter the balance of social and political power. Immigration is changing the political arithmetic, propelling parties and politicians who jockey for advantage to adjust campaign strategies to reflect evolving electoral conditions. Several landmark pieces of legislation have been enacted at the national and state levels affecting the economic, social, and political status of immigrants.[21]

Political Implications

Immigrants have reemerged as pivotal players in contemporary American politics, but their numbers far exceed their political representation and clout. These demographic changes hold significant political implications, especially in the states and metropolitan areas where immigrants are concentrated, several of which now have majority minority populations. Because noncitizens are counted for districting purposes, they affect the apportionment of seats in the House of Representatives. This can, in turn, have an impact on presidential elections, as those all-important electoral votes are determined based on representation in Congress.

At the state and local levels, where they make up a larger proportion of the potential electorate, immigrants can have an even greater impact. Immigrants who have naturalized already hold the capacity to determine winners and losers in close contests. Noncitizen adults comprise over 10 percent of the voting-age population in seven states and the District of Columbia, and 19 percent of all Californians of voting age. If these noncitizens were enfranchised, they could wield decisive power in state races. On the local level, noncitizens are even more highly concentrated. Adult noncitizens in Los Angeles make up more than a third of the voting-age population; in New York City, they are 22 percent of adults. In some cities and towns, adult noncitizens make up 40 to 50 percent—or more—of all voting-age residents.

Because of the high number of noncitizens, the overall proportion of Latinos and Asians in the population who vote is sharply lower than that of whites: in 2000, Latinos represented 12.6 percent of the total U.S. population but only 5.3 percent of all votes cast. Similarly, Asians were 4.2 percent of the population but cast only 1.9 percent of the votes. Whites, on the other hand, were 70 percent of the total population but cast over 81 percent of all votes. Put another way, 62 percent of Latinos were either not of voting age or were noncitizens and thus could not register to vote in 2000; the same was true for 59 percent of all Asians. These figures dropped to 35 percent for African Americans and 25 percent for whites.[22] Thus, the electorate is sharply skewed by these demographic factors.

The level of political exclusion in these jurisdictions approximates the level of disenfranchisement associated with the exclusion of women and African Americans. In many places, a quarter to a half of the population is excluded from selecting representatives who make the policies that affect daily life.[23]

What do these conditions mean for such basic democratic principles as "one person, one vote," "government rests on the consent of the governed," and "no taxation without representation"? Immigrant political exclusion challenges the ideals of a modern democracy, cutting to the heart of our political practice.

A Nation of Immigrants

There are moral and practical reasons to restore immigrant voting rights. The acquisition of political rights—including voting rights—has been a vital tool for every disempowered group in America's history to achieve economic, social, and civil rights and equality.[24] Because legislative bodies confer rights and make public policy, it is critical to possess the capacity to influence and select representatives. Legal barriers to political participation, however, have historically hampered the attainment of such rights by distinct classes of citizens, including African Americans, women, and young people.

Previously excluded groups have gained access to the franchise principally through political struggle. They fought their way into the polity through political agitation, sometimes with the support of factions within political parties or via third parties, through social movements and independent organizations, or by using the courts as a tool. Ultimately they needed the support of other sectors in society to win political rights. The agitation of the property-less encouraged sectors of the propertied to extend the franchise; the abolitionist movement and civil rights movements led whites to enfranchise blacks; the suffragettes compelled men to include women among the voting citizenry; and younger adults, after participation in the social movements of the 1960s and 1970s, were granted voting rights by older adults when the voting age was lowered from twenty-one to eighteen in 1971 with the passage of the Twenty-sixth Amendment.

Why not for immigrants too?

Without the vote, noncitizens are at risk of discrimination and bias because policy makers can, and often do, ignore their interests. Discriminatory public policy and private practices—in employment, housing, education, health care, welfare, and criminal justice—are the inevitable by-products of immigrant political exclusion, not to mention xenophobic political campaigning and racial profiling.

Noncitizen voting would extend the visibility and voices of immigrants, which in turn could make government more representative, responsive, and accountable. Winning voting rights could help advance other struggles important to immigrants, from obtaining drivers' licenses to speeding up the naturalization process, enacting real amnesty, and eliminating racial profiling and hate crimes.

Creating universal suffrage would facilitate immigrant political incorporation and ultimately bring benefits to the larger society as a whole. We should encourage all residents of our cities and towns to participate in the life of their communities regardless of whether they come from Delaware or the Dominican Republic. We all have the same interests in ensuring good schools, safe streets, and affordable health care and housing. We're a stronger society when everyone participates, because everyone benefits if decisions are made democratically.

Most immigrants want to become citizens but are often deterred for little reason other than bureaucratic roadblocks that have been erected. The average time it takes many immigrants to become a U.S. citizen—or to "naturalize"—is ten years or longer after they arrive to America, up from eight years in 1960. Technically, immigrants that obtain legal permanent residency (green cards) can apply for citizenship after five years. But the path to legal permanent residency can take several years for many immigrants. In addition, immigrants face daunting obstacles in the process, including application fees $400, lack of access to the English and civics classes needed to prepare for the naturalization examination, and application backlogs that can range from six months to nearly two years.[1]

---

[1]Spiro, Peter J. 1999. "Questioning Barriers to Naturalization." Georgetown: Georgetown Immigration Law Journal. 13; Michael Fix, Jeffrey Passel and Kenneth Sucher. "Trends in Naturalization." The Urban Institute. September, 2003; Wernick, Allan. *U.S. Citizenship and Immigration*. New York: Prima Publishing (Random House), 2004.

Moreover, millions of immigrants are not eligible to become U.S. citizens because the pathways to citizenship are restricted to certain categories of individuals, such as family members, asylum seekers, military personnel, etc. Thus, it is not only undocumented or "illegal" immigrants who are not eligible for citizenship but also the millions of documented or "legal" immigrants who may possess any one of the nearly two dozen types of visas (including worker and student visas) that also are precluded from becoming citizens.

In the meantime, these newest Americans are subject to all the laws, work in every sector of the economy, own businesses, send their children to school, have revitalized neighborhoods in every city in the country, contribute billions of dollars in taxes each year, serve in the military, and even die defending this country. Yet they cannot vote on issues crucial to the quality of their daily lives. Excluding such a significant portion of the population from political participation closes off a proven pathway to promote civic education and citizenship. Worse, it undermines the health, representativeness, and legitimacy of our laws and public policies. Rather than undermining democracy, as some will argue, resident voting could lead to more robust democratic politics and policy making. And instead of diluting the concept of citizenship, as its critics maintain, resident voting can enrich citizenship by encouraging immigrants to participate in the political life of their communities.

Most importantly, it is legal and feasible. The U.S. Constitution does not preclude voting by noncitizens, and both state and federal courts have upheld noncitizen voting. In *Minor v. Happersett*, for example, the Supreme Court ruled in 1874, "Citizenship has not in all cases been made a condition precedent to the enjoyment of the right of suffrage."[25] Other federal and state court rulings have upheld voting by noncitizens. The decision about who holds the franchise has always rested with states and localities.

Campaigns to Restore Immigrant Voting

Even while anti-immigrant sentiments have reigned in public discourse and policy, particularly after September 11, a mobilization among immigrant groups and their political allies is evident, including campaigns for noncitizen voting rights. We see a burgeoning immigrant rights movement, one that has tremendous political savvy. Witness the proliferation of immigrant rights organizations that engage in a broad range of advocacy and activism and that build multiracial alliances with other groups on a range of issues, including labor, housing, education, health, welfare, and foreign policy. Immigrants walk picket lines and lobby legislatures with greater frequency and force. Indeed, labor unions, housing organizations, and welfare rights groups have reached out to immigrants where they have common ground and shared interests. For example, many such groups—spearheaded by labor unions—mounted an Immigrant Workers Freedom Ride in 2003 that sent busloads of immigrants from nine cities; converged on Washington, D.C.; and ended up with 100,000 people marching in New York City. Inspired by the "freedom rides" during the civil rights movement, the planners hoped to focus public attention on immigrants' rights—particularly as workers—and show immigrant strength. Immigrant groups have also mobilized voter registration and get-out-the-vote efforts. Such activity reveals a growing awareness among new immigrants that they possess legitimate claims on the American polity, and they are commanding greater attention.

One form that immigrant mobilization has taken is in campaigns to gain the vote. Several characteristics stand out in nearly every campaign in the contemporary period: demographic shifts propelled immigrant mobilization; proponents of noncitizen voting engaged in effective grassroots organizing, coalition building, and lobbying; and sympathetic politicians, mostly liberal Democrats and some Green Party members, enacted or supported legislation. In every case, these campaigns were contentious.

Opponents of noncitizen voting have countermobilized. Generally, opponents have been conservative Democrats and Republicans, representatives of all political stripes who view noncitizen voters as a potential threat to their incumbency, community residents and groups that express anti-immigrant sentiments, and others who object to immigrant voting on other grounds. And opponents have often thwarted immigrant voting rights initiatives, most recently in San Francisco.

There are many objections to immigrant voting raised by its opponents: it would diminish the value and meaning of citizenship, blur the lines between citizens and noncitizens, and reduce incentives for immigrants to naturalize. Some object that immigrants already have a pathway to voting—by becoming a citizen. Individuals wishing to vote should take the step to naturalize, like everyone else. People should have loyalty to one country, not two. Granting immigrants voting rights would lead to less informed voters, increase vote fraud, make the difference in close elections, and affect contentious public policy issues, or, worse still, as one critic has audaciously objected, enfranchise terrorists like Osama bin Laden.[26] Immigrant rights advocates have their own concerns. Some worry that immigrants would become further exposed and made more vulnerable if voting rights laws were not crafted carefully, protecting registrants' confidentiality. Some African Americans and other minority groups worry their voting power and number of representatives would be diluted at a time when they are reaching parity with whites in many areas and levels of governance. These objections are answered in the rich debates between advocates and opponents, which typify every initiative to restore or grant voting rights to noncitizen immigrants contemporarily and historically.

In writing *Democracy for All,* my aim is to provide a comprehensive look at a neglected issue facing our democracy, noncitizen voting. In chapter 1, I analyze the rise and fall of immigrant voting rights in the U.S. from 1776 to 1926, paying close attention to the politics of its expansion and contraction at particular times in the states. In chapter 2, I examine arguments for and against immigrant voting, and attempt to make a compelling case for immigrant voting rights. Chapter 3 looks at the jurisdictions where noncitizens currently vote in the United States, including Maryland and Chicago, as well as the recent experience of noncitizen voting in New York City school board elections. I explore how immigrant voting rights became an issue, how they were won, and how they operate in practice. I provide insight into the groups and political actors who fought for and against such efforts, what factors contributed to the success of these campaigns, and the impact of noncitizen voting in elections of these cities and towns. In chapter 4, I present contemporary campaigns to restore immigrant voting in the U.S., including those in California, Washington, D.C., New York, and Massachusetts. The book concludes with a look at the future of immigrant voting rights and its implications for politics and democracy in the United States.

Expand the Franchise

In highlighting successful efforts to restore noncitizen voting rights, I will show how campaigns based upon democratic and moral claims can mobilize immigrants and their allies. Such campaigns provide immigrants with important means to defend themselves against nativist attacks, and also give other minority groups greater means to forge winning voting blocs that can advance their mutual interests. Immigrant taxation without representation not only challenges the legitimacy of America's mantle of democratic governance but also provides a rationale and opportunity for organizing a progressive political majority.

Just as the civil rights movement sought to extend the franchise to African Americans and others who had been barred from voting to attain equitable representation, a renewed movement for human rights would further extend the franchise to new Americans. True universal suffrage could boost possibilities for working-class electoral majorities and strengthen chances for winning progressive policies.[27] Of course, progressives run the risk—one they willingly accept for the sake of democratic principles—that enfranchised immigrants might vote for conservative candidates and issues.

Essentially, the issue is about fairness. It is only fair that persons who are part of a local community and contribute to its tax base and economy should have a say in the formulation of laws and policies that will have a direct bearing on their well-being. Excluding persons from voting because of their lack of citizenship is to exclude them from the body politic. As we move forward in this new century, we must continue to make the political process more accessible to everyone. By doing so, we will help politically integrate individuals who have a vested interest in our collective future. Equally important, all community members will benefit. Everyone has common interests in good public services and in accessible and affordable public goods from quality education and health care to jobs. Such outcomes are likely to be more widely available if all community members participate in decision-making processes.

As Jamin Raskin, one of the most outspoken and prominent intellectual voices of the contemporary movement for noncitizen voting rights in the U.S., said, "immigrant rights are the civil rights" of the day and "by that logic, noncitizen voting is the suffrage movement" of our time.[28] The burgeoning movement to create a truly universal suffrage calls forth America's past and future as an immigrant nation. Restoring voting rights to all its residents would update our democracy for these global times.

CHAPTER 2

The Rise and Fall of Immigrant Voting in U.S. History: 1776 to 1926

The world is my country, all mankind are my brethren, and to do good is my religion.

—Thomas Paine, *Common Sense*[1]

There is no such thing as impartial history. The chief problem in historical honesty isn't outright lying. It is omission or de-emphasis of important data.

—Howard Zinn, *You Can't Be Neutral on a Moving Train*[2]

Writing for the *American Political Science Review* in 1931, Leon Aylsworth noted, "For the first time in over a hundred years, a national election was held in 1928 in which no alien in any state had a right to cast a vote for a candidate for any office—national, state, or local."[3] Although it may come as a surprise to many, "aliens" voted in local, state, and even national elections in as many as forty states and federal territories from the founding of the United States until 1926, and noncitizen immigrants held public office such as alderman and coroner.[4] But, as discussed in the previous chapter, this 150-year practice came to a grinding halt in the early twentieth century.

There is discrepancy in the scholarship about how many states, which states, and at what times states allowed noncitizens to vote. Several scholars, who calculate the figure using the date on which noncitizen voting rights ended, estimate that "at least twenty-two states and territories allowed noncitizens to vote and hold office."[5] Raskin rightly questioned the accuracy of this figure.[6] More recent scholarship shows "an upper limit of 35" states and territories that "ever permitted noncitizens to vote," according to Marta Tienda.[7] My research, drawing upon secondary and primary sources with the assistance of law students at New York University, shows that as many as forty states and federal territories at one point or another allowed noncitizens to vote, as detailed below. Regardless, the fact remains that a majority of states and territories in the United States have at some point permitted noncitizens to vote. The idea that noncitizens should have the vote is older and has been practiced longer than the idea that they should not.

Contrary to the dominant narrative about a consistent expansion of democracy and political participation in the United States, the history of immigrant suffrage provides a more accurate lens to expose a recurring pattern that runs throughout the history of American voting rights: one step forward and two steps back. An influx of newer immigrants at a point in time sparks a wave of nationalism and nativism—often associated with war or political conflict—and a rollback of voting rights. Alternatively and sometimes simultaneously, struggles to expand democratic participation and economic imperatives—such as westward expansion and the need for labor—spur further cycles of migration and conflict, which have led to additional changes in electoral arrangements.[8]

What was the basis of noncitizen voting? How extensively was it practiced? Why were noncitizen voting rights eliminated? Which groups fought for and against this practice? What impacts did this shift have on political participation and politics? This chapter addresses these questions and related issues.

The Rise and Transformation of Immigrant Voting

From the colonial period, voting by noncitizen immigrants was widely practiced and not extraordinarily controversial.[9] The emerging republicanism and liberalism embodied in slogans such as "No taxation without representation" made noncitizen voting a logical democratic practice tied to notions of "inhabitants" and difficult to challenge.[10] Voting rights were instead predominantly tied to property, gender, and race.[11] Alien suffrage was compatible with the exclusion of other categories of residents (men without property, women, and blacks), and actually buttressed the privileging of propertied white male Christians.[12] From the late 1770s until the 1820s, voting requirements were not tied to citizenship.

Massachusetts provides a typical example. Its 1780 Constitution reads, "Every male person, being twenty-one years of age, and resident in any particular town in this Commonwealth for the space of one year next preceding, having a freehold estate within the same town, of the annual income of three pounds, or any estate of the value of sixty pounds, shall have a right to vote in the choice of a Representative, or representatives for the said town."[13] That is, all male "inhabitants" who met these financial qualifications were permitted to vote, regardless of citizenship status.[14]

National figures no less than George Washington affirmed such principles. In 1783 he said, "The bosom of America is open to receive not only the opulent and respectable stranger, but the oppressed and persecuted of all nations and religions; whom we shall welcome to a participation of all our rights and privileges."[15]

Congress itself promoted noncitizen voting in the Northwest Ordinance of 1789, which gave "freehold aliens" with two years of residency the vote for territorial legislative representatives. Furthermore, it granted "wealthier" resident aliens with three years of residency the right to serve in territorial legislatures.[16] In subsequent acts, Congress granted voting rights for immigrants in the new territories of Washington, Kansas, Nebraska, Nevada, the Dakotas, Wyoming, and Oklahoma. In addition, Congress explicitly authorized the right of aliens to vote for representatives to statewide constitutional conventions in Ohio, Indiana, Michigan, and Illinois.[17]

Historically, Michigan, like other Northwest Territory states, permitted noncitizen voting. After entering the union in 1835, Michigan's state constitution allowed noncitizens to vote and to participate in state constitutional conventions. In 1885, the Michigan Supreme Court reaffirmed this practice when it was challenged, stating that "if the intention to become a citizen is declared in due form of law, and the other conditions of age, residence within the state and voting precinct for the proper length of time, are found to exist, the constitution (article 7, § 1) confers the right of suffrage."[18]

Alien suffrage was widely practiced throughout the nineteenth century, though it ebbed and flowed during particular periods. During the antebellum period and westward expansion, the issue of immigrant voting increasingly became more contentious. The War of 1812 slowed and even reversed the spread of alien suffrage—in part by raising the specter of foreign "enemies."[19] Northern states generally held that alien suffrage fell in line with basic rights of the Republic, while Southern states saw immigrants as a threat because the newcomers were generally hostile to slavery. Immigrant voting was a significant issue leading up to the Civil War, as reflected in debates in Congress and in the Confederacy. In fact, when the South seceded, the first plank of the Confederate Constitution explicitly stated that only citizens of the Confederacy would have voting rights, precluding alien suffrage at all levels of government.[20] Nearly 25 percent of the Union Army was foreign-born during the Civil War.[21] After the Civil War and Reconstruction, alien suffrage spread to the South and West, reaching its peak in 1875. But during the decades surrounding the turn of the twentieth century, immigrant voting rights were rolled back and ultimately eliminated by 1926. The appearance, transformation, and disappearance of alien suffrage—and related policy—occurred at critical junctures in American history.

For example, the Alien and Sedition Acts of 1798 were passed by the Federalists partly in response to fears that Frenchmen entering America would infect the people with radical revolutionary ideas.[22] The Federalists hoped to retain control of the presidency (John Adams) and used the acts to appeal to conservatives and nativists. In addition, the Federalists passed a Naturalization Act that made it more difficult to attain citizenship by raising the residency requirements from five to fourteen years.[23] However, after the Federalists lost the 1800 election the Alien and Sedition Acts were not enforced; they expired in 1801. Shortly afterwards, in 1802, under President Thomas Jefferson, the residency requirement for naturalization was returned to its original five years.[24] Later, some would push for easier and faster naturalization laws. In 1842, for example, J. P. Walker, a Democrat from Wisconsin, proposed shortening naturalization by reducing the five-year residence requirement to three years. But Walker met with stiff opposition from some of the Southern states, and the bill was defeated.[25]

Similarly, the War of 1812 stirred nationalism and anti-alien sentiment. Some states that permitted alien suffrage began to revoke the practice, usually by changing the "constitutional definition of voters from 'inhabitants' to 'citizens,'"[26] and some other states enacted laws requiring U.S. citizenship as a prerequisite to vote. Some have speculated that another factor may have also been at work: the gradual reduction and elimination of property qualifications for voting. Because alien suffrage was "ideologically consistent" with property qualifications, when agitation increased to abolish property qualifications—which began just after the War of 1812 ended—support for alien suffrage decreased. By eliminating the property qualification, all immigrant men would have the vote, which posed a threat to the status quo.[27] To help follow these changes, table 2.1 and figure 2.1 present the timeline of state practices.

To maintain a measure of control on the electorate, states added other qualifications to vote, including citizenship.[28] In a few years, several states enacted citizenship requirements proximate to the times they reduced or

TABLE 2.1 Noncitizen Voting Rights in the United States

State	Time Period when Noncitizens Held Voting Rights
Alabama	1868–1901
Alaska	none
Arizona[a]	none
Arkansas[b]	1874–1926
California	none
Colorado	1876–1902
Connecticut	1776–1819
Delaware	1776–1831
District of Columbia	none
Florida	1868–1894
Georgia	1868–1877
Hawaii	none
Idaho	1863–1890
Illinois	1818–1848[c]
Indiana	1851–1921
Iowa	none
Kansas	1854–1918
Kentucky[d]	1789–1799
Louisiana	1879– ?
Maine	none
Maryland	1776–1851 for state and federal elections; six towns allow noncitizen voting in local elections.[e]
Massachusetts	1780–1822
Michigan	1835–1894
Minnesota	1849–1896
Mississippi	none
Missouri	1865–1921
Montana	1864–1889[f]
Nebraska	1854–1918
Nevada	1848–1864
New Hampshire	1792–1814
New Jersey	1776–1820
New Mexico	none
New York	1776–1804

(Continued)

TABLE 2.1 Noncitizen Voting Rights in the United States *(Continued)*

State	Time Period when Noncitizens Held Voting Rights
North Carolina	1704–1856
North Dakota	1861–1889/1909[g]
Ohio	1802–1851
Oklahoma	1850–1907
Oregon	1848–1914
Pennsylvania	1790–1838
Rhode Island	1762–1842
South Carolina	1790– ?
South Dakota	1850–1918
Tennessee	1796–1834
Texas	1869–1921
Utah	none
Vermont	1767–1828
Virginia	1776–1818
Washington	1850– ?
West Virginia	none
Wisconsin	1848–1908
Wyoming	1850–1899

Source: Adapted from Marta Tienda, "Demography and the Social Contract," *Demography* 39, no. 4 (2002): 587–616; Alexander Keyssar, *The Right to Vote: The Contested History of Democracy in the United States* (New York: Basic Books, 2000); Virginia Harper-Ho, "Noncitizen Voting Rights: The History, the Law and Current Prospects for Change," *Law and Inequality Journal,* no. 18 (2000); Gerald L. Neuman, "'We Are the People': Alien Suffrage in German and American Perspective," *Michigan International Law* 13 (1992): 259; Jamin B. Raskin, "Legal Aliens, Local Citizens: The Historical, Constitutional, and Theoretical Meanings of Alien Suffrage," *University of Pennsylvania Law Review* 141 (1993): 1401ff.; Paul Kleppner, "Defining Citizenship: Immigration and the Struggle for Voting Rights in Antebellum America," in *Voting and the Spirit of American Democracy: Essays on the History of Voting and Voting Rights in America,* ed. Donald W. Rogers and Christine Scriabine (Urbana: University of Illinois Press, 1992); Gerald Rosberg, "Aliens and Equal Protection: Why Not the Right to Vote?" *Michigan Law Review* 75 (April–May 1977): 1092–36; Kirk H. Porter, *A History of Suffrage in the United States* (1918; reprint, Chicago: University of Chicago Press, 1971); New York University Law Students for Human Rights; New York University Law Students for Human Rights included Ying Chi, Jessica Chicco, Caroline Cincotta, Rachel Coen, Hannah Gladstein, Po-Siann Goh, Sarah Parady, Eric Ruben, Zoe Salzman, and Ellen Van Scoyoc. Suffrage Universal, "Le droit de vote aux Etats-Unis (Voting Rights in the USA)," http://users.skynet.be/suffrage-universel/us/usvo.htm; and the Immigrant Voting Project, "Immigrant Voting Project: Democracy for All."

[a] Kleppner, "Defining Citizenship: Immigration and the Struggle for Voting Rights in Antebellum America," in *Voting and the Spirit of American Democracy: Essays on the History of Voting and Voting Rights in America,* ed. Donald W. Rogers and Christine Scriabine (Urbana: University of Illinois Press, 1992).

TABLE 2.1 Noncitizen Voting Rights in the United States *(Continued)*

ᵃ Although the United States took possession of the territory, including present-day Arizona, following the Treaty of Guadalupe Hidalgo in 1848, Arizona was not organized as a territory separate from New Mexico until 1863. During the territorial period, it appears that some noncitizens may have voted at the local level. Historian Lawrence Michael Fong explains that Anglo settlers in Arizona primarily feared the political power of a consolidated Mexican vote and, perhaps as a consequence, paid comparatively little attention to immigrant groups such as the Chinese. While Fong's examination of the Pima County register for 1882 reveals that only one Chinese resident, Chan Tin-Wo, a naturalized citizen, voted, he concludes that it "appears that in Pima County there were no social or political barriers for Chinese who wished to participate in deciding county or municipal issues. Of course, one had to be able to speak the institutional language, English." A handful of other Chinese immigrants registered to vote prior to the turn of the century, including one Chan Tin-Wo, who "cast the decisive vote in favor of a bond issue for the construction of Drachman School in the 1890s." Although it is unclear whether those voting had naturalized, it is probable that at least some were noncitizens, given that the Chinese Exclusion Act of 1882 had called a halt to the naturalization of Chinese immigrants. New York University Law Students for Human Rights; Lawrence Michael Fong, "Sojourners and Settlers: The Chinese Experience in Arizona," *Journal of Arizona History* 21 (1980): 1–30.

ᵇ Although Arkansas's Constitution of 1836 provided suffrage only to "free white male citizen[s] of the United States," the postwar Constitution of 1874, in addition to enfranchising nonwhite men, allowed noncitizen men to vote, granting suffrage to every "male person who has declared his intention of becoming a citizen" of the United States and met the age and residency requirements. Arkansas Constitution of 1874, art. III, sec. 1.

ᶜ Noncitizens, who were present in 1848, were grandfathered in.

ᵈ In *Cowan v. Prouse*, 93 Ky. 1956 (1892), the Kentucky Court of Appeals permitted a noncitizen to vote in Christian County in the election of the clerk of the court. His vote had been challenged in a dispute over the outcome of the election, but the court did not disqualify him because he had declared his intent to become a citizen and had served in the armed forces, receiving an honorable discharge. He apparently had voted in previous elections. 93 Ky. at 167–68.

ᵉ Since 1918, Barnesville has permitted noncitizens to vote; Martin's Additions and Somerset have permitted noncitizens to vote since 1976; Takoma Park since 1992; and Garrett Park since 1999.

ᶠ Noncitizen voting was phased out over a five-year period after the enactment of the Constitution that prohibited it, so as to grandfather in declarant alien voters to achieve U.S. citizenship and thus retain their suffrage uninterrupted. The Montana Constitution read, "Every male person of the age of twenty-one years or over . . . [who] shall be a citizen of the United States. . . . *Provided* [t]hat nothing herein shall be construed to deprive any person of the right to vote who has such right at the time of the adoption of this constitution; *Provided*, that after the expiration of five years from the time of the adoption of this constitution no person except citizens of the United States shall have the right to vote." Montana Constitution of 1889, art. IX, sec. 2. Reproduced in William F. Swindler, *Sources and Documents of United States Constitutions*, vol. 6 93 (Dobbs Ferry, N.Y.: Oceana Publications, 1976).

ᵍ At some point before 1909, North Dakota amended its Constitution to remove the declarant alien provision. Francis Thorpe, *The Federal and State Constitutions, Colonial Charters, and Other Organic Laws of the States, Territories, and Colonies Now or Heretofore Forming the United States of America* (Washington, D.C.: Government Printing Office, 1909), 2895. Thorpe does not give a year for the amendment to the state's constitution that eliminates the declarant alien provision.

eliminated property qualifications. In 1804, for example, New York enacted one of the first citizenship requirements, partly due to the anti-French sentiment following the 1789 French Revolution, which spread radical ideas that alarmed elites. Although New York's Constitution never

Fig. 2.1 Marta Tienda, "Demography and the Social Contract," *Demography* 39, no. 4 (2002): 604. Reprinted by permission of Population Association of America and Marta Tienda.

explicitly limited voting to U.S. citizens, in its 1821 Convention, some delegates referred to noncitizen voting when discussing their opposition to a proposal to grant blacks voting rights. As one delegate put it, "It is not thought advisable to permit aliens to vote, neither would it be safe to extend it to the blacks. We deny to minors this right, and why? Because they are deemed incapable of exercising it discreetly, and therefore not safely, for the good of the whole community."[29] In 1814, New Hampshire enacted a citizenship requirement.

Connecticut disenfranchised noncitizens in 1818 during a time that fear of immigrant voters was on the rise and manifested in public debates. For example, Federalist Noah Webster proposed that a greater number of votes be allotted to ministers and those with greater taxable wealth so as to ensure that newer immigrants would have comparatively less influence. The Constitution of 1818 disenfranchised noncitizens at the same time it explicitly excluded blacks and women from voting.[30] Other states that soon followed suit for similar reasons included Virginia (1818), New Jersey, (1820), Massachusetts (1822), Vermont (1828), and later Delaware (1831), North Carolina (1856), Tennessee (1834), and Rhode Island during the following two decades. (Ohio did not adopt citizenship requirements until 1851.) Only Georgia and North Carolina did not follow suit and link voting with citizenship prior to 1860.[31] Similarly, Illinois maintained alien suffrage (for those with six months' residency) until 1870.[32] And most of the newly admitted states to the U.S. "confined the franchise to citizens", beginning with Louisiana (1812), and then Indiana (1816), Mississippi (1817), Alabama (1819), Maine (1820), and Missouri (1821).[33] Between 1820 and 1845, however, the focus on alien voting rights receded as debates about property qualifications and the "Negro" came to occupy center stage.[34]

But with the great waves of immigrants from Ireland and Germany, nativism rose and spread. The reaction was not so much against people of Irish and German descent per se; rather, what provoked nationalism and nativism was their religion, Catholicism in particular. Some perceived the invading hordes to be part of a larger plot: Reverend Lyman, for example, in his 1835 sermon *A Plea For the West*, saw the new arrivals as an attempt by the pope to conquer America. Similarly, Samuel F. B. Morse wrote a series of letters in the *New York Observer* "warning that the Catholic monarchies of Europe were sending immigrants to take over this country and force it to succumb to the doctrines of despotism and popery."[35] In response, nativists would form the Know-Nothing Party.

The Know-Nothings saw these immigrants as a threat because of their ideas and voting trends. In 1856, the Know-Nothing Party's platform denounced alien suffrage and also called for a twenty-one-year residency requirement for naturalization. Legislation to allow noncitizens to vote in the new territories became hotly contested. In 1854, for instance, John M. Clayton, a Whig, introduced an amendment to deny alien inhabitants suffrage in Nebraska, which drew the ire of Democrats.[36]

The kinds of nativist concerns expressed at this time are strikingly similar to those of contemporary nativists: immigrants were uneducated, would steal jobs from "real" Americans, would become paupers and live off of taxpayers' money, were immoral, and would undermine the civil and social institutions of the country. Other nativists worried about the politics of the new immigrants and their potential impacts on elections and policy. For example, New York Senator James Brooks said it was not religion "we make war [upon]" but "the politics of men whose principles are alien to the institutions of our country."[37]

In 1841, Senator Alexander Porter, a Whig, petitioned the Louisiana House of Representatives to increase the residency period to fourteen years as a requirement for becoming a citizen and obtaining voting rights. The Louisiana House went further, passing a resolution by a vote of 20 to 10 to increase the naturalization period to twenty-one years of residence.[38] Similarly, Governor Henry J. Gardner of Massachusetts made several proposals in his third term (in 1856) aimed at excluding Catholics and foreign-born residents from voting and holding office. One was for a twenty-one-year residency requirement before immigrants could gain the franchise, which did not pass, but another successful proposal did impose a literacy requirement for suffrage.[39]

Alien suffrage became increasingly contested in struggles between the North and South between 1850 and 1860. Northerners tried to expand the political power of immigrants largely because the newer immigrants were opposed to slavery (even if they were not friendly to blacks), which of course spurred Southerners to further resist and oppose alien suffrage. Similarly, alien suffrage was increasingly contested in Congress as it weighed legislation regarding new states and territories. During the Civil War only eight of the Northern states allowed aliens to vote, which meant that the North lost a significant number of votes proportionate to their population given the influx of immigrants at that time.[40]

Yet, alien suffrage spread in the South and West with the growing need for new labor, particularly after the Civil War and during Reconstruction. Many new states and territories used alien suffrage as an incentive to attract settlers. The general practice was to require residency from six months to one year before voting rights were granted.

Wisconsin developed a formula in 1848 that allowed aliens who "declared" their intent to become citizens the right to vote. The Wisconsin formula became a model for other states and Congress. Jamin Raskin describes how this model—the declarant alien qualification—helped to weaken the objections of nativists and nationalists who opposed alien suffrage "by recasting" how alien suffrage was conceived and practiced. Alien suffrage was now seen more clearly to be "a *pathway* to citizenship" rather than a substitute for it—a kind of "pre-citizen voting."[41] Declarant aliens were now presumed to be on the "citizenship track."[42] The Wisconsin proposal provided a strong rebuttal to opponents of alien suffrage. It was articulated during the Constitutional Convention by delegates who were foreign born, most notably Franz Huebschmann and Charles Burchard, who "argued that when a foreigner left his old life behind and traveled thousands of miles to start a new life in Wisconsin, that effort alone was more than adequate to demonstrate his loyalty and commitment to Wisconsin."[43] In this way, Wisconsin provided a reply to adversaries that proved to be effective. Thus, in Wisconsin and other states, declarant aliens won the right to vote in local, state, and national elections.[44] As we shall see in later chapters, this line of reasoning has proven effective for contemporary advocates of immigrant voting rights, and has similarly deflected opponents' objections that immigrant voting would deter newcomers from naturalizing.

Similarly, soldiers returning from the Civil War demanding the right to vote provided another argument that proved to be effective for supporting alien suffrage, one that has been likewise employed by advocates today. During and following the Civil War, immigrant soldiers argued for and obtained what many perceived as their just reward for their service, particularly given that they fought for the freedom and voting rights of blacks.[45] Another Civil War–related reason was also at work: the need to attract cheap labor, particularly in the South and West after the abolition of slavery.[46]

Before the Civil War, none of the Southern states permitted noncitizen voting, but under Reconstruction declarant aliens were allowed to vote as specified in the constitutions of Alabama, Arkansas, Florida, Georgia, South Carolina, and Texas. In addition, Congress passed acts enabling the territories of Oregon, Minnesota, Washington, Kansas, Nebraska, Nevada, the Dakotas, Wyoming, and Oklahoma to allow noncitizen voting, and after achieving statehood, most preserved the practice. At least thirteen new states adopted declarant suffrage. Noncitizen voting was practiced to its greatest extent by about 1875.[47] By the time of the close of the nineteenth century, nearly one-half of all the states and territories had some experience with voting by aliens, which lasted for more than half a century for most of them. However, a gradual decline in the number of states that allowed noncitizen voting began at the close of the nineteenth century even while several states (such as the Dakotas) passed noncitizen voting rights in 1889.

Alabama represents an interesting example of the shifting politics of immigrant voting rights. After the War of 1812, Alabama restricted the vote to citizens.[48] But after the Civil War and during Reconstruction, Alabama was one of several states to reverse course and grant voting rights to noncitizen males, hoping to draw new settlers. In 1901, however, Alabama rescinded voting rights for noncitizens by constitutional amendment, except for male noncitizens who previous to the 1901 Constitutional Convention declared their intention to become citizens. This "grandfathering" in of resident aliens who intended to naturalize was meant to avoid disenfranchising white men, while preventing future nonwhite immigrants from gaining the vote.[49] Indeed, race played a critical role in the ebb and flow of immigrant voting rights.

The Fall of Immigrant Voting

The massive influx of Southern and Eastern European immigrants during the decades surrounding the turn of the twentieth century fueled anti-alien passions and halted and reversed noncitizen voting practices.

The largest wave of immigrants into the U.S. occurred between 1880 and 1910: 12.5 million people streamed into the country from Southern and Eastern Europe. Immigrants comprised about one-third of the total population of the country during those years. This tremendous increase of darker Mediterranean and politically suspect immigrants sparked a nativist reaction, which produced several significant changes that have had lasting impacts on the American polity.

The elimination of noncitizen voting rights during the first decades of the twentieth century—coupled with the malapportionment of cities—came at the same time as the population of urban America rivaled the populations in much of the rural and suburban parts of the country. By 1920, 51 percent of the total population in the U.S. resided in cities.[50]

Immigrants became the subject of, and embroiled in, sharp social, economic, and political conflict during the Progressive Era, which cut to the heart of notions of citizenship and democracy. Rapid industrialization and urbanization—and the wrenching social and economic changes they brought—fueled social protest movements of Labor, Populists, and Socialists and the third parties they formed.

These developments in turn provoked countermobilizations. Mass immigration sparked intense debate about the impacts of immigrants on nearly everything. The Progressive Era also witnessed explosive conflicts among immigrants and the native-born. Nativistic responses led to proposals that restricted immigration and to public policies that consigned immigrants to second-class status. Since the founding of the U.S., nativist groups have perpetrated certain themes about immigrants: they have portrayed newcomers as being genetically and morally inferior, possessing cultural "habits" and language barriers that make them unable or unwilling to "assimilate" into the "mainstream" of American culture, and being prone to criminal activity or just plain lazy—all of which have pervaded the rhetoric and policy surrounding immigration.[51]

As a result, a host of laws was enacted that addressed these issues in ways that constricted the franchise and had profound impacts on public policy and American political development. For example, eighteen states adopted literacy requirements aimed at restricting the flow of immigrants and their political participation, as well as that of other working-class constituencies and African Americans.[52] By 1900, only eleven states retained immigrant voting rights. In the years leading up to and with the advent of World War I, these remaining states moved to end alien suffrage, usually by constitutional amendment. The states were Alabama (1901), Colorado, (1902), Wisconsin, (1908), Oregon, (1914), Kansas, (1918), Nebraska

(1918), South Dakota, (1918), Indiana, (1921), Texas, (1921), Missouri, (1921), and Arkansas (1926).[53]

The case of Minnesota provides insight into both the rise and fall of noncitizen voting, particularly that of other Midwestern and northwestern states. The federal Organic Act of 1849 created the territorial government of Minnesota, which allowed declarant aliens the right to vote. It stated the following:

> That every free white male inhabitant above the age of twenty-one years, who shall have been a resident of said Territory at the time of the passage of this act, shall be entitled to vote at the first election, and shall be eligible to any office within the said Territory; but the qualifications of voters and of holding office at all subsequent elections shall be such as shall be prescribed by the legislative assembly; provided, that the right of suffrage and of holding office shall be exercised only by citizens of the United States and those who shall have declared on oath their intention to become such, and shall have taken an oath to support the constitution of the United States and the provisions of this act.[54]

When Congress was considering legislation that would enable the territory of Minnesota to be admitted to statehood in 1857, a contentious debate ensued. Senator Asa Biggs stated that "the right of suffrage ought to be confined to citizens of the United States," and he introduced an amendment that would have required voters on the statehood issue to be U.S. citizens. Other supporters of the Biggs amendment defended this position by pointing out the dangers of foreign influence in elections, even while they claimed no affiliation with the nativist Know-Nothing Party.[55] One supporter, Senator Albert Brown, proclaimed his disdain of immigrants and a fear that new immigrants would be susceptible to manipulation by political parties: "There may be in this Territory Norwegians, who do not read one word of English. . . . What a mockery, and what a trifling with sacred institutions it is to allow such people to go to the polls and vote! Who does not know that they are led up like cattle to the ballot-boxes, and vote as they are told to vote?"[56] Moreover, Senator Brown claimed it was important to set limits in order to prevent claims that suffrage should be extended to "both sexes, male and female . . . to black and red as well as white."[57] Equally important and revealing, some representatives from slave states feared that abolitionist noncitizen voters might tilt the delicate balance that existed between North and South on slavery.[58] For example, Senator John Bell of Tennessee worried that looking to the general aspect of the party divisions by which the country is distracted, and more particularly to the point of the intensity and magnitude of the interests depending on our national elections, you will see that foreigners not naturalized constitute an element of strength, distributed as they are in several of the northern and northwestern States, destined often to control our national elections, if they shall be allowed the privilege of voting; and thus they may, in the end, exert a powerful influence in changing the policy and even the vital principles of our Government.[59]

Supporters of declarant alien voting, such as Senator William Henry Seward, countered that noncitizens were capable of exercising self-government just as were citizens, and that alien suffrage was desirable "precisely for the reason that these new States are to be made chiefly by aliens and foreigners."[60] Although the Senate did adopt Senator Biggs's amendment in the bill, the final act allowed any "legal voter," which included qualified aliens, to vote on statehood.[61] Minnesota subsequently reaffirmed its commitment to declarant alien suffrage in its first state constitution, adopted in 1857.[62]

But in 1896, after the influx of more and newer immigrants, Minnesota discontinued its practice of noncitizen voting by referendum, whereby a vote of 97,980 to 52,454, Minnesota voters approved a constitutional amendment that prohibited noncitizen voting.[63] A 1902 editorial in the *Washington Post* captured the prevailing attitude of the times. It criticized the states that had not yet repealed alien suffrage, referring to the "marked and increasing deterioration in the quality of immigration" and saying, "Men who are no more fit to be trusted with the ballot than babies are to be furnished with friction matches for playthings are coming in by the hundred thousand."[64]

Similarly, Nebraska provides insight into how concerns about who would wield the vote—particularly women and immigrants—affected franchise laws. During Nebraska's Constitutional Convention of 1871 it was female suffrage, not alien suffrage, that generated the most controversy. One delegate, Mr. Estabrook of Douglas County, proposed to add to the Nebraska Bill of Rights the following provision: "Every human being, of full age, and resident for a proper length of time on the soil of the nation and State, who is required to obey the law, is entitled to a voice in its enactment, and every such person whose property is taxed for the support of the government, is entitled to a direct representation in such government."[65] Presumably, Estabrook proposed this amendment to secure a broader suffrage provision. And although the amendment was designed to enfranchise women, opponents revealingly objected on the grounds that it would make suffrage an inalienable "natural" right rather than a discretionary "political" right, thus enfranchising not only women—who were deemed to be incompetent to exercise the franchise wisely—but also "barbarian" aliens. Using racist rhetoric, opponents of broader suffrage objected,

> The Chinaman who scoffs at your religion; who bows down and worships blocks of wood and stone; and who defiles your temples of Christianity with his blasphemy and who refuses to declare that he is a liege subject of your government—he is to be allowed to exercise the elective franchise. . . . Are you willing that every barbarian as soon as he shall land here, shall exercise full political power? I think that this move is a dangerous one.[66]

Thus, it was fear of the "barbarian" aliens voting combined with anti–female suffrage attitudes that led to the defeat of Estabrook's proposed amendment. It would take the force of the federal government's constitutional amendment in 1920 to give women the vote in Nebraska. Two years earlier, in 1918, Nebraska changed its constitution to eliminate declarant alien voting.[67] Apparently, rising hostility to new immigrants and xenophobia generated by World War I led to the elimination of noncitizen voting. Hostility to Greek immigrants who came to Omaha to work on the railroads and in the meat-packing industry was common.[68] For example, an editorial in the *Omaha Daily News* expressed the commonly held sentiments of the day: "Herded together in lodging houses and living cheaply, Greeks are a menace to the American laboring man—just as the Japs, Italians, and other similar laborers are."[69] The examples of Nebraska and Minnesota provide insight into the rationale embodied in legal changes to the franchise, most often embodied in state constitutions.

The timing of the disenfranchisement of immigrants—and of other poor and minority groups through other means such as literacy tests, poll taxes, restrictive residency requirements, and voter registration procedures—does not appear to have been coincidental. Such disenfranchising measures were promoted and enacted by powerful economic and political elites just when the electoral potential for working-class constituencies, progressive social movements, and third party mobilization was growing.[70] The impact of noncitizens in elections increased with their numbers—making the difference in several state elections, and feeding critics of "the weight of a foreign element" in politics.[71] Elites viewed noncitizen voters as a threat because of the appeal that third party challenges had on immigrants and the working class more generally. Moreover, elites reacted to big-city political machines that were tied to immigrants. Elites were also alarmed at the fact that 70 percent of total government spending was done at the state and local levels before 1929.[72]

These disenfranchising measures and the elimination of noncitizen voting rights contributed to the precipitous decline in voter participation during the Progressive Era. From 1830 to 1900 voter turnout nationally in presidential elections ranged from 70 to 80 percent, but dropped to 49 percent by 1924. Voter turnout in state and local elections was also significantly higher during the nineteenth century compared with the twentieth century. In some urban centers, such as New York City (where most immigrants in the state resided), nineteenth-century voter turnout ranged upward to between 85 and 90 percent.

Additional anti-immigrant federal legislation was enacted to limit the influx of immigrants to the U.S. From 1882 until 1924, national anti-immigrant laws were enacted to exclude the entrance of persons on qualitative grounds—the Chinese, criminals, prostitutes, the physically and mentally ill, and, in 1917, the illiterate (a literacy test was established for immigrants), who were considered likely to become "paupers." In 1903, "anarchists" were added to the list of excludables.[73] The 1924 National Origins Act drastically reduced the flow of immigrants into the U.S. and limited the proportion of non–Western European immigrants.[74] Nativist groups, including the Ku Klux Klan, played a role in the passage of the National Origins Act.[75]

Taken together, these developments limited democratic politics and progressive possibilities in the United States for years to come. The legacy of these changes had significant implications for public policy and American political development throughout the twentieth century to this day.[76]

Race, Ethnicity, and the Politics of Immigrant Policy

At the root of these developments were racial and ethnic conflicts. The newer immigrants who arrived during the Progressive Era affected deeply held racial and national identities, which cut to the core of notions of American citizenship and democracy. Who can become an American—and, equally important, at what level in the social hierarchy they be incorporated—are processes that have long been imbued by racial considerations.[77] Race and ethnicity have always played a critical and often decisive role in shaping immigration and immigrant policy and politics throughout U.S. history. The main contours of U.S. immigration and immigrant policy reveal distinct racial and ethnic conflicts (along with social, economic, and political dynamics), and have been a site of political struggle throughout American history.[78] Moreover, voices for and against immigration and immigrant rights have coexisted since the founding. Yet there are periods when anti-immigrant sentiments have tended to be stronger.

For example, anti–Irish Catholic sentiment, which surfaced especially around the time of the War of 1812 and during the 1840s, led to rollbacks in noncitizen voting, particularly in the Northeast. The antipathy of many old-stock New Englanders toward the Irish and Germans is well documented, and it manifested in efforts to impose a variety of restrictions on immigrants—including voting—during these periods. For example, foes of Tammany Hall in New York pressed for changes in the state's constitution to establish literacy requirements and property qualifications.[79] Similarly, other states such as Massachusetts, Connecticut, and Maryland attempted to restrict immigrant activity and to reel in the growing power of political machines during much of the nineteenth century.[80]

In 1854 in Massachusetts, nativists who had formed the Know-Nothing Party won statewide offices and a majority of the state legislature, and subsequently passed anti-immigrant legislation. One of their legacies was embedded in the Massachusetts Constitution, which stated, "No person of foreign birth shall be entitled to vote or shall be eligible to office, unless he shall have resided within the jurisdiction of the United States for two years subsequent to his naturalization, and shall be otherwise qualified, according to the constitution and laws of this Commonwealth."[81] Thus, immigrants were prevented from voting for two years even after they naturalized.

The case of Wisconsin is particularly revealing. As aforementioned, Wisconsin forged a model for enfranchisement of immigrants that many states followed—by granting voting rights to aliens who declared their intention to become naturalized citizens. Declarant immigrants who resided in the state for six months were permitted to vote beginning in 1848. But controversy surrounding the merits of this policy, evident in debates of the state legislature and during constitutional conventions, points to specific factions that came down on opposite sides of the issue. For example, during the constitutional debate in the 1840s, delegates from southwestern Wisconsin opposed alien suffrage due to the fact that most immigrants were settling in the eastern counties. These regions had different ethnic bases. Wisconsin politics was dominated by Yankees from New York and New England who initially settled the territory. Beginning in the 1840s, however, large numbers of European immigrants—particularly from Germany and Norway—settled in Wisconsin. During the next seventy-five years, Wisconsin became one of the most heavily ethnic states in the U.S. Ethnic conflicts percolated during several periods that affected noncitizen voting rights.

Older blueblood Wisconsin residents fought German immigrants on such issues as liquor consumption and Sunday practices, issues that also played out with Irish immigrants in Wisconsin and elsewhere. Concern about alcoholism ran high amongst Yankees, who associated it with a host of social ills and believed that Sundays should be devoted to worship. German culture and practice, on the other hand, entailed the consumption of beer and use of Sundays for recreational purposes. In 1872, the Wisconsin legislature passed a more stringent version of the 1849 antiliquor law known as the Graham Law. Germans in Wisconsin felt this was a direct attack on them and went to court to contest the new law. Although their court fight was unsuccessful, they went to the voting booth in 1873 and helped defeat the Republican administration that had passed the Graham Law. In 1874, the legislature "replaced the Graham Law and the Sunday blue law with a considerably milder law."[82]

Similarly, schools that taught material in the German language were subject to legislation mandating the use of English in the 1890s. Wisconsin ended declarant noncitizen voting in 1909. World War I further sharpened anti-German (and other immigrant) sentiment and elicited frequent calls to eliminate immigrant voting rights throughout the U.S. As one *Washington Post* article framed the sentiment during the period,

> The political campaigns in Wisconsin and elsewhere, in which the issue is narrowing down to Americanism versus Germanism, or victory versus defeat, may bring out in sharp outlines the mistake made by Wisconsin and some other states in permitting aliens to vote. . . . The enemy is not to be trusted, here or in Europe. No temptation should be placed in the way of aliens to do mischief to the American cause. The enemy will make enough mischief without being assisted by American neglect. The State legislatures should amend the election laws as promptly as possible to provide that no person shall be qualified to vote unless he is a citizen of the United States.[83]

Ohio offers similar insights about ethnic prejudices of the day. Ohio was one of the few Midwestern states that did not permit noncitizen voting. During the Ohio Constitutional Convention of 1873–1874, Democrats and some foreign-born members proposed enfranchising declarant aliens, arguing that such legislation would foster migration into the state, attach immigrants to American institutions, reward loyal aliens who fought in the Civil War, and destigmatize aliens who by implication were now inferior to recently enfranchised blacks.[84] But opponents successfully marshaled nativist arguments, including fear of foreign influence in domestic policy making and anxieties about racial equality.

In the late nineteenth and early twentieth centuries, Italians and Jews in particular were the object of much scorn and discrimination. Moreover, they were not universally viewed as "white." In fact, Italians and Jews were sometimes referred to as "colored." For example, in 1891 the *New York Times* and local Louisiana newspapers referred to several Italians who were lynched in New Orleans as "colored" while at the same time mentioning that "Negroes" were also present. Such incidents were not isolated. Officially, however, the U.S. Census categorized Europeans as white, as did some newspapers of the time.[85]

Interestingly, contemporary parallel characterizations—and fears—appear in current popular debate. Emerging patterns of immigrant social and political incorporation hold great significance for future race relations and political alignments, particularly regarding which immigrant groups are becoming "white" and which groups are becoming "black" as they are ascribed a place in a racial hierarchy, just as was done in the past.

Additional Anti-immigrant Measures

Further obstacles were erected to limit immigrant voting power. In the name of guarding against fraud, naturalization processes were made more onerous, literacy requirements imposed were made more stringent, and residency laws were enacted. Most of these changes were usually supported by Republicans and middle- and upper-class elites and opposed by Democrats and working-class ethnic groups.[86]

But traditional categories of "liberal" and "conservative" or "left" and "right" are ill equipped to adequately discuss or explain U.S. immigration and immigrant policies, including noncitizen voting rights. For example, throughout much of U.S. history organized labor has been anti-immigrant (although labor is usually characterized as being progressive in general) yet has actively organized immigrants into unions. Still, U.S. workers and unions composed of dominant ethnic groups have often perceived newer immigrant laborers as undercutting their hard-won gains.[87] Business groups, on the other hand, have historically been more pro-immigration in general. They generally view particular types of labor as valuable resources, whether as cheap and abundant labor or highly skilled labor (depending on changing economic conditions). But while business groups have generally supported immigration for economic reasons, members of the upper and middle classes often held anti-immigrant sentiments and actively contributed to campaigns to not only limit immigration but also enact policies hostile to immigrants and immigrant rights including the abolition of noncitizen voting rights. Analysis of immigrant policy is complicated.

Nevertheless, nativist groups have been consistently anti-immigration and anti-immigrant. During the Progressive Era, a broad range of nativist groups increasingly perceived newer immigrants as a threat to them: in economic terms, particularly in periods of economic recessions, but also on social and moral grounds.[88] Immigrants were often characterized by nativists as low-skilled, ignorant, criminals, pestilent, anti-American, unable to properly and successfully assimilate, generally socially and politically suspect, and morally ill fitted to American culture. Catholic immigrants, for example, were seen by many Protestants as being prone to alcoholism, crime, disease, and poverty, which they contended would lead to economic, social, and moral decline for the nation. Jews and other Eastern Europeans were similarly branded. At the time, the bulk of Eastern and Southern European immigrants arriving were not considered "white" by popular and academic taxonomy.[89] The racism behind such views and sentiments was often highly vitriolic.

Other nativists—particularly elite "reformers"—utilized a more veiled racism. For example, at the turn of the twentieth century they helped popularize population projections showing that America would become mostly nonwhite (or non-"Aryan" and non-Protestant) within fifty years.[90] Such scare tactics were used by elite reformers and nativist groups (such as the Immigration Restriction League) to influence and sway officials to pass legislation during the Progressive Era that restricted immigration and perpetuated other anti-immigrant policies, including the elimination of noncitizen voting. As aforementioned, from 1882 until 1924, national immigration policy excluded people accused or suspected of being criminals, prostitutes, physically or mentally ill, illiterate, paupers, and anarchists.[91] Similar to the wave of anti-immigrant hysteria that swept the country in 1812, the "Red Scare" during World War I led to a sweeping retreat of the remaining alien suffrage policies that had characterized the nineteenth century. One prominent example is that of U.S. Attorney General A. Mitchell Palmer, who rounded up over 4,000 suspected radical foreigners, deporting hundreds. From the Know-Nothings in the early nineteenth century to the KKK in the early twentieth century, these nativist and xenophobic groups were among the critical players in shaping U.S. immigration and immigrant policy. As mentioned, the KKK played an important role in the 1924 National Origins Act, which dramatically curtailed immigration and tied it toward European immigrants.[92] That is, race and ideology—along with economics, religion, and politics—drove the curtailment of immigration and the constriction of the franchise. Alabama changed its constitution in 1901 to eliminate noncitizen voting; it was followed by Colorado in 1902; Wisconsin in 1909; Oregon in 1914; Kansas, Nebraska, South Dakota, and Texas in 1918; Indiana in 1921; Mississippi in 1924; and, lastly, Arkansas in 1926.

Ultimately, the distribution of rights to racial and ethnic immigrant groups reflects the biases and strategies of dominant political actors who enacted immigrant policies and citizenship laws. Political actors and interests aligned themselves with different groups at different times—depending on their calculations about the consequences of particular policies on their political fortunes—shaping laws governing immigrants, including noncitizen voting rights. Rogers Smith maintains that lawmakers structured U.S. citizenship in terms of illiberal and undemocratic racial, ethnic, and gender hierarchies—white male Anglo-Saxon Protestant—for reasons rooted in basic, enduring imperatives of political life.[93] Political elites forge citizenship laws and policies—including noncitizen voting rights—which legally incorporate and empower (or exclude and disempower) their likely constituents. They also offer symbolic support for civic ideologies and identities that foster a sense of peoplehood for dominant groups. Thus, the most successful political actors have been those who mix liberal (individual personal freedoms) and democratic (prosperity for all citizens) ideologies with ascriptive notions of which groups are most American and "worthy." Political actors have used these traditions of political discourse about civic identity to protect or alter citizenship arrangements, or to justify or oppose laws in light of changing political conditions. These dynamics were particularly evident during the Progressive Era. The establishment and then the elimination of noncitizen voting rights provide further evidence for this perspective.

Progressive Era Reformers: A Mixed Bag

One way to view American civic life is through distinct periods of party realignment.[94] Political conflicts emerge in each period and reflect the balance of power among the system's participants, who, in turn, structure the terrain and content of later conflicts. Such an approach is useful in understanding forces arrayed against immigrants who led the fight and eliminated noncitizen voting rights during the Progressive Era. Partisan conflict among three basic groups is critical to understand these changes: urban political machines (usually Democratic), rural and suburban politicians (usually Republican, particularly in the North), and Progressive Era upper- and middle-class reformers (often independents, allied with the Republican Party or dissident factions of the Democratic Party). Not only does examination of partisan conflict among these groups illuminate who eliminated noncitizen voting rights and how, but it also points to key linkages among the class, racial, ethnic, and political constituencies involved.

Perhaps nothing characterizes the Progressive Era better than the impulse to reform. But many Progressive Era reform groups had different interests and notions of reform, thereby promoting their own ideal. Most progressives attacked corruption in government, but different groups focused on particular elements of the political system. For example, many elite progressive reformers attacked urban political machines and sought to make government more efficient and economical. By "throwing the rascals out," these reformers hoped to "clean up" government. They held that good government was possible by rationalizing and democratizing politics. To achieve these ends, such Progressives inaugurated a broad range of reforms—including important electoral changes—that have had significant and lasting impacts on our political system.

"Progressivism" was an uneasy coalition at best—it was not a cohesive movement. Progressive Era reform movements operated at the local, state, and national levels, but many of the diverse groups in what is characterized as Progressivism were actually antagonistic to one another.[95] Historians have often divided Progressives into two camps in attempts to sort out the complexity of the period. For example, some dichotomize progressives into "social" reformers versus "structural" reformers,[96] while others posited groups of "social justice" progressives versus "social order" progressives,[97] and still others focused upon "new-stock urban liberals" versus "old-stock patrician reformers."[98]

While there was a significant democratic tendency within Progressivism, one where laborites and socialists found common ground with Progressives (as in the first groupings listed above), there was another strain that is the focus of attention here. These latter groups of Progressive Era reformers (in the second categories listed above) tended to be more conservative. For example, their attempt to overthrow urban political machines—which often had the loyal following of ethnic immigrant working-class voters—involved imposing elite institutions in their place (such as boards and commissions where decision-making power was further removed from the hands of voters and their local representatives, such as city council members or aldermen). Moreover, many such progressives held more veiled forms of nativist animus against immigrants, arguing, for example, for various means of "social uplift." In another parallel to the present day, this refrain can be heard among contemporary social reformers.[99]

Most importantly, some reforms that conservative Progressives advocated for included electoral changes that constricted working-class immigrant political participation. The elimination of noncitizen voting rights was among these. A host of other electoral reforms—including restrictive residency requirements for voting, cumbersome registration procedures, literacy tests, and antifusion laws and other ballot access measures that limited third party challenges—effectively barred poor and working-class immigrant citizens as well as insurgent parties and candidates from participating in elections. These electoral changes, in turn, reduced party competition (along with the North/South sectional political realignment following the election of 1896)—all of which combined to sharply reduce voter participation.[100]

For example, one common reform—requiring immigrants to show their naturalization papers in order to vote—proved to be a significant hurdle, much as lawmakers knew it would be. As the *New York Herald* reported, "A sad feature [of this requirement] was that many persons will be deprived of their vote, as their papers are either worn out, lost, or mislaid."[101] Similarly, the *New York Times* reported that a committee of twenty prominent civic organizations recommended changes to the naturalization process that would impose literacy requirements and place the process in the hands of "proper administrative officials" (and away from the courts).[102] Both of these changes, which were enacted during the early twentieth century, decreased the rate and total number of immigrants who were naturalized. Similarly, a *Washington Post* article argued, "Until we have laws in all the States providing an educational qualification for suffrage, we ought to deny citizenship to applicants who cannot speak English."[103] Thus, by increasing the difficulty for immigrants to naturalize and by linking literacy tests to both the naturalization process and the voting process, voter participation rates of working-class immigrants decreased.

Such changes were enacted in the name of preventing fraud. In fact, Progressive Era charges of corruption and fraud—prevalent among this more conservative group of reformers—were important tools in their arsenal to enact political change. Allegations of what they claimed was rampant fraud were also integral to their explanation about why voter turnout declined precipitously after the turn of the twentieth century. Progressive Era reformers claimed that the decline in voter participation was due to the elimination of fraudulent ballots, particularly by immigrants tied to urban party machines.[104] They contend that these electoral changes, such as stricter voter registration laws and the establishment of bipartisan boards of elections, reduced control over the electoral process by urban political machines and reduced illegal voting by immigrants.

But these assumptions are flawed and unsupported by compelling counterevidence. Burnham, for example, argues that allegations of electoral fraud reflected elite motivations and interests of those who inaugurated and implemented Progressive Era electoral changes, and contends that other factors—such as the decline in party competition—account for a greater proportion of the decline in voter turnout.[105]

Perhaps most revealing is that charges of fraud—and the laws they helped create—reflected a nativistic animus aimed at the new urban immigrants who were tied to party machines, which many reformers reviled.[106] Moreover, partisan considerations also appear to have been involved. Most allegations of fraud originated within Republican Party organizations, oppositional or insurgent factions within Democratic Party ranks, or upper-class reform organizations and groups, who charged dominant regimes (generally urban political machines, usually controlled by Democrats with strong ties to working-class immigrants) with fraudulent activities. The most frequent charges were made during the years of heaviest immigration (1870s through the 1920s). Much writing was "openly condescending, moralistic, and prejudiced toward the new arrivals. . . . The literature on election fraud, in sum, corresponded roughly with the years of the mugwump-progressive reform movements and can be seen as a manifestation of the middle and upper-class reform of these years."[107] Charges of fraud originated in muckraking magazines (such as *Harper's Weekly, Outlook, McClure's, Century,* and *Forum*) whose writers were native-born, white, Protestant, middle- and upper-class Progressive reformers. The accounts were largely anecdotal and based on accounts of highly motivated observers and participants.

The pattern of partisan wrangling over legal and institutional changes is repeated regarding immigrant voting rights. These same reformers (from the late Gilded Age through the Progressive Era) pressed for and won the elimination of noncitizen voting in state after state from the 1880s to the 1920s. Many pressed these changes into their states' constitutions, while others eliminated immigrant voting rights through changes in statutes. In either case, elite reformers and other opponents to noncitizen voting used racial and ethnic appeals and scare tactics to attain passage of these electoral and legal changes. Some of the most influential critics of universal manhood suffrage—who published critiques of the growing influence of immigrants in politics in the *Atlantic Monthly,* the *Nation,* and the *North American Review*—included such notables as historian Francis Parkman, editor E. L. Godkin, and other elite, Protestant, generally Republican-leaning, upper-class opinion makers.[108] Such Progressive Era reformers argued that if immigrants were allowed to continue to select representatives sympathetic to their concerns and interests, the political system would grow more corrupt and American society would decline. The *New York Sun,* which supported the repeal of alien voting, alarmingly led off a 1909 story by noting that nine states still allowed noncitizens to vote: "It is possible that the balance of political power in the United States is lodged with foreigners owing no allegiances to this government, or, in fact, to any government on the face of the globe."[109] Eventually, these reformers succeeded in overturning noncitizen voting rights.

Thus, the interests of those who won such political struggles are embedded in these new electoral arrangements. These changes to election laws, in turn, produced other reinforcing electoral dynamics. For example, the elimination of noncitizen voting rights affected the nature of party competition and issue appeals: the parties were freer to ignore newcomers who were now barred from voting. Moreover, the elimination of noncitizen voting further allowed state legislatures to draw district lines for the selection of representatives in such a way as to shortchange urban-centers. The malapportionment of cities, where the majority of noncitizens resided, resulted in the further marginalization of immigrant interests. These electoral changes set the path of public policy making in the direction away from the interests of noncitizens and immigrants more generally and decidedly toward rural and growing suburban constituencies.

In the name of reforming corrupt political machines, elite political interests successfully established an election system—whether by design or default—that fostered undemocratic electoral dynamics and political outcomes by disenfranchising millions of Americans, particularly immigrant voters. These electoral arrangements skewed political power away from the needs and interests of the working class for years to come. Keyssar sums up the impact of the massive disenfranchisement enacted by Northern and Southern elites:

> Millions of people—most of them working class and poor—were deprived of the right to vote in municipal, state and national elections. Their exclusion from the electorate meant that outcomes of innumerable political contests were altered, different policies were put into place, different judges appointed, different taxes imposed. Third-party insurgencies were deprived of a potential electoral base, and the relative strength of the two major parties, in at least some cities and states, was reversed. Many of the core institutions of the modern American state—institutions built and solidified between Reconstruction and World War I—were indeed shaped and accepted by a polity that was far from democratic.

Even when the Great Depression launched the New Deal, it was blunted of greater political support from below than it might otherwise have received, which probably contributed to its limited nature and eventual undermining by economic and military elites.

Conclusion

The political biases of the past continue to plague the contemporary electoral system. There is good historical reason to believe not only that these electoral changes helped depress voter turnout, especially of low-income and minority groups, but also that the class- and race-skewed contemporary electorate continues to reflect the legacy of these laws and institutions that still remains largely unreformed today. Restoring immigrant voting rights has the potential to rectify some of these conditions and could help to reinvigorate the American polity.

As we shall see, today's immigrants—whose numbers rival those at the turn of the twentieth century—owe a great debt to the civil rights movement. Civil rights activists not only helped open the door to newcomers from around the world, a door that had been shut tightly after 1924, but also flung it open to immigrants from every part of the globe to enter the United States. One year after the Civil Rights Act was signed into law (July 2, 1964) and just months after the Voting Rights Act became law (August 6, 1965), the Immigration and Nationality Act of 1965 was enacted in October 1965, which prohibited immigration and naturalization on the basis of race, sex, or nationality. The Hart Celler Act, as it was popularly called and which took effect on June 30, 1968, abolished the nation-of-origin restrictions that were imposed in the 1920s and that had previously limited immigration to Europeans. The Hart Celler Act established new immigration criteria based on kinship ties, refugee status, and "needed skills." Henceforth, America has been open to receive immigrants from Africa, Latin America, and Asia, places that had previously been largely excluded or severely restricted. Thus, the reason most contemporary immigrants are people of color is because the civil rights movement pried open America's door that had been closed to them. It is to these changing demographics—and their political ramifications—that we now turn our attention.

CHAPTER 3

The Return of Immigrant Voting: Demographic Change and Political Mobilization

Contemporary initiatives for immigrant voting rights grow out of several related factors. One is the changing political arithmetic for elected officials—and would-be elected officials—who are forced to reckon with growing numbers of immigrant voters (and potential voters) where they comprise an increasing share of the whole. Another factor is the growing number and political activity of immigrants themselves, who walk picket lines and lobby legislators in greater number and with more force, even in the post–September 11 world. Immigrant mobilization—coupled with renewed efforts by a broad range of labor, civil rights, and other organizations to fight for economic and social justice, which sometimes lead to the formation of effective coalitions and alliances—can advance progressive agendas in particular locales. Finally, there are political entrepreneurs—of all stripes—seeking issues and mechanisms to forge winning electoral majorities. These factors and trends have combined to propel such groups to explore the expansion of the franchise to noncitizens in local elections as a means to make government more representative, responsive, and accountable. In sum, noncitizen voting rights are seen as one pathway to democratize governance, and for those excluded to gain political power. Progressives hope the expansion of the electorate will help advance progressive candidates and policies; conservatives and libertarians who endorse noncitizen voting believe it will help their cause. In both cases, they believe it is the right thing to do.

One thing is clear: it is undeniable that immigrants have reemerged as pivotal players in contemporary American politics. Their increasing numbers give them greater presence and make immigrants critical to political calculus. Although the number of immigrants who have naturalized and can (and do) vote has rapidly increased, their overall numbers far exceed their political representation and clout.[1] In New York City, for example, nearly 40 percent of the 2.2 million total votes cast in the 2000 elections were by naturalized immigrants.[2] Yet, another 1.3 million adult residents remain noncitizens and make up about 23 percent of New York City's total adult population of over 6 million.[3] Similar patterns are evident in many other jurisdictions in the U.S.

Growing Numbers and Kinds of Immigrants

The last four decades of mass migration have produced the largest immigrant population in the United States since the turn of the last century. Since 1965, the number of immigrants living in the U.S. has tripled; more than one in ten individuals is foreign born (11.1 percent), the highest level since 1910, when over 14 percent were foreign born.[4] As discussed earlier, nearly one in ten families in the U.S. is a "mixed" family, having at least one parent who is a *noncitizen* and at least one child who is a *citizen*. That means that one out of five U.S. residents is the child of an immigrant.[5]

Moreover, an increasing proportion of immigrants are noncitizens: over 18 million of the 31 million immigrants were noncitizens in 2000. Because it can take up to ten years on average for immigrants to naturalize—coupled with a relatively steady influx of newcomers—more and more of the foreign-born population in the U.S. remains noncitizens. Over time a smaller proportion of immigrants have naturalized, resulting in a larger proportion and total number who have remained noncitizens. In 1970, fewer than 3 million of the over 9 million immigrants were noncitizens (26 percent); in 1980, the number grew and approximately 5 million of the over 14 million immigrants were noncitizens (38 percent); in 1990, the number of noncitizens jumped to a majority of all immigrants—roughly 11 million of the nearly 20 million immigrants were noncitizens (55 percent); and in 2000, over 18 out of the 31 million immigrants were noncitizens (60 percent). (See figure 3.1).

The picture is more striking at the state and local level. Because of such demographic change—along with the growth of naturalized immigrant citizens and the political coming of age of second-generation

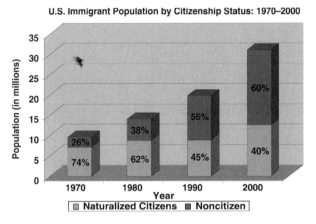

Fig. 3.1 Source: U.S. Census Bureau.

immigrants—foreign-born residents (both citizens and noncitizen) are beginning to make their mark. The sleeping giant, as many commentators refer to the burgeoning number of newcomers, is experiencing a political awakening.

Immigrants are dispersing, making their way into every part of the country. Nearly every census tract in the U.S. now contains foreign-born residents. In many states, they constitute a significant and growing proportion of the total adult population. Over twenty-one states have adult noncitizen populations that comprise more than 5 percent of the state's total adult population (see table 3.1). Seven states and the District of

TABLE 3.1 States with High Percentage of Noncitizens

State	Percent of Adult Population Who Are:			Citizenship Rate of Foreign-born Adults (%)
	Native-born Citizens (%)	Naturalized Citizens (%)	Noncitizens (%)	
California	67.6	13.6	18.8	42.0
New York	75.3	12.0	12.8	48.4
Nevada	81.1	7.5	11.5	39.5
Texas	83.0	5.8	11.2	34.2
New Jersey	78.8	10.3	10.8	48.8
Florida	80.2	9.5	10.3	48.1
Arizona	85.0	4.9	10.1	32.7

Source: U.S. Census Bureau.

Columbia have an adult noncitizen population that is over 10 percent of the total.

From 1970 to the early 1990s, almost 75 percent of all immigrants settled in six states (California, New York, Texas, Florida, New Jersey, and Illinois). But from the mid-1990s on, immigrants settled in greater numbers in other states, primarily in the South and Midwest, where 35.7 percent of the total foreign-born population of the U.S. lived by 2000. In fact, these regions became the home for 45.7 percent of all newcomers between 1995 and 2000.[6] Although California remained the largest recipient of new immigrants (22 percent) and other large immigrant-receiving states continued to get about 40 percent of new arrivals, many of the newcomers instead went to the middle of the country. Between 1990 and 2000, the foreign-born population in three states—Nevada, Georgia, and North Carolina—grew by more than 200 percent, and it grew by over 130 percent in Arkansas, Utah, Tennessee, Nebraska, Colorado, Arizona, Kentucky, South Carolina, and Minnesota. Thus, in the 1990s the foreign-born population in these states grew twice as fast than in the usual immigrant-receiving states.[7] (See figure 3.2).

New Immigration Growth Centers

Immigration Categories
Major Destinations (70% of Immigrants) (6)
Traditional States (>250K in 1920) (8)
New Growth States (1990–99 > 50%) (19)
Other States (18)

Source: Passel and Zimmerman, 2001.

Fig. 3.2 Jeffrey S. Passel and Wendy Zimmermann, Are Immigrants Leaving California? Settlement Patterns of Immigrants in the Late 1990s, April 1 (Washington, D.C.: Urban Institute, 2001), 8. Reprinted by permission of by the Urban Institute.

Proportion of States with Noncitizen Rich (20% or More) Cities

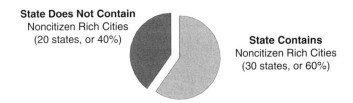

State Does Not Contain
Noncitizen Rich Cities
(20 states, or 40%)

State Contains
Noncitizen Rich Cities
(30 states, or 60%)

Fig. 3.3 Source: U.S. Census Bureau.

The picture is even more striking in local communities. In fact, most states have cities with large populations of noncitizens. Thirty states (60 percent) contain cities with populations that are 20 percent or more noncitizens (see figure 3.3).

Even the states with a relatively low percentage of noncitizens overall often contain cities that do have large noncitizen populations. Of the forty-two states with noncitizen populations below 10 percent, twenty-nine states contain cities with noncitizen populations above 10 percent of the voting-age population. In immigrant-rich states, the proportion of noncitizen residents is significantly larger, particularly at the local level. In California, for example, where nearly 19 percent of the state's total population is composed of noncitizens, over 25 percent of the adult population in California is noncitizens in at least eighty-five cities; eighteen municipalities have noncitizen adult populations of between 40 and 49 percent; and noncitizens comprise a majority of the adult population (50 to 63 percent) of another twelve municipalities. The noncitizen population in Los Angeles is approximately one-third of the total.[8]

Eight hundred and seventy-four cities across the country have an adult noncitizen population of more than 10 percent of the city's total adult population. The city having the most noncitizens is Chamblee City, Georgia, with 64.5 percent. There, close to seven out of every ten adult persons in Chamblee City cannot vote because of citizenship restrictions. Similar disparities can be found across the country. One hundred and ninety-three cities have a noncitizen population of more than 25 percent of the city's total adult population (one out of four), and twenty-one cities have an adult noncitizen population of 50 percent or more (one out of two). (See table 3.2).

The ten most populated cities in the United States have a large percentage of adult noncitizens. Los Angeles has close to a 33 percent adult noncitizen population, followed by San Jose at 25 percent and New York, Houston, and Dallas at 23 percent (see table 3.3).

TABLE 3.2 Selected Cities with High Proportion of Noncitizens

	Selected Cities	State	% Noncitizen Eighteen Years Old and Over
1	Chamblee, DeKalb County	Georgia	64.5
2	Cactus, Moore County	Texas	63.7
6	Bell Gardens, Los Angeles County	California	56.5
7	Royal City, Grant County	Washington	56.3
14	Wendover, Tooele County	Utah	52.2
15	Santa Ana, Orange County	California	51.9
18	El Cenizo, Webb County	Texas	51.3
19	Somerton, Yuma County	Arizona	50.9
22	Greenfield, Monterey County	California	49.8
24	Sweetwater, Miami-Dade County	Florida	48.5
25	Bridgeport, Douglas County	Washington	47.9
26	Hialeah Gardens, Miami-Dade County	Florida	47.6
27	Coachella, Riverside County	California	47.5
29	Parlier, Fresno County	California	47.2
31	Cockrell Hill, Dallas County	Texas	46.3
33	Hialeah, Miami-Dade County	Florida	45.7
34	Lynwood, Los Angeles County	California	45.6
38	Roberts, Jefferson County	Idaho	43.8
39	Union City, Hudson County	New Jersey	43.7
41	Gervais, Marion County	Oregon	43.1
44	Hidalgo, Hidalgo County	Texas	42.9
46	Doraville, DeKalb County	Georgia	42.5
47	Brewster, Okanogan County	Washington	42.2
48	Rio Bravo, Webb County	Texas	42.1
49	Passaic, Passaic County	New Jersey	42.0
50	Wilder, Canyon County	Idaho	41.9
51	Paramount, Los Angeles County	California	41.5
52	Mesa, Franklin County	Washington	41.3
53	San Fernando, Los Angeles County	California	41.1
54	Norcross, Gwinnett County	Georgia	41.1

(Continued)

TABLE 3.2 Selected Cities with High Proportion of Noncitizens *(Continued)*

	Selected Cities	State	% Noncitizen Eighteen Years Old and Over
56	Fellsmere, Indian River County	Florida	40.8
58	Sullivan, Hidalgo County	Texas	40.6
59	Firebaugh, Fresno County	California	40.3
60	Sunland Park, Dona Ana County	New Mexico	40.3

Source: U.S. Census Bureau.

Similar patterns appear in towns, townships, and villages. There are 250 towns and townships nationwide where the adult noncitizen population constitutes 10 percent or more of the total adult population. In the most disparate, Mattawa, Washington, the adult noncitizen population constitutes 77.7 percent of the town's total adult population. (See table 3.4 for other examples).

Villages also follow this pattern of distribution and concentration. There are 129 villages throughout the country that cross the 10 percent adult noncitizen threshold, with the highest being Stone Park Village in Illinois at 47.4 percent.

There is another category, "census designated places" (CDPs), which refers to unincorporated areas that contain significant concentrations of

TABLE 3.3 Large Cities with High Proportion of Noncitizens

Top Ten Most Populous Cities	% of VAP Who Are Noncitizens
Average	22.5
New York City	22.9
Los Angeles	32.5
Chicago	16.4
Houston	22.9
Phoenix	17.5
San Diego	16.6
Dallas	22.7
San Francisco	16.7
San Jose	24.9
Austin	13.8

Source: U.S. Census Bureau.

TABLE 3.4 Selected Towns

Town	Number of Noncitizen Adults	% of Noncitizens	Total Adult Population
West New York, New Jersey	16,601	46.6	35,644
Cicero, Illinois	23,051	41.2	55,998
Addison, Texas	2,521	21.5	11,738
Madison, Wisconsin	1,155	19.2	6,030
Pembroke Park, Florida	1,392	30.5	4,565
Herndon, Virginia	5,400	34.1	15,827
Rye, New York	8,905	26.5	33,601
Center Town, Colorado	430	28.3	1,520
Stillmore, Georgia	137	25.6	535

noncitizens. Over 700 CDPs nationwide contain 10 percent adult nonciti-zens. The highest CDP adult noncitizen population concentration is in Muniz CDP, Texas, at 76.4 percent. Most significantly, there are thirty-five CDPs at a 50 percent or greater adult noncitizen population threshold.

Impact on Racial Composition of the U.S. and Future Trends

Since 1965, most immigrants have come from Latin America, Asia, and the Caribbean, changing the ethnic and racial composition of the U.S. popula-tion. The U.S. Census reports that several states and locales now have a majority minority population—such as California—led by Hispanics who have surpassed African Americans as the single largest "minority" group in the U.S. Moreover, the Census Bureau projects that the U.S. will become a country of "minorities" in the next forty-some years. Latino and Asian populations in particular will grow rapidly. Latinos are expected to reach 25 percent of the population by 2050, and Asians are expected to reach 10 percent of the population by 2050. African Americans are projected to grow slightly, to about 15 percent. By 2025, close to 50 percent of Latinos and Asians will be eligible to vote.

Naturalization and Immigrant Voter Participation

Despite increases in the number of immigrants who have naturalized in recent years, the average time it takes to obtain citizenship is nearly ten years. According to the United States Citizenship and Immigrant Services (USCIS, formerly the Immigration and Naturalization Service, or INS), the time it takes all immigrants to naturalize has increased over the past 30 years. In 1965, for example, it took seven years for immigrants to become citizens but by 2000 it took ten years. In addition, not all immigrants naturalize at the same rates: in 2000, immigrants Europe, Africa, Asia obtained citizenship fastest (8 years), followed immigrants from South America (9 years), and North America (11 years).[9] The time it takes to become a "permanent resident," a prerequisite to apply for citizenship, can take even longer. Backlogs in processing applications and increased requirements—largely due to a host of anti-immigrant legislation, among other things—produce a cumbersome naturalization process that is significantly more difficult, time consuming, and costly than it was in earlier times in the U.S. In some parts of the country, the processing time for citizenship applications is over two years, and in twenty-nine of the thirty-three district offices of the USCIS the processing time is over one year.[10] In addition, the number of naturalization applications that are denied has risen, and many others are deterred from applying altogether.[11]

Still, the number of immigrants who naturalized rose from 6.5 million in 1995 to 11 million in 2002.[12] Several factors have driven up the number of immigrants who have naturalized and/or applied for citizenship. For example, one of the consequences of the Immigration Reform and Control Act of 1986 (IRCA) was that more immigrants became eligible for citizenship. About 2.7 million undocumented immigrants were legalized by this federal law and became eligible for citizenship by 1994. In addition, a host of anti-immigrant legislation at the federal and state levels led to an unprecedented number of applications for citizenship, because the legislation denied immigrants a range of public benefits from education and health care to public assistance. Sparked by Proposition 187 in California in 1994, several federal anti-immigrant measures ensued, including the Personal Responsibility and Work Opportunity Reconciliation Act of 1996 (the federal welfare reform law) and the Illegal Immigration Reform and Immigrant Responsibility Act of 1996. The latter allowed the federal government to deport legal immigrants for minor offenses, even if they were committed decades ago. By naturalizing, immigrants could retain access to social programs and be safer to respond to anti-immigrant sentiments and policy.[13] Over a four-year period—between 1996 and 2000—the number of new adult citizens rose by 30 percent.[14] The post–September 11 antiterrorist legislation—such as the USA PATRIOT Act—further stripped immigrants of due process and led to the detainment and deportation of tens of thousands of immigrants. Since 1996, a million immigrants have been deported. Taken together, they drove up naturalization applications and the number of new citizens.

As the foreign-born naturalize and the native-born children of immigrants come of age, their growing numbers increasingly make them potentially decisive players in politics. In 2000, 6.2 million new citizens were registered to vote and 5.4 million of them actually cast ballots. In fact, new citizens accounted for more than half the net increase in registered voters in 2000. In several immigrant-rich states, including California, Florida, New York, and New Jersey, new citizens comprised more than 10 percent of all voters.[15] In 2004, the number of new citizen registrants and voters was even greater. Although immigrant influence in electoral politics is growing, immigrant political power lags far behind their numbers. Even when immigrants do naturalize, they tend to vote at lower rates than native-born citizens. Variation exists, however, among different immigrant groups.[16]

The overall proportion of Latinos and Asians in the voting population is sharply lower than that of whites. In 2000, Latinos represented 12.6 percent of the total U.S. population but only 5.3 percent of all votes cast. Similarly, Asians were 4.2 percent of the population but cast only 1.9 percent of the votes. Whites, on the other hand, were 70 percent of the total population but cast over 81 percent of all votes.[17] Latino immigrants generally take longer to naturalize than Asian immigrants, but register and vote at higher rates than Asians. Foreign-born whites and Asians vote at lower rates than their native-stock counterparts, but foreign-born naturalized black and Latino citizens vote at higher rates than their native-born counterparts.[18]

The Representation Gap

Equally important, the number of Latino and Asian elected officials lags far behind that of other groups (particularly whites and African Americans). The largest group, Latinos, has a significant representation gap. Latino elected officials almost never exceed the percentage of Latinos who can vote. Although gerrymandering, racial bloc voting, and single-member districts may contribute to the representation gap, lack of voting rights for noncitizens is a significant factor. Figure 3.4 shows the gap between the proportion of Latinos and the total number of Latino elected officials in selected states, which are representative of other states as well.

This gap is also apparent in state legislatures. In these seven immigrant-rich states, on average 8.4 percent of Latinos are noncitizens, while only 5.6 percent of all non-Latinos are noncitizens. This might explain, in part, why Latinos only get 12 percent of the legislative seats on average (see figure 3.5), even though they are 22.1 percent of the total voting-age population.

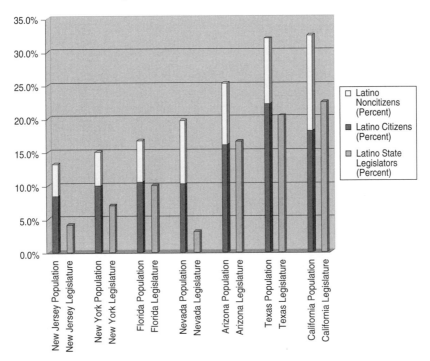

Fig. 3.4 Source: Census 2000 Summary File 1, Table GCT-P6, Race or Hispanic or Latino - 2000; The Council of State Governments, The Book of the States, 2004 Edition, Vol. 36, at 82 (2004); National Association of Latin Elected Officials, 2004 National Directory of Latino Elected Officials (2004). Data provided by Joaquin Avila and Chart produced by Ari Weisbard.

But the representation gap is nowhere more apparent than in the nation's largest metropolitan areas, the very places where new immigrant groups comprise significant and increasing proportions of the population (see figure 3.6). For example, as Mollenkopf and Logan point out, "Whites hold political office in both Los Angeles and New York City at far higher rates than their population share and blacks hold offices at about parity with their population or a little more, but Latinos and Asians hold much less representation than their population share. Indeed, their current level of representation matches their much smaller population share twenty years ago."[19]

The cumulative lack of political power—from few votes to few representatives—translates into fewer immigrant pathways to opportunity, worse socioeconomic conditions, and government policies that slight them.

Striking parallels exist for two additional large disenfranchised groups: the 4.5 million mostly black and Latino ex-offenders who are denied voting

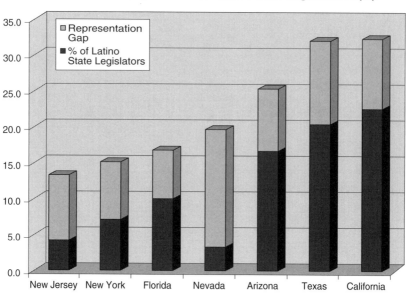

Fig. 3.5 Source: Census 2000 Summary File 1, Table GCT-P6, Race or Hispanic or Latino - 2000; The Council of State Governments, The Book of the States, 2004 Edition, Vol. 36, at 82 (2004); National Association of Latin Elected Officials, 2004 National Directory of Latino Elected Officials (2004). Data provided by Joaquin Avila and Chart produced by Ari Weisbard.

rights by state felony disenfranchisement laws; and the approximately 4.5 million residents in U.S. Territories who cannot vote in U.S. federal elections.

The Socioeconomic Status of Immigrants

Immigrants are disproportionately relegated to the lower socioeconomic order. One in four low-wage workers is foreign-born, and one in four low-income children is the child of an immigrant.[20] Despite the fact that immigrants work more than most other Americans—for more hours and often at two or more jobs—large numbers of immigrants and their families have low incomes, lack health insurance, and are food insecure.[21] "Immigrants compose an increasingly large share of the U.S. labor force and a growing share of low-wage workers."[22] Hourly wages of immigrants are lower on average than native-born citizens' wages by a significant margin; nearly one-half of immigrants earn less than 200 percent of the minimum wage as opposed to one-third of low-wage, native-born workers. In 2002, 22 percent—over one out of five—children of mixed-status

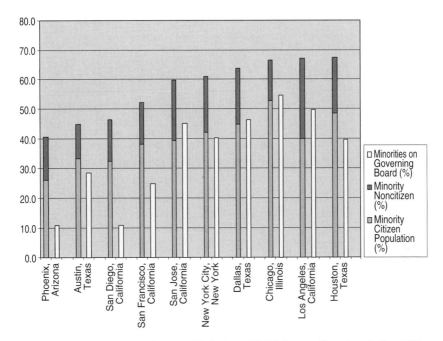

Minority Representation Gap in Ten Largest Cities (%)

Fig. 3.6 Source: Census 2000 Summary File 1, Table GCT-P6, Race or Hispanic or Latino–2000; Major City Websites; National Association of Latin Elected Officials, 2004 National Directory of Latino Elected Officials, Passim (2004); UCLA Asian American Studies Center, National Asian Pacific American Political Almanac, 2003–2004; Telephone Survey (Week of September 5–10, 2004) for Black Elected Officials (Includes Office of Mayor for Some Cities). Data provided by Joaquin Avila and figure produced by Ari Weisbard.

families lacked health insurance, compared with 12 percent of children with citizen parents.[23]

Yet, immigrants play a vital role in the economy and public revenues. The Cato Institute, for example, reported that in 1997, immigrant households in the United States paid an estimated $133 billion in taxes to federal, state, and local governments—from property, sales, and income taxes. The National Research Council of the National Academy of Sciences reported that typical immigrants pay an estimated $80,000 more in taxes than they receive in federal, state, and local benefits over their lifetimes.[24]

Contrary to popular belief, the majority of immigrants are documented, or "legal." As of 2002, approximately 12.2 million immigrants were "legal permanent residents" (35 percent) of all 34 million immigrants residing in the U.S.; about 9 million were undocumented immigrants (27 percent). The remaining 11.3 million foreign-born were naturalized citizens

(32 percent).[25] Thus, of the 34 million foreign-born people that currently live in the U.S., over 12 million *legal* permanent residents are noncitizens and are barred from voting—more than one-third. If we include "undocumented" or "illegal" immigrants, the number of noncitizens rises to 18 million, or nearly 60 percent of all immigrants.

Political Mobilization: Renewed Nativism and Efforts to Build Progressive Politics

The demographic changes have significant political implications, especially in the states and metropolitan areas where immigrants are concentrated. Six states are the home for the overwhelming majority of new immigrants—California, New York, Florida, Texas, Illinois, and New Jersey (in that order)—and within these states immigrants are concentrated in eight metropolitan regions: Los Angeles; New York City; Miami; Anaheim; Chicago; Washington, D.C.; Houston; and San Francisco. These immigrant-receiving states and locales, several of which now have majority minority populations, play an important role in choosing representatives for Congress—affecting the apportionment of seats in the House of Representatives—and hold critical electoral votes for the presidency. At the state and local level, where they make up a larger proportion of the potential electorate, immigrants can have an even greater impact. Emerging patterns of immigration are creating new political fault lines with the potential to alter the balance of social and political power. Immigration is changing the political arithmetic, propelling parties and politicians who jockey for advantage to adjust campaign strategies to reflect evolving electoral conditions. As immigrants naturalize and native-born children of immigrants come of age, their growing numbers increasingly make them potentially decisive players in politics. Yet a sizeable number of adult noncitizens remain locked out of formal political processes.

Demographic changes have prompted cross-cutting currents. On the one hand, there is intensified debate about the newcomers and a rising nativism, particularly after September 11 and the beginning of the War in Iraq. Consequently, conflict over U.S. immigration and immigrant policy has intensified, heightening tensions between contending social and political groups. Nativistic responses have led to legislation that restricts immigration and tightens border control as well as increases domestic surveillance, including rounding up immigrants suspected of criminal activity and a sharp increase in deportations. Legislation has been passed and/or proposed that limits illegal immigrants' access to drivers' licenses and a wide variety of social services such as education, health care, and welfare.[26]

On the other hand, we see a growing immigrant rights movement that has forged alliances with a broad range of social justice activists. Even while anti-immigrant sentiments have reigned in public discourse and policy, a mobilization among immigrant groups and their political allies is evident. Witness the proliferation of immigrant rights organizations that engage in a broad range of advocacy and activism and who build alliances with other groups on a range of issues, including labor, housing, education, health, welfare, and foreign policy. Immigrants lobby legislators and engage in protest politics with greater frequency and force. Indeed, labor unions, housing organizations, and welfare rights groups have reached out to immigrants where they have common ground and shared interests. For example, many such groups—spearheaded by labor unions—mounted an Immigrant Workers Freedom Ride in 2003 that sent busloads of immigrants from nine cities, then converged on Washington, D.C., and ended up with 100,000 marching in New York City. Inspired by the "freedom rides" during the civil rights movement, the planners hoped to focus public attention on immigrants' rights—particularly as workers—and show immigrant strength. Immigrant groups have also mobilized voter registration and get-out-the-vote efforts. In 2002, for example, Arab American groups registered 250,000 new voters and ran forty candidates (twenty-six of whom won).[27] In 2004, immigrant political mobilization reached new heights. Such activity reveals a growing sense among new immigrants that they possess legitimate claims on the American polity, and they are commanding greater attention. Yet, immigrant political power lags behind their numbers. Initiatives for immigrant voting rights flow from these trends. Essentially, they are seen as a pathway to political power.

As we shall see, several key characteristics are present in these campaigns to expand the vote to all residents of communities: demographic shifts propelled immigrant mobilization; proponents of noncitizen voting engaged in effective grassroots organizing, coalition building, and lobbying; and sympathetic politicians, mostly liberal Democrats, enacted or supported legislation. Opponents of noncitizen voting have been more conservative Democrats and Republicans, representatives of all political stripes who view noncitizen voters as a potential threat to their incumbency, community residents and groups that feel threatened by the influx of newcomers, and those who object on many other grounds, which will be described in the next chapter. In every case, immigrant voting rights campaigns have been highly contentious.

Now that we have looked at the history of immigrant voting and the contemporary relevance of this issue, let us now turn our attention to the arguments for and against immigrant voting rights.

CHAPTER 4

The Case for Immigrant Voting Rights

The cornerstone of democracy is the right of voters to elect the decision-making bodies of political assemblies at regular intervals. If the right to vote is to be truly universal, it must be granted to all residents of the territory concerned. . . . Universality, in the original sense of the word, would imply that all residents, irrespective of nationality, are included in the electorate.

—European Commission to the European Parliament[1]

The global push to confer local voting rights on all municipal inhabitants underscores the significance of similar efforts in the United States. As the world grows closer in terms of population mobility, capital investment, labor markets, cultural production, and high technology, it is imperative that we create political norms to make these processes of integration consistent with democratic values. The possibilities for exploiting displaced persons are too great if we make capital and labor mobile but political rights immobile. We cannot treat the world as a global economic village but define it as a collection of remote islands for the purposes of political participation. Eventually we may define a human right to democratic participation.

—Jamin Raskin[2]

The United States has long been a beacon of democracy to the world. In fact, the U.S. has prided itself as a promoter and protector of democracy, whether rightly or wrongly. Yet, Americans bristle at the reminder that "for over 80% of U.S. history, American laws declared most of the people in the world legally ineligible" to vote "solely because of their race . . . nationality or gender."[3] Although the civil rights movement swept away many of the remaining barriers to voting that buttressed white privilege and relegated African Americans and other minorities to second-class status, the rising tide of immigrants outlined in the previous chapter today again challenges the meaning and practice of democracy in America. The democratic ideal is challenged by the rising numbers of foreign-born persons who are not U.S. citizens, not only because they are excluded from participation, but also because they are all too often relegated to the lower social orders. Democratic notions of inclusion and equality, which were core goals of the civil rights movement, now appear in the form of a growing immigrant rights movement.

Contemporary campaigns for immigrant voting rights are part of the broader immigrant and civil rights movement. The effort to create a truly universal suffrage, which would include all members of a community, is one tactic in the struggle for human rights and to achieve economic and social justice. Toward these ends, immigrant rights' advocates utilize moral and political claims to achieve voting rights for noncitizens. In fact, advocates often employ many of the same moral and political arguments used in past struggles to expand the franchise to previously excluded groups, including blacks, women, and youth. There are three basic arguments: the social contract, in which a just government rests on the consent of the governed; discrimination and bias, which are often a consequence of being politically excluded; and the mutual benefits that would accrue to all community members who share common interests.[4]

Marta Tienda reminds us that democratic theorists such as Jean-Jacques Rousseau cautioned against the creation of "partial societies," where some members lack full rights, privileges, and obligations. To protect against the emergence of such partiality—and thereby inequities—Rousseau argued for democratic equity. Today, the U.S. is home to more partial members than at any time in its past, creating a crisis in our democracy. Because noncitizens do not possess the same rights, privileges, and obligations as citizens, reconciling immigrant rights and citizen rights has become "central to the project of democracy for the twenty-first century." Tienda convincingly argues, "As long as membership confers different rights to different groups, future progress toward reducing social and economic inequality will be stymied." Therefore, she concludes, "the diversification of the population warrants a realignment of democratic ideals with demographic realities."[5]

Opponents of immigrant voting raise several objections, including that granting voting rights to noncitizens would diminish the value and meaning of citizenship, reduce incentives for immigrants to naturalize, create divided loyalties, lead to less informed voters, skew the results in close elections, increase vote fraud, and affect contentious public policy issues. Even some immigrant advocates and civil libertarians worry that immigrants, particularly undocumented ones, would be further exposed and made more vulnerable if voting rights laws were not crafted carefully. And some African Americans and other minority groups worry that their hard-won gains in voting power and increased number of representatives could be diluted at a time they are reaching parity with whites in many areas and levels of governance.

There are no easy answers. Reconciliation of these contending positions seems impossible. Both sides present legitimate concerns and potent arguments. Still, deeper examination sheds light on the merits and flaws of the various claims and reveals much about the nature of the debates about immigrants and noncitizen voting.

The Arguments for Noncitizen Voting

The Social Contract

One of the basic tenets of democratic theory is found in the notion of the social contract: the legitimacy of government rests on the consent of the governed. Members of democratic communities are rightfully obliged to obey the laws they are subject to if they possess a means to participate in governance, such as by voting. Citizens consent to be governed in exchange for the power to select their representatives, a mechanism that can hold elected officials accountable to the people. The Founding Fathers enshrined this notion in the phrase "No taxation without representation," which provided a rallying cry for the American Revolution. This argument emphasizes the rights of all members of communities—including immigrants—in a democratic polity.

Early American notions of democracy were influenced by the political theories of John Locke and other social contract theorists, including Thomas Hobbes and Jean-Jacques Rousseau, who posited that individuals give up their natural rights in exchange for security and other social benefits. In the first instance, individuals move from a "state of nature" by agreeing to make a compact with each other to form civil society. In so doing, they collectively consent to grant personal rights to a political sovereign, a government, which insures their safety and other shared goods. This is the basis of a republic, a representative government, where the people give their rule-making power to elected officials who make decisions on their behalf. Of course, the people retain some individual rights and indirectly play a role in lawmaking by selecting representatives who make the rules. Although voting is a relatively crude instrument, it is a power that the people can wield to keep government responsive and accountable.

Although ancient democratic theory and practice, such as in Athens, Greece, maintained a sharp distinction between citizens and foreigners,[6] modern liberal democratic theory generally assumes that everyone has formal access to citizenship rights. In short, modern democratic theory posits that all members of a society have equal rights and responsibilities. When noncitizens are contemplated at all, liberal theory generally assumes that an immigrant who chooses to move to another country is implicitly consenting to be governed by the laws of that new regime. If the regime is based on democratic principles, noncitizens should have access to most of the same rights, privileges, and civil guarantees granted to citizens, particularly immigrants who are legally admitted. In other words, noncitizens should be more, rather than less, identical to citizens—except perhaps in regard to voting privileges, and naturalization would provide for those.[7] Again, the assumption is a mutual reciprocity between the government and the governed.

However, many liberal theorists do not adequately contemplate how real world differences in social group status can create second-class members. The historic struggles for political inclusion and equal rights of African Americans and women, including for voting rights, moved the society closer toward the ideal of equality. But political inclusion did not bring equal treatment and equal outcomes. Thus, African American men who were legally enfranchised after emancipation could be subject to segregation and oppression, women could be subordinated even after their enfranchisement, and poor and working people could be relegated to the lower social orders. Moreover, since not all noncitizens can become citizen members, liberal democratic theory and practice have been further confronted by this new reality, particularly since noncitizens—like other subordinated groups—affect citizen members of the host society: "Because aliens are a significant part of many contemporary political communities, their presence inevitably shapes the nature and practice of citizenship within."[8]

In the case of immigrants in a democratic polity, there are two typical answers to this problem. One is to draw a sharper line between immigrants and citizens. Noncitizens are not entitled to the same rights and privileges as citizens, it is argued, because certain immigrants are not eligible to become full citizen members of their host society. In the case of undocumented immigrants, their violation of U.S. law makes them ineligible for any such rights.[9] Even for legal immigrants, Peter H. Schuck (for example) identifies five exceptions to the principle of equity embodied in the Fourteenth Amendment, whereby a government is justified in differential treatment of citizens and noncitizens, including the following: legal residents are subject to deportation; legal aliens do not have as great an ability as citizens to have their relatives immigrate to the U.S.; and legal residents cannot serve on juries, vote, run for office, or be appointed to certain government jobs.[10]

Another answer moves in the opposite direction, which is to expand the equal protection principle and to adjust democratic norms to the new demographic realities. For example, Tienda argues:

> The citizen-alien distinction can be blurred because both citizens and aliens are entitled to representation in Congress [via apportionment], both are required to pay taxes, both serve in the armed forces, and both are bound by the same laws and obligations. . . . That states retain the authority to grant noncitizens the right to vote in state and local affairs is a socially meaningful way to fade the distinction between aliens and citizens. Some have argued that the citizen-alien distinction should be blurred because it is morally consistent with the values of equality and inclusiveness professed by a liberal democracy and because political participation in local affairs ostensibly can prepare aliens for statutory U.S. citizenship.[11]

Varsanyi also argues that "tacit acceptance of a disenfranchised, vulnerable and second class, working class is a direct challenge to justice in a democratic system." These scholars argue that a reconfiguration of the boundaries surrounding voting and citizenship is needed. Similarly, Aleinikoff and Klusmeyer argue, "Any discussion of the franchise for immigrants must consider the basic democratic premise that what concerns all should be decided by all . . . laws of democratic states apply not only to their citizens, but to all who live in the territory."[12]

Lisa Garcia Bedolla takes the argument a step further. She contends that liberal democratic theorists, like Schuck and Smith, who focus "solely on the actions and responsibilities of individual immigrants . . . ignore the role of the state, and state-sanctioned economic actors, in facilitating, subsidizing and making possible, migration." In fact, Bedolla argues, migrants have the "tacit consent" of powerful economic and governmental actors that benefit—even require—a cheap and pliable labor supply to fuel global capitalism, particularly guest worker schemes such as the Bracero program and President Bush's recently proposed temporary work program that allows immigrants to reside in the U.S. only for a limited period of time with no pathway to citizenship. Instead of viewing migrants as coming here on their own, which ignores "the web of economic interdependence that connects all of us," Bedolla views migration as the result of "structural, rather than individual, processes." Immigrants are important and permanent parts of our political community, she argues, and we have a reciprocal responsibility based on "moral obligations" for noncitizens whose presence is integral to the functioning of our economy and society.[13] Thus, noncitizen residents as a social class render "citizenship-as-rights" and "citizenship-as-status" problematic. A solution is to grant political rights to all noncitizens under a broader notion of citizenship as members of a society with standing so as to move toward integration, incorporation, and equal treatment.[14]

Immigrants themselves echo many of these ideas and sentiments. Take the case of Salvador Hernandez, an immigrant from El Salvador and a member of an organization called Centro Presente in Cambridge, Massachusetts, that promotes and supports immigrant civic activism: "My children attend the public schools, so I should have a say in choosing those people who oversee how the [sic] school system is run. Similarly, I have the responsibility to pay taxes, so why can't I have the privilege of contributing to how those taxes are spent?"[15]

Increasingly, we hear similar voices across the country. Berta Hernandez, a resident of San Francisco who has two kids (in the third and seventh grades), said, "I pay taxes and want to vote for school board because they make policy that affects my children's education. I want to have a say in my children's education."[16] Margaret Fung, executive director of the Asian American Legal Defense and Education Fund, contends, "These people should not be disenfranchised. If you're paying taxes, you should be able to vote. . . . They should have a voice about how decisions are made, especially on the neighborhood level where issues affect them directly."[17]

Some academics also concur. For example, Michael Jones-Correa of Cornell University says, "It's problematic for any democratic society to have a large portion of its population outside of political participation. It undermines democracy."[18] Similarly, Joaquin Avila of Seattle University School of Law argues that

> noncitizens have the same obligations as citizens and should therefore enjoy some of the same privileges. . . . A society's

interests are not furthered when a substantial number of its inhabitants are excluded from the body politic and have no meaningful way to petition for a redress of grievances through the electoral process. Such a continued exclusion from political participation is detrimental to achieving a more cohesive society. The ultimate product of such exclusion is a political apartheid.[19]

Indeed, federal, state, and local governments already treat noncitizens—both legal permanent residents and undocumented individuals—like other community members. The most obvious example is that all residents must pay income taxes regardless of their immigration status. In fact, contrary to popular belief, an overwhelming proportion of immigrants pay more in taxes than they receive in benefits (except refugees) and more than the average American, while contributing positively to the nation's economy on the whole.[20] Immigrant households paid an estimated $133 billion in taxes in 1997 to federal, state, and local governments—from property, sales, and income taxes—and the typical immigrant pays an estimated $80,000 more in taxes than they receive in federal, state, and local benefits over their lifetimes.[21]

Similarly, elected officials employ the same arguments to buttress their support of immigrant voting rights. "They're paying taxes, they're working, they're contributing to our prosperity. And yet they're not able to exercise the franchise," said Jim Graham, a Washington, D.C., councilman who introduced a bill in June 2004 that would allow immigrants to vote in local elections in our nation's capital.[22] California Assembly Member Leland Yee, who represents San Francisco, said, "America has a long and rich immigrant history and for its first 150 years allowed immigrants to vote, and even hold office. . . . It's time we got back to the true principles of our founding fathers, who encouraged democratic participation, knowing that newcomers would be further encouraged to put down roots, build a stake, and invest in local communities."[23]

Noncitizens have the same stake and interest in a community's political decisions and civic responsibility as that of any citizen. Like other citizens, immigrants tend to become involved and invested in their communities and the nation when given a voice and means of participating in social and political processes. Indeed, voting is an important means of becoming incorporated and engaged in a polity, not merely the outcome of becoming assimilated. According to this line of reasoning, the proper measure of membership in democratic communities is residency, not nationality per se.[24]

The main point—one that runs through all three arguments—is fairness. Vladimir Morales, a member of the local governing body and a leader of the campaign in Amherst, Massachusetts, argued, "Resident aliens own houses and businesses in Amherst, pay property taxes and send their children to school, but they cannot participate in the democratic process. We have a lot of citizens who pay taxes who make decisions for other people who pay taxes. . . . It's about expanding democracy."[25]

Similar arguments made in Cambridge, Massachusetts, led its city council to extend voting rights to resident aliens in 1999 and again in 2003, first for school committee elections and then for all local elections. "The true values of citizenship are not measured by a piece of paper but by actions that speak of personal responsibility. The vast majority of immigrants work, pay taxes, send their children to school, and worship in churches. They even die in wars defending a country that too often rejects and ignores them. In the recent U.S. conflict in Iraq the first casualty was a Guatemalan immigrant who was not yet a U.S. citizen, who could not vote yet was willing to give his life to this country."[26] More than 70,000 immigrants serve in the U.S. armed forces, where they represent around 5 percent of enlistees; among them, about 40,000 are "green card" soldiers who are not yet citizens.[27]

A sixteen-year-old daughter of an immigrant told the Cambridge City Council

> It's simply not fair that people who have lived here for so long, who have paid taxes and contribute to the community do not have a right to speak about their own children's education [speaking about her mother]. These people are constantly being affected by all the various laws that are being passed but are not allowed to voice their opinions at all. These are people who are part of the society and are influenced by changes made, whether in housing, taxes, or security. Therefore, they should be included in the process of making change. They live in the society and look upon it as their home. They certainly deserve a voice in how it is run.[28]

Not surprisingly, advocates draw upon American history in making the case for noncitizen voting. Kathy Coll, a Harvard University professor and a member of the coalition in Massachusetts, stated, "What we're doing is something that has a long tradition of inclusion and expansion of the franchise for all people that live in this country."[29] Similarly, New York City Councilman Bill Perkins said, "This effort is as American as apple pie. The tradition of expanding the franchise is one that has been seen over and over again in this country."[30] Perkins noted that, historically, "All they had to do was to get off the boat and they could vote. It's time for us to bring back that aspect of our democracy."[31]

Cheryl Wertz, the director of government access at New Immigrant Community Empowerment (NICE), a grassroots, community-based organization based in New York City, said,

> Democracy is, after all, about representation. The one in five New Yorkers who are disenfranchised are not a random one in five. It is not as though we were to disempower 20 percent of the people in this room. We are leaving out a very specific and targeted group of people—immigrants. As a direct result, there are issues that are not being discussed, and voices that are simply not being heard in City Hall. If New York City had a functioning democracy there should be vigorous debate in City Hall about multi-lingual city services, improvements in public education, funding for ESL classes, and a strong confidentiality policy that makes sense. But there is no public outcry for these services because noncitizen voices have been so effectively silenced.[32]

Cambridge City Councillor Denise Simmons addressed a concern that incumbent politicians of all stripes may have: "One could say, 'why would you vote . . . [to] give people the opportunity to run against you?' Because taxation without representation is not fair. These individuals [immigrants] who have entrusted us to educate their children, not so well I might add in a lot of instances, and this [passing the bill to extend the franchise to noncitizens] will increase their rights and responsibilities and contributions."[33]

All of these themes have been articulated by advocates in jurisdictions where voting rights were extended to noncitizens (such as Maryland, Chicago, and New York) and in places that are considering following suit (including Washington, D.C.; San Francisco; Los Angeles; New York; Portland, Maine; Madison, Wisconsin; Minnesota; New Jersey; North Carolina; and Texas).[34]

Bias

A second argument refers to discrimination and bias. Noncitizens are at risk of bias in majoritarian electoral systems because politicians can ignore their interests. Discriminatory public policy and private practices—in employment, housing, education, health care, welfare, and criminal justice—are the inevitable by-products of immigrant political exclusion, not to mention xenophobic political campaigning and racial profiling.

Foreign-born workers, for example, earned about 76 cents for every dollar earned by U.S.-born workers in 2000.[35] One in five children in the U.S. and, as mentioned in the previous chapter, one in four low-income children is the child of an immigrant; as also aforementioned, one in four low-wage workers is foreign-born.[36] Even though immigrants work more hours than most other U.S. citizens, an alarmingly large number of immigrants and their families lack health insurance and are food insecure. Children of immigrants are more likely to have poor health, lack health insurance, and lack access to health care than natives.[37]

Again, advocates of immigrant enfranchisement marshal standard democratic and civil rights principles for their cause. Noncitizens have legitimate interests in a community's political processes and need protections within it. As Jamin Raskin, a law professor at American University who led the successful campaign to enact noncitizen voting in Takoma Park, Maryland, stated, "If you can't vote, you tend to be disregarded politically. It [voting rights] has extended real visibility to a formerly invisible population."[38] In short, the problem is not merely that immigrants pay taxes and don't have the vote; the problem is that the U.S. is undergoing another nativist period that threatens the rights and civil liberties of immigrants who have no formal voice to protect themselves. Witness the violation of civil liberties evident in the arbitrary discriminatory detention of many mostly Middle Eastern and South Asian immigrants, the host of restrictionist legislation proposed and/or enacted at the federal level and in several states, the risking number of racially motivated bias attacks on immigrants, and the vigilante activities of "minutemen" in Arizona, California, and Texas.

Drawing a parallel between the presuffrage plight of women and African Americans and the conditions of immigrants today, one advocate for noncitizen voting rights argued, "We should think of voting rights as being connected to being free."[39] That is, groups can be more easily subordinated and discriminated against by depriving them of the vote, and, conversely, can attain greater freedoms when they possess the right to vote. The Campaign for Immigrant Voting Rights in Cambridge, Massachusetts, effectively used such arguments with politicians on the city council and in the state legislature to win their support for noncitizen voting rights. In advocacy materials they included documents such as the Nineteenth Amendment to the U.S. Constitution, which granted women the right to vote, and statements by various suffragettes. "Massachusetts has long been a leader in electoral reforms aimed at increasing civic participation in local elections. National women's suffrage leaders from Massachusetts included Susan B. Anthony and Lucy Stone. In 1879, forty years before the Nineteenth Amendment granted women the right to vote, women in

Massachusetts were allowed to vote in school committee, tax and bond elections."[40] Similarly, they point to parallels between the historic struggles for voting rights of African Americans (and other minorities) and those of immigrants.

Advocates for noncitizen voting also point to the Twenty-sixth Amendment, which lowered the voting age from twenty-one to eighteen: "A key argument on behalf of this amendment, ratified during the heyday of youth protest against the Vietnam War, was . . . that those who were old enough to fight were old enough to vote. . . ."[41] This time-honored argument about enfranchising classes of people asked to serve in the military should apply equally as well to 'aliens,' who have been subject, in various degrees to military conscription ever since it began during the Civil War."[42] Such tactics have been employed in nearly every campaign for noncitizen voting across the country, particularly since the start of the War in Iraq.

In San Francisco, immigrant rights advocates launched an initiative in 1996 that would have allowed noncitizens to vote in local elections, partly based on the discrimination argument. The immigrant rights movement hoped to place a measure on the ballot that would "create a movement around the real issues concerning immigrants: the need to include them and make them participatory of our society rather than the scapegoats."[43] This initiative grew out of an effort to fight the backlash against immigrants typified in Proposition 187 in California, which would have denied them access to public benefits such as education, health care, and so on. However, the San Francisco initiative met strong opposition and was never allowed to come to a vote. Then–Secretary of State Bill Jones fought the proposal to enfranchise immigrants, contending that it violated the California Constitution and arguing that "voting is a privilege open only to legal citizens, and that this initiative will increase incidences of voting fraud."[44]

More recently, however, Matt Gonzalez, president of the San Francisco Board of Supervisors, promoted the idea of immigrant voting when he ran for mayor in 2003, and in 2004 successfully introduced a proposal that appeared on the November 2004 ballot to amend the city charter to allow immigrant parents of children in the public school system to vote in school board elections.[45] A broad coalition of immigrant rights and civil rights advocates, lawyers, parents, youth, educators, community groups, labor, faith-based organizations, and elected officials formed an organization, A Voice for All Parents, to promote the proposal. One of their contentions has been that immigrant parents are slighted in school policy and that granting voting rights to parents of children in the public schools could help produce more equitable treatment and better education for all. Gonzalez argued, "Giving immigrant parents voting power will foster greater parental involvement in their children's affairs and heighten the likelihood that elected representatives of the district address their needs."[46]

A member of the San Francisco coalition argued that she—and other parents—should have a say in school policy.

> Parents are scared to engage with the school. The Board doesn't tell parents that schools don't collect Social Security numbers, or that parents don't need to be documented to come to school for their kids. I want a Board that values educating immigrant parents about these truths. And because the school system in other countries can be different, immigrant parents often don't know how to engage the school system. For example, immunizations are required for students for public school enrollment. Not only are low-cost immunizations difficult to find for noncitizen parents, but they often don't' realize they are even required, and children often stay at home for several days after school starts. The Board of Education has a responsibility to educate and integrate immigrant parents into the system. And I should be able to decide who those Board members are.[47]

Sergio Luna, an immigrant from Guatemala and a resident of Washington, D.C., supports the initiative there that would grant voting rights to legal permanent residents in all municipal elections because he believes it will lead to improvements in the city's struggling schools, where his son is a student, among other things. "If we have the opportunity to vote for the school board, the Council and the mayor, we'll be making some changes."[48]

"Voting rights for residents will help protect immigrants, give them better access to government, and make government more accountable," argues Bryan Pu-Folkes, the executive director of NICE, one of the leading advocates of the New York City initiative.[49] Cheryl Wertz, also of NICE, noted that there are many New York City Council districts that have a high percentage of noncitizens. For example, in "council member Hiram Monserrate's district, 45 percent of the population, or 72,000 of his 164,000 constituents, can't vote for him." Wertz noted that although council member Monserrate "is fantastic [and] does everything he can to represent the needs of all of his constituents in City Hall, not all New York City residents are as lucky. There are council members in changing districts that actively choose to represent the needs of voters in their district, to the detriment of their constituents. Fairness demands that those two groups should never be distinct and luck should never have a role."[50] Indeed, as Pu-Folks has argued, a neighboring city council district in Queens has been represented by council member Helen Sears, who has repeatedly voted for legislation that directly counters the interests and wishes of her noncitizen population, which comprises about 41 percent of her constituents. Pu-Folks argues that Sears's lack of responsiveness and accountability to her noncitizen members is a by-product of the fact that she can essentially ignore their interests without worrying of retribution at the polls, and he argues that the proposed legislation in New York City would make it difficult for representatives such as Sears to ignore the interests and wishes of noncitizen constituents.

Mutual Benefits

A third argument stresses the benefits that would accrue to other community members who have common interests. Working-class individuals and people of color—particularly in metropolitan regions—face many of the same problems that immigrants do, including discrimination in employment, housing, education, and so on. Common interests can forge common ground, reduce competition and strife, and enhance mutual understanding and cooperation. On the other hand, cultural differences, the struggle for scarce economic resources, and prejudice can breed intergroup conflict. Universal voting rights can provide a buffer against potential social strife or segmented assimilation. Alliances among competing minority groups in struggles for fair employment practices, living wage campaigns, access to affordable housing, and quality education have formed the basis of such effective coalitions. Noncitizen political participation could help strengthen potential alliances in electoral contests and public policy formation. Indeed, an enlarged electorate might have changed the outcome of some close elections.[51]

For example, San Franciscan advocates argued that parent involvement in school elections is beneficial to children and communities. Groups like Parent Voices worked to empower parents. Maria Luz Torre, founder of Parent Voices, argued that building parent leadership among immigrants is a good way to support parent accountability in education systems, and at the same time, immigrant parents should have an "opportunity to weigh in" on decisions affecting their children. "We ask parents to hold their youth accountable. And I train parents to better do this. Why can't we ask the same of our School Board, to be accountable to all of the parents in the District?"[52]

In this way, advocates contend that immigrants strengthen communities. Immigrants not only contribute materially but also enhance the quality of life in communities and add richness to neighborhoods. "Immigrants are very much a part of the fabric of [Cambridge, Massachusetts] and make it strong and healthy and wonderful place to live . . . who attend school meetings, who care about affordable housing, who care about strengthening our economy, who in fact participate in strengthening the economy . . . who want to play an active role. We need to do everything we can to encourage their participation in the electoral process."[53]

Immigrant voting advocates also make connections to global events and trends, which have local impacts. As Raskin notes, "While nationalism prevailed in defining citizenship for voting purposes in the earlier part of the twentieth century, the unification of national economies into a global market system at the end of this century undermines the salience of national identity and increases the historical importance of defining a citizenship of place and locality. . . . Wherever human beings find themselves living, they face the consequences" of globalization.[54] Globalization has unleashed new forces that push and pull people across borders, just as capital now flows more readily and rapidly, which in turn also creates new possibilities for cross-border activism.[55] Such global changes are redefining relationships between local communities and international actors and processes, including notions of citizenship and voting rights.

Debates about immigration often center on the actions and responsibilities of individuals rather than on the role of governments and government-sanctioned economic actors, which also facilitate, subsidize, and propel mass migration.[56] For example, U.S. guest worker programs have long drawn immigrants, especially from Mexico. In this way, American companies can use immigrant labor without granting them rights and privileges in the U.S. Similarly, changes to immigration law, which often reflect U.S. foreign policy and political considerations, affect migration patterns. The U.S. has allowed Cubans nearly automatic asylum since the Cuban revolution in 1959 and done the same for Nicaraguans during the 1980s, when the U.S. actively opposed the Sandinista regime, while refugees from El Salvador and Guatemala, whose repressive regimes were backed by the U.S., were generally often sent back. In fact, many of the latter groups have been long-term "legal" residents, have U.S.-born children (citizens), and own homes and businesses, but are now being brought into deportation hearings, in part due to changes in immigration law.[57] This is borne out in overall patterns of recent immigration regarding other countries and migrants, which has several main features: (1) the proximity to the U.S., (2) the penetration of the sending country's economies by the U.S. economy, (3) U.S. foreign policy, and (4) historical patterns of chain migration. Over a third of recent immigrants come from Mexico, Central America, Cuba, and the Dominican Republic; another 20 percent come from Asia, China, and the Philippines especially; Western Europe and Canada still send a significant number (more than 15 percent); while Caribbean countries and the former Soviet bloc send over 5 to 10 percent each.[58] These migrants are, in part, encouraged by the U.S., which rewards corporations and businesses that employ these newcomers in low-wage jobs to clean offices and homes, take care of lawns and children, prepare food in restaurants, and so on. At the same time, companies that invest in foreign countries also help produce mass migration by commercializing agriculture and industrializing cities in developing countries, which drives people from rural to urban spaces and into developed First World countries. Thus, increased interdependence and immigration, which characterize globalization, are as much a product of structural forces as of individual processes.[59]

Noncitizen voting rights advocates (and other activists) contend these global changes propel localities to respond to forces they are increasingly affected by, such as by pressing for basic economic and democratic rights, including voting rights for noncitizens.

> While the globalizing process is fraught with danger for local communities, a great many cities have taken the offensive by asserting their right to be involved in the conduct of foreign policy and govern the local effects of international relations. . . . One important example of such action in the United States is the grass roots movement to offer sanctuary to refugees from war-torn countries like El Salvador and Guatemala. The move towards local citizen voting can be seen as part of the trend of communities accepting responsibility for participating in the enforcement of global human rights norms. In this regard, Takoma Park, Maryland, which enacted noncitizen voting in 1992, was only following up on its earlier decision to make itself a sanctuary city. After securing Salvadoran and Guatemalan immigrants to live free from political persecution, it extended to them the right to participate in the political life of their hometown.[60]

Similarly, Cambridge, Massachusetts, made itself a sanctuary city before enacting noncitizen voting legislation. Cambridge had previously passed legislation declaring their city a sanctuary for refugees (particularly from Central America). Elena Latona, executive director of Centro Presente in Cambridge, Massachusetts, stated at a public meeting of the Cambridge City Council, "Cambridge has a proud tradition of protecting immigrants as evidenced by the fact that Cambridge is a sanctuary city and has already pronounced itself against the U.S. Patriot Act."[61]

Objections to Noncitizen Voting

Citizenship First, Voting Rights Second

Opponents to noncitizen voting raise several objections. The most common objection is that immigrants already have a means of obtaining voting rights: by becoming citizens. Rodolfo de la Garza of Columbia University and the Tomas Rivera Institute put it in typical fashion: "It's a relatively easy process [to become a citizen]. Immigrants should become citizens and then vote. Otherwise you create the possibility of people voting who have no stake in society. . . . I don't think it's a good thing to have immigrants voting immediately."[62] New York City Mayor Michael Bloomberg said that "the essence of citizenship is the right to vote, and you should go about becoming a citizen before you get the right to vote."[63] Representative Tom Tancredo (R-CO) asks, "Is it really too much to ask that American citizenship be a prerequisite for voting in American elections?"[64]

For many opponents, allowing noncitizen immigrants to vote would demean citizenship, blur the lines between citizens and immigrants, essentially make citizenship meaningless, and reduce incentives for immigrants to naturalize. Representative Tancredo, who rallied members of Congress in opposition to immigrant voting initiatives, continues, "One of the things that differentiates American citizenship from simple residency is the right to vote. The passage of this [D.C.] measure would not only blur that distinction, it would erase it."[65] Similarly, Daniel Stein, executive director of the Federation of American Immigrant Reform, a Washington D.C.–based organization that supports stricter immigration controls, put it in stronger terms: "No one should be given the franchise without taking the Pledge of Allegiance. If you divorce citizenship and voting, citizenship stops having any meaning at all."[66] Mark Krikorian, the executive director of the Center for Immigration Studies, a Washington group that favors greater restrictions on immigration, argues, "Extending voting rights to noncitizens eliminates the last distinction between people who have accepted permanent membership in the American people and those who have not."[67]

Cambridge City Councillor Anthony Gallucio opposed passage of a bill to extend voting rights to noncitizens on the ground that it would "diminish citizenship principles."[68] The American Legion and the Hudson Institute formed "an alliance" called the Citizenship Roundtable to halt "attacks on the citizenship process," which include "changing laws to encourage noncitizen voting."[69] In 2002, San Franciscans voted on a related issue: whether to allow noncitizens to be appointed to city boards, commissions, and agencies (known as Proposition C). The measure lost. Some contend that voters "believed it would remove any incentive for immigrants to become citizens."[70] Furthermore, it is argued, immigrants must earn the right to become citizens and vote just like previous generations. Such views and sentiments are routinely marshaled by opponents of initiatives to grant voting rights to noncitizens in local elections.

Stanley Renshon, a professor of political science at Lehman College, for example, wrote, "Voting is one of the few, and doubtlessly the major, difference between citizens and non-citizens. Citizenship itself, and open access to it, is one of the major unifying mechanisms of E Pluribus Unum. When citizenship loses its value—and it would if voting were not an earned privilege—a critical tie that helps bind this diverse country together will be lost."[71] At a public forum, Renshon elaborated that it takes time to learn about a society, and granting voting rights before "crucial political socialization" would not only cheapen citizenship but also damage it. The five-year waiting period for naturalization is a "reasonable amount of time to wait" to gain voting privileges. Like a relationship, there are different "degrees of commitment," and it is not unreasonable to ask and expect immigrants to wait and develop a deeper relationship to and knowledge of U.S. culture and politics.

Noncitizen voting rights advocates counter by pointing out that the relationship between voting and citizenship is a product of politics; it is not intrinsic. Historically, voting was not tied to citizenship, which is why blacks and women who were citizens could be denied the vote, and why noncitizen men could vote. For example, Cheryl Wertz (of NICE) argued, "The right to vote was not, and is not now, about citizenship. It is about who has a right to have a say." She points to the fact that only white men with property were initially permitted to vote, excluding women and people of color, who later fought their way into the polity. "It was only during the Vietnam War, when young men were dying in a war in which they had no voice, that people between the ages of 18 and 21 were able to get the vote. Who has a right to have a say is an evolving process and non-citizen voting in local elections is the next step."[72]

Opponents argue that the fact that noncitizens were historically permitted to vote traditionally "doesn't make it right." Take a look at why noncitizen voting was eliminated, opponents argue. Following the great waves of immigration in the late nineteenth and early twentieth centuries, the nation debated what it means to be an American. Our history evolved and so did our thinking and laws. The idea that voting should be tied to citizenship increasingly was seen as a crucial, "primal" link.[73]

Voting rights, advocates maintain, have much more to do with power. This is why they support expanding the franchise to include all residents of a community. Then those in power will not be able to relegate immigrants as second- or third-class status, much as women and blacks were treated. Historically, pseudo-scientific eugenics justified rampant xenophobia and nativism that flourished at the turn of the twentieth century and during World War I. Wars have often been times when the flames of fear are fanned and prejudice can be institutionalized, such as with the internment of the Japanese and the mistreatment of Germans and Jews during World War II; Koreans in the 1950s and beyond; Vietnamese, Cambodians, and Laotians who came from war-torn Southeast Asia in the 1960s and 1970s; Central Americans who came from war torn Nicaragua, El Salvador, and Guatemala in the 1980s; and Arabs and Muslims from the Middle East and Southeast Asia today.

As further evidence, advocates say, take a closer look at what objections opponents raise. First, opponents' rhetoric about how granting voting rights to noncitizens would dilute and damage citizenship—read, the citizenship of "real" Americans—reveals a veiled racism and anti-immigrant sentiments. It is not just about preserving the sanctity of citizenship per se; it is about making sure that American culture and values are not sullied by foreigners.[74] Second, consider the fears that opponents express about the possible political impacts of enfranchising noncitizens in elections. Many opponents perceive initiatives to grant immigrants voting rights as a cynical way of cultivating Democratic Party votes, since immigrants and minorities are often more likely to vote Democratic than Republican. Essentially, these opponents see these campaigns as plot to advance Democrats over Republicans and a liberal agenda over a conservative one. For example, Ira Mehlman, a spokesman for the Federation of American Immigration Reform (FAIR), which favors stricter immigration laws, said, "They see (immigrants) as likely Democratic voters. Clearly, their motivation is to get these people to the polls."[75] Daniel Stein of FAIR similarly characterized what the group perceives to be the underlying motivation for initiatives to grant noncitizens voting rights: "It's always interesting. The genesis of these proposals seems to be there are people on the city council who see a lot of people in their communities who would probably vote for them but aren't citizens."[76]

They may have a point, although it is far from clear how noncitizen immigrants as a whole will vote if given the chance. In fact, survey research shows that immigrants who naturalize and vote are hardly monolithic. Some groups, such as Cubans, some Asian groups, and many Arabs, have tended vote for Republicans. But these same groups—and other immigrant groups—have shifted their political preferences in some cases, depending on the election, candidates, time frame, and locale. Immigrants appear to be less attached to the parties and more volatile in their political preferences, which is not dissimilar to the voting behavior of much of the native-born electorate in recent times.[77]

Politics aside, advocates contend that the vast majority of immigrants do in fact intend to become U.S. citizens but that the naturalization process has become so cumbersome it acts as a barrier. Some analysts argue that the naturalization process has become so complicated that it is "a real instrument of exclusion and subordination."[78] Mario Cristaldo, who was born in Paraguay and has been a resident of the District of Columbia since 1994, said, "I invite anyone who says we don't want to become citizens to navigate the [immigration] system. It is not easy." Adding that foreign-born residents are "not going anywhere," Cristaldo argues that legal permanent residents should be able to "elect our council members, ANC commissioners, school board representatives and the mayor."[79] Similarly, Elena Latona presented the case of Jose Perez to the Cambridge City Council: it took "Jose Perez almost twenty years to become a U.S. 'permanent resident,' a prerequisite to apply for citizenship. Now, Jose must wait another four years to become a U.S. naturalized citizen. He is not the only one. At Centro Presente, we have at least 300 constituents that face the same fate."[80] Cambridge City Councillor Henrietta Davis said such facts proved decisive in her decision to support legislation allowing noncitizens to vote in local elections.[81]

The backlog of naturalization applications at the United States Citizenship and Immigration Services (USCIS) has been one to two years or more in recent times. In fact, such delays have increased since September 11 because of increased security and antiterrorism measures, shortage of staff and redeployment of staff for security work, and mismanagement.[82] As the 2004 presidential election approached, backlogs ranged from a low of six to seven months to over twenty-one months. For example, the Miami office of USCIS, which is now part of the Homeland Security Department, had a twenty-one-month backlog; in Arizona, it took thirteen months; and the 19-month backlog in New York was among the worst.[83] Some opponents of noncitizen voting acknowledge these problems but say the solution lies in reducing the backlog, not in enfranchising noncitizens in local elections.

Advocates maintain that these are not mutually exclusive goals and, in fact, that noncitizen voting is a pathway to citizenship, not a substitute for it. What noncitizen voting does, advocates contend, is to promote civic education and participation among incipient Americans. Gouri Sadhwani, the executive director of the New York Civic Participation Project, one of the groups that endorsed the campaign in New York City, argued, "In many ways, this prepares people. They start local, and then they become citizens and vote in national elections."[84] This logic is similar to nineteenth-century practice, when it was widely believed that noncitizen immigrants who declared their intent to naturalize should be allowed voting rights because it would encourage acquisition of knowledge about the U.S. and hasten integration and political incorporation. As Michele Wucker, a senior fellow at the World Policy Institute and a codirector of the Immigrant Voting Project, has argued, "Voting in local elections gives immigrants an unbeatable education in the American political system. There's no better preparation for eventual citizenship. We all benefit when new Americans think of themselves as full members of civil society."[85] Most campaigns for noncitizen voting rights employ this line of reasoning. For example, Angelo Ancheta of the Asian Law Caucus and one of the members of San Francisco's immigrant rights movement, launched in 1996, argued that allowing noncitizens to vote "would actually encourage people to naturalize and eventually vote in federal elections."[86]

In 1968, New York City granted noncitizens who were parents of schoolchildren the right to vote in community school board elections and to hold office on school boards.[87] Guillermo Linares, the first Dominican ever elected in the U.S. (initially as a New York City community school board president, and then as a New York city councilman), argued, "The parent–voter provision facilitates parents' ability to assist their children's education, strengthens families' ties to the U.S. and speeds integration of immigrants into the larger society." Such actions, he continued, "benefit the city" and "celebrate and assist the newest wave of immigrants, who are as vital to New York City's future as their predecessors."[88] Moreover, New York's school boards have been the most "representative" governmental bodies in New York City, in terms of race and ethnicity.[89]

In the end, advocates contend, granting local voting rights to noncitizens would not remove the many reasons that remain for immigrants to naturalize. These campaigns are for local voting rights; immigrants would still be precluded from voting in state and federal elections. Moreover, as Cheryl Wertz argued, immigrants "do not qualify for many government jobs, scholarships, or social service programs." Even legal permanent residents (i.e., "green card" holders) "can only spend a certain number of days a year outside of the United States. Depending on one's nationality, international travel may be easier with a U.S. passport." Noncitizens always face the possibility of being deported. Wertz concludes by pointing out that "none of these reasons for gaining U.S. citizenship will be at all diminished by allowing noncitizens the right to vote in municipal elections."[90] Similarly, Gregory Siskind, an immigrant rights attorney, lists ten reasons to become a citizen, one of which is voting, in addition to many of the ones mentioned above.[91]

*Divided Loyalties: Noncitizens Do Not Have American
Interests at Heart*

Another objection that opponents raise is that since noncitizens have not sworn a loyalty oath to the U.S., they cannot be trusted to vote in the best interests of this country. Opponents contend that immigrants will vote their own interests or those of their country of origin. Ostensible proof of an immigrant's commitment and loyalty to the U.S. would be their naturalization. Dual citizenship, which allow immigrants to vote in the U.S. and in their home countries, undermines "integration," "cultural coherence," and "loyalty."[92] Approximately one hundred nations allow dual citizenship, with some allowing migrants the right to vote from abroad. Critics of dual citizenship argue it diminishes loyalty to the U.S. "Every effort ought to be made to integrate legal immigrants into our national community. Yet, isn't it fair to ask that they know something about it before they fully take up the responsibilities, and not just the advantages, of what has been the core of citizenship?"[93] Critics of noncitizen voting contend that loyalty is a legitimate claim to make on newcomers, and the test for loyalty is immigrants' willingness to become U.S. citizens.

> Our Constitution begins 'We the people of the United States' not "We the inhabitants' or 'We the taxpayers' or 'We the consumers.' Our political institutions therefore ought to be reserved for the American people—citizens either by birth or by choice, joined in the common goal of forming a more perfect union. . . . Think of becoming a citizen as similar to getting married to America. The oath of citizenship even sounds like a wedding vow: 'I absolutely and entirely renounce and abjure all allegiance and fidelity to any foreign prince, potentate, state, or sovereignty.' Until he or she becomes a citizen, the immigrant and America are just living together, learning about each other before considering a permanent commitment. . . . Voting—in any kind of election—is the culmination of that process, not just a step along the way.[94]

But such arguments ignore the fact that people born in the United States are not required to swear allegiance to the Constitution. Not only is it flawed to assume that native-born residents are "loyal," but it is equally untrue that noncitizens are not "loyal."[95] This argument overlooks that immigrants are, in fact, already community members. A measure of noncitizen commitment and loyalty is evident in their choice of coming to the United States and, perhaps more tellingly, in their continued presence here. Noncitizens demonstrate their commitment and loyalty daily, such as in participating in voluntary organizations or opening a small business. To make their right to participate in the management of public affairs dependent upon renouncing citizenship to their home country—which might preclude their right to return or to hold property in their country of origin—amounts to denial of the latter rights. Given the magnitude of such consequences, including not seeing family and loved ones, many immigrants don't naturalize yet live in the U.S. for decades.

Advocates argue that the fact that over one hundred countries allow dual citizenship "renders moot the question of loyalty to either the source or the host country,"[96] just as naturalized persons ostensibly can maintain ties and loyalties to their home country but vote in elections in their adopted homes. Proponents of noncitizen voting further counter that "migrant workers are able to earn more money and better protect their rights if they are citizens of both their native land and their newly adopted homeland. A good citizen is one who participates in civic life, not one who merely feels patriotic affinity."[97] Ashira Pelman Ostrow notes that "dual residents are subject to local taxes and ordinances and are profoundly affected by policies that concern their second-home communities. Yet, in most states, individuals are prohibited from voting in more than one location through voting statutes that equate residence with domicile."[98] Ostrow argues that dual citizens should have dual resident voting rights, from both an "equal protection" legal standpoint as well as "normative arguments arising from the democratic tradition of government by the consent of the governed and against taxation without representation."[99] Finally, advocates argue, there is a double standard being applied. The U.S. sanctions and encourages U.S. citizens living abroad to vote in U.S. elections by using absentee overseas ballots, and many U.S. citizens vote as foreign nationals in their host countries' elections that permit noncitizen voting. These policies and practices are hypocritical, advocates contend.

Noncitizens Lack Sufficient Knowledge to Make Informed Decisions

Another argument that opponents make is that noncitizens lack sufficient knowledge of and feeling for American political institutions and issues to make informed voting decisions. "[N]o law bars non-citizens from learning democracy in civic organizations or political parties. No law keeps them from joining unions or speaking out in public forums. Indeed, no law bars them from holding positions of responsibility within all these groups. In all of these many ways, legal residents can learn about their new country and its civic traditions. Voting is not the only means to do so, and may not even be the best; it can be done from start to finish with the pull of a lever."[100]

But specific knowledge is not a prerequisite for political participation. If it were, many native-born citizens would fail tests of even basic political knowledge, as survey research has consistently shown. Moreover, such notions come dangerously close to those previously used to impose literacy tests, or to exclude or expel people on the basis of ideological beliefs. Opponents who argue that immigrants need time to become politically socialized are making the same kind of arguments that justified the exclusion of blacks and women from the vote: they do not know enough, we have to train them, and so on. Advocates decry these arguments as paternalistic. In addition, advocates contend that immigrants who would vote in local elections are not much different from citizen residents who move from one place in the U.S. to another—both would need to learn about the political system, candidates, issues, and so on of their new home. Whether it is a student who moves from Kalamazoo, Michigan, to Los Angeles; an artist who moves from Austin, Texas, to New York City; or an immigrant who moves from Cambodia to St. Paul, Minnesota, all will need to learn about the government, candidates, and issues of their new local communities. The point here is that opponents of noncitizen voting assume that citizens are capable of such learning but immigrants are not. Advocates argue this is a double standard that smacks of justifications to keep immigrants oppressed.

As Cheryl Wertz of the New York Coalition to Expand Voting Rights put it,

> I have also heard many times that immigrants don't understand enough about U.S. government or our electoral process to be informed voters. But let's be honest here, the vast majority of New Yorkers couldn't tell you what the Public Advocate does. So why do we have this double standard for non-citizens? Before the Civil Rights movement, the idea that African-Americans weren't informed about the electoral process was frequently used as an excuse to keep people out of the polls. We have ended literacy tests. Knowledge-based tests for inclusion in the franchise are no less reprehensible.[101]

In addition, most "education" on campaign issues often occurs in the few weeks and months before an election, not years prior, and is all too often done by the media and candidates anyway. Even conceding that political education has long-term components, it is not safe to assume that large differences would exist between the two populations. In fact, because noncitizens have chosen this country rather than been born into it, and are in the process of learning English and about U.S. culture, they often pay more attention to the events around them than many disaffected citizens do. Furthermore, foreign-language television, radio, and newspapers in many immigrant communities keep people up to date on politics here as well as abroad. If it is the politics of immigrants that opponents dislike or fear, that is a different matter, and one that deserves to be publicly debated.

Natalie Smith of the Campaign for Immigrant Voting Rights presented Cambridge city councillors copies of a U.S. naturalization form and citizenship test to illustrate how the federal government "holds immigrants to standards that most U.S. citizens are not held to. . . . Some say, 'you need to be here [in the U.S.] a while to see how it works.' But someone can come here [Cambridge] from Arizona and not be civically engaged, but someone can come from France and be very civically engaged, so that doesn't hold very much water. Some immigrants are better informed, educated, and care [more] about public affairs [than native-born Americans]."[102]

Noncitizens Could Influence Outcomes of Contentious Policy Debates

Opponents of noncitizen voting also argue that noncitizens would tip the political balance in a state or community by voting in their own interest. For example, noncitizens could vote to grant state public assistance to undocumented people, or permit bilingual instruction in the public schools.

While it may be true that many noncitizen immigrants might vote for such policies, native-born citizens also vote their own interests. Neither group, however, is homogeneous. It is not exactly clear how noncitizens would actually vote and what impacts they would actually have on the political balance of power. Indeed, this is an area that requires more research. There is some evidence about the voting patterns of newly naturalized U.S. citizens—as well as noncitizen voting in Europe—which suggests that only modest shifts, if any, would occur.[103] However, newly naturalized immigrants do tend to be more sympathetic toward other noncitizen immigrants than native-born citizens.[104]

What lies at the heart of opponents' concerns appears to be their objections to specific policies. Indeed, opponents' worries seem to be more about how immigrant voting will affect electoral outcomes and public policy. Essentially, what is at issue are questions about who will control government and whose interests will be represented.

Advocates counter by arguing that the enfranchisement of immigrant voters could invigorate electoral dynamics and produce a general increase in the democratic participation of all classes of voters. Indeed, social and political conflicts might be able to be worked out at the ballot box instead of on the streets. This was one of the arguments used in the Washington,

D.C., campaign for noncitizen voting, which began following riots in 1991 in the neighborhoods of Adams Morgan and Mount Pleasant, majority Latino neighborhoods.[105] City Councilman Frank Smith Jr., who represented Mount Pleasant, introduced a bill that would have allowed noncitizens to vote in municipal elections.[106] Similarly, New York's campaign to extend voting rights to noncitizens in the early 1990s came at a time when protests and rioting swept through Washington Heights, a largely Dominican community. These events propelled a twenty-four-member Task Force on New Americans in the Democratic-dominated New York State Assembly to introduce legislation that would have enabled municipalities to extend voting rights to noncitizens.[107] In the case of New York, a multiracial coalition of legislators and advocates sponsored the legislation. But interracial competition mired an effort to extend noncitizen voting rights in Los Angeles in 1992. In this instance, Leticia Quezada, the first Latina president of the school board in Los Angeles, proposed a bill that would have allowed noncitizen parents to vote in school board elections. Some African Americans opposed the measure, seeing it as a veiled attempt to expand her base. When a school board meeting was postponed, Latino parents threatened to pull their children out of school in protest.[108] The measure lost.

Granting Noncitizens Voting Rights Would Increase Election Fraud

Opponents of noncitizen voting contend that allowing immigrants to vote would open doors to electoral fraud. Critics argue that unethical immigrants or dishonest politicians might use corrupt voting practices to compromise the integrity of the ballot. Hearkening back to the historical period, where allegedly rampant electoral fraud was committed by political machines and new immigrants, opponents worry that such practices—from vote buying and selling to voting more than once—would return. In fact, concerns about immigrant voting fraud in the 2004 presidential election reached new heights, leading to unprecedented ballot security operations mounted by Republicans and Democrats and their allies.[109]

Logically, however, immigrants are no more likely to be bought or sold than citizens. Moreover, there is little hard evidence of voter fraud, both historically and contemporarily.[110] Furthermore, strong antifraud measures are already in place that can detect and deter fraud.

To be sure, there are practical administrative problems of managing the simultaneous registration and voting of different classes of electors while preventing potential double voting or other fraud. Jurisdictions will have to determine whether voters must provide identification at poll sites and/or during the registration process. Decisions will also need to be made about whether to restrict voting to legally admitted noncitizens who have been residing in a jurisdiction for a certain period of time (such as Amherst, Massachusetts, did, as opposed to Cambridge, Massachusetts, and towns in Maryland that extended voting rights to all noncitizens). In order to reduce the potential for erecting cumbersome barriers to participation—as well as costs and confusion—the fewer the distinctions made between classes of voters and procedures that are required, the better.

Thankfully, existing systems that allow noncitizens to vote illustrate the viability of such reforms. For example, Takoma Park, Maryland, allows all noncitizens—legal permanent residents and undocumented immigrants—to vote in local elections. Maryland's election administrators keep two separate lists: one for both citizens and noncitizen voters to vote in local elections; and a separate list for citizens to vote in state and national elections. Election administrators have developed two types of voter registration forms and use them to draw up the two different lists. For local elections—where both citizens and noncitizens vote—the clerks merge the two lists. In this way, the only people who know citizens from noncitizen voters are the election clerks. From the vantage point of an observer, all voters look the same. After a local election, however, noncitizen voter cards are removed from the voter lists and kept separately. Only citizens will appear on the voter lists for elections of state and federal offices. In Massachusetts, the city of Cambridge conducts an annual census. The city census form contains a box that asks whether the resident is a citizen or not. Advocates argued that the Elections Commission could draw up a list of noncitizen voters from this existing process.[111] They also argued such a mechanism would impose few additional costs. The Election Commission did not oppose this proposal, and it was approved by the Cambridge City Council on May 5, 2003. Voters would still have to register to vote—both citizens and noncitizens. To guard against possible fraud, the Elections Commission sends a nonforwardable mail check to registered voters to verify residency. If the form is returned to the Elections Commission as undeliverable, registered voters are removed from the voter rolls (within certain prescribed procedures and proper follow-up verification). Such mechanisms could be implemented in nearly all communities in the U.S. because election officials routinely send mail notifications to registered voters during an election year, which municipalities could expand to all residents with appropriate language and procedural changes. Europe also provides viable examples.[112]

Politics of Noncitizen Voting Campaigns

Which groups and political actors fought for and against such efforts? What factors contributed to distinct outcomes? Several key characteristics stand out in nearly every campaign: demographic shifts propel immigrant mobilization; proponents of noncitizen voting engaged in effective grassroots organizing, coalition building, and lobbying; and sympathetic politicians, mostly liberal Democrats or Green Party members, enacted or supported legislation. Campaigns for immigrant voting rights often emerge in conjunction with related struggles, such as for affordable housing, equal treatment, and so on. In some cases, grassroots mobilizations have raised the specter of potential challengers to incumbent politicians of all political stripes. In each case, granting voting rights to noncitizens was seen as an extension of active efforts to foster an inclusive and participatory democratic polity.

On the other side, opponents of noncitizen voting have been conservative Democrats and Republicans and representatives of all political stripes who view noncitizen voters as a potential threat to their incumbency, community residents and groups that feel threatened by the influx of newcomers, and others who object on other grounds described above. In every case campaigns were contentious and hotly debated. In the end, the divide comes down to who will hold power and have sway in policy making.

Immigrant voting is seen by advocates as one means to defend against nativist attacks and advance a progressive agenda. Immigrants' taxation without representation not only challenges the legitimacy of America's mantle of democratic governance and political tolerance, but also provides a rationale and foundation on which to organize progressive politics. Noncitizen political participation could help strengthen progressive alliances in electoral contests and public policy formation. For advocates, immigrant voting can give other minority groups greater means to forge winning voting blocs that can advance their mutual interests. Indeed, immigrant votes historically often accounted for the difference between the winners and the losers in elections.[113] Advocates hope to replicate such results today.

Of course, immigrant rights advocates are simultaneously pursing other avenues to advance such goals, including improving the naturalization processes and reducing the backlog of citizenship applications, advocating for dual citizenship, pursuing pathways to regularize the status of undocumented immigrants (such as the Dream Act or other proposals for amnesty), and struggling for a range of public policies that could improve the economic and social conditions of working people more generally. To be sure, these strategies and tactics are not mutually exclusive. Indeed, many see them as compatible and reciprocally reinforcing.

Just as the civil rights movement sought to extend the franchise to African Americans and others who had been barred from voting, a renewed movement for human rights would further extend the franchise to new Americans. As the U.S. population becomes more diverse, forging electoral coalitions beyond a "politics of black and white" and "black versus brown" will be necessary to achieve a progressive majority. To the extent this might be accomplished along working-class lines, racial and ethnic conflict could be mitigated. One step that could help forge progressive alliances is the establishment of a truly universal franchise, which would provide for noncitizen voting.[114] Benefits would accrue to all community members, particularly to communities of color, poor and working-class communities, and urban and metropolitan residents more generally. Underscoring the common social and economic interests that exist between such groups suggests a political agenda that could unite them, especially in the face of the present conservative reaction; growing economic, social, and political polarization; and the declining standards of living that an alarming and growing number of Americans face.

Making common cause among immigrants—and with other people of color, particularly African Americans—is crucial to forge a progressive agenda. Together they are, after all, the emerging working-class majority. Of course, invoking the need for working-class solidarity across racial and ethnic lines will not by itself overcome the multiple and significant challenges that progressives face in forging and sustaining such alliances. The palpable discomfort—and outright conflict—of African Americans with many of the newcomers who they perceive as undermining hard-won gains are no small obstacles.[115] Still, infusing immigrant issues as human rights issues into the ongoing work of real, effective, and sustainable multiracial coalitional efforts is a start. For example, groups working to restore the voting rights of ex-felons have increasingly teamed up with advocates of immigrant voting rights. Essentially, such groups are attempting to expand the franchise and increase the voting power of disenfranchised groups.

Creation of a truly universal suffrage could foster conditions conducive to forming progressive coalitions. Imagine the progressive political possibilities in jurisdictions with high numbers of immigrants such as New York City; Los Angeles; Washington, D.C.; and Chicago—as well as in such states—if noncitizens were re-enfranchised. Political parties and candidates—not to mention insurgent parties, factions, and contenders—would have greater pressure to be responsive to the issues and interests of these new voters. Just as labor has made overtures to organize immigrants, dominant political parties and candidates are increasingly turning their attention toward immigrants. It would be desirable for progressives to lead the way. Even if it turns out that most immigrants do not vote for progressive causes, it is a risk that progressives should be willing to take for democratic principles. For this and other reasons, advocates draw upon the civil rights tradition to advance immigrant rights, making noncitizen voting akin to a contemporary suffrage movement. Jamin Raskin, for example, argued a dozen years ago that "immigrant rights are the civil rights" of the day and "by that logic, noncitizen voting is the suffrage movement" of our time.[116]

By the same token, opponents object to what they perceive as a slippery slope: granting noncitizens voting rights in even school board and local elections would open the way to immigrant—and liberal influence—in other realms. Moreover, instead of closing U.S. borders and stemming the influx of the newcomers—particularly "illegal" immigrants from developing countries such as Mexico—which is one of the main goals of opponents who see such immigrants as diluting and undermining the essence of American culture and society, immigrant voting threatens to tip policy in the other direction. Indeed, some opponents see immigrant voting merely as a ploy by immigrant rights advocates to obtain amnesty and open the floodgates wider. Furthermore, they view such initiatives as an effort by Democrats to gain more votes and political power. This is the not-so-subtle subtext of opponents' objections: the unmaking of America by immigrants and the political challenge of liberals.

We now turn to the campaigns and places in the United States where noncitizen voting rights have been won, are being waged, and were lost, in order to further examine the people and politics of such initiatives.

CHAPTER 5

Contemporary Immigrant Voting: Maryland, New York, and Chicago

Today, noncitizen voting rights have been restored in several jurisdictions in the United States. Noncitizen immigrants currently vote in local elections in six towns in Maryland, in Chicago, and, until recently, in New York City. The laws and practices governing these places are explored in this chapter. We examine how immigrant voting became an issue in these jurisdictions, how immigrant voting rights were won, how the elections work in practice, as well as immigrant voter participation patterns and their impact. We begin with Maryland, the state that has the longest experience with immigrant voting in recent times.

Maryland

Six municipalities in Maryland permit noncitizens to vote in local elections: Takoma Park, Barnesville, Martin's Additions, Somerset, Garrett Park, and Chevy Chase Section 3. Most of these towns, all in Montgomery County, have allowed noncitizen voting for over a decade, some for several decades. More recently, there have been efforts to restore voting rights to noncitizens in several towns in Prince George's County. How did noncitizen voting get onto the political agenda in these towns? How was it won? Who fought for and against it? How does it actually work? What impacts, if any, has it had on elections and policy? Before addressing these questions, we begin by exploring the demographics and other background information that set the stage.

Montgomery County

In the past two decades, Montgomery County's population has grown considerably and diversified rapidly. The total population in 2003 was 918,881, and in 2000 it was 873,341, a 5.2 percent increase; from 1990 to 2000 the population grew by 14.5 percent.[1] The total foreign-born population in 2000 was 232,996 (26.7 percent) with 132,338 being noncitizens (15.2 percent). In 2000, the total Latino population in Montgomery was 100,604 (11 percent), and a sizable share of all Latinos were foreign-born, 81,911 (35.2 percent). Asians also comprise 11 percent of the total population in Montgomery County and an even greater share of the foreign-born at 38.3 percent. In addition, there is a large and growing immigrant population from Eastern Europe and the former Soviet Union (13.9 percent of the foreign-born population is from Europe), and from Sub-Saharan Africa (11.1 percent). Large numbers of noncitizens live in unincorporated parts of Montgomery County (called census designated Ppaces, or CDPs). For example, 28.6 percent (or 16,913 out of 59,140) of the total population over 18 years of age in the Silver Spring CDP is noncitizens, and 26.3 percent (or 11,385 out of 43,361) of the Wheaton-Glenmont CDP is noncitizens. The impetus to extend the right to vote to noncitizens in local elections in some Montgomery municipalities is due, in part, to this growing immigrant population.

State and Local Law

One of the factors that made it possible for noncitizen voting to be enacted and implemented is Maryland state law:

> Maryland cities and towns enjoy considerably more discretion in conducting their local elections than the State and counties. Each municipality promulgates its own election procedures through its charter, ordinances and regulations. . . . Under state universal registration law found in the State Election Code, a city or town resident that registers with the county also automatically is registered for municipal elections. A municipality may choose to use a supplemental voter registration list to extend the right to vote to municipal residents who do not wish to register with the county/ state or do not meet the state's minimum requirements. At least one municipality in Maryland, Takoma Park, allows non-U.S. citizens the right to vote in city elections.[2]

In addition, a municipality may choose to use a supplemental voter registration form to extend the right to vote to residents who do not wish to register with the county or do not meet the state's requirements.[3] If a municipality's charter allows for noncitizens to vote, they can register using a separate municipal registration form. The six Maryland towns used their charter powers to permit noncitizens to vote in local elections. The largest and best known is Takoma Park.

The Case of Takoma Park

According to the U.S. Census, 20.2 percent of the adult population in Takoma Park was noncitizens in 2000. Specifically, 2,652 were adult noncitizens out of a total of 13,123 adults; the total population was 17,299. Noncitizens are predominantly Latino, but include substantial numbers of immigrants from nearly every continent.

Takoma Park has a history of progressive politics. For example, in 1983 Takoma Park made itself a nuclear-free zone and in 1985 declared the city a sanctuary for refugees (particularly from Central America, including El Salvador, Guatemala, and Nicaragua). Leaders in these efforts—and in the noncitizen voting rights initiatives—have been liberals, progressives, immigrants, and civil rights advocates. Not surprisingly, the City Council has been comprised primarily of liberal Democrats. In these campaigns, advocates forged political alliances with key legislators. Many of the legislators that supported noncitizen voting framed it as an extension of a politics of inclusion and protection of civil rights. Some such legislators saw their own political destinies as linked to the plight of new immigrants, or at least felt a need to be responsive to mobilizations of immigrants that engulfed them.

How It Was Won A 1990 city census found large numbers of noncitizen residents in districts. When the Takoma Park Elections Task Force completed its 1990 city council redistricting process, it found that some of the wards—particularly new wards—had more eligible *voters* because some wards contained large numbers of noncitizens.[4] In other words, although each ward had roughly equal numbers of residents, there was an imbalance of eligible voters and therefore unequal political clout among wards.

In the course of discussion, Task Force members wondered if the city could grant voting rights to noncitizens. One of the Task Force members, Jamin Raskin, a law professor and advocate, researched the question and concluded that Takoma Park could legally allow noncitizens voting rights in local elections.[5] In addition, the Task Force consulted with City Clerk Paula Jewel about how the elections could be administered if noncitizens were permitted to vote, concluding that a separate municipal voter roll could be maintained distinct from the Montgomery and Prince George's County Boards of Elections voter rolls and that the additional administrative work and expense "would be within reasonable limits."[6]

The Task Force emphasized the difference between local elections and those for state and federal office: "[A] non-U.S. citizen resident of Takoma Park has just as much interest in how his or her garbage is collected and what level of police protection is provided to his or her home as a U.S. citizen has. Non-U.S. citizens live, work, own and/or rent property and pay taxes in Takoma Park, just as U.S. citizens do."[7] Based upon these conclusions, and the general sense that it would be "consistent with Takoma Park's historic commitment to activist democracy and its status as a Sanctuary City, the Task Force supports the concept of allowing all residents of Takoma Park, regardless of citizenship, to vote in City elections."[8] The Task Force, however, recognized that the issue would be controversial and recommended a question be placed as a referendum on the November ballot to gauge public sentiment.

The City Council approved a nonbinding referendum that read, "Should the Takoma Park City Charter be changed to permit residents of Takoma Park who are not United States Citizens to vote in Takoma Park elections?" The referendum, which was advisory, passed by 92 votes (1,199 to 1,107) on November 5, 1991. The city's six wards, however, varied in the proportion of total votes cast, along with those who voted in favor of the referendum and against the referendum. Ward 1, for example, cast 362 votes for and 276 against, while Ward 4 cast 91 for and 76 against. Three wards (3, 4, and 5) cast fewer total votes, in part because of a larger number of noncitizens who were not qualified to vote. Two wards (2 and 6) cast a majority of votes against, while a majority of voters in the other four wards supported the measure.[9]

Over the course of the next several months, two public hearings were held by the City Council to solicit commentary and to debate the issue. Not surprisingly, the debate was often heated. Citizen opponents raised several objections. For example, Margie Garey said that 368 people did not vote on the referendum and may not support noncitizen voting. She also noted that "an eligible alien may apply for citizenship" after five years of residency in the U.S. and could make a "conscious commitment to join in the political and social life of their community." She said the legislation would grant political power to people "who have made no commitment or legal ties to this country or the community." James Jeffas said his relatives became citizens, and based on his experience helping people become citizens, it was "a small effort to become a citizen" and to swear allegiance to the U.S. and "not to some other country."[10]

The referendum garnered attention from nearby Washington, D.C., and nationally. During the debate in Takoma Park, former INS Commissioner Alan C. Nelson denounced the initiative in a way that captured many of the objections voiced by opponents:

> In many countries of the world, an alien is always an alien. In our country, we are proud of our laws and social policies that encourage aliens of all races and cultures to become citizens. In recent years, however, an increasing number of aliens have not pursued citizenship. . . . This trend is disturbing, because it could seriously affect the assimilation process immigrants have pursued in this nation for 200 years. . . . This important value of becoming a citizen is lost if an alien can vote without becoming a citizen. Any legal resident alien can become a U.S. citizen in five years. That is not an unreasonable time to wait to be able to participate in our democracy. The five-year wait emphasizes the value of citizenship as a requirement to vote and to becoming a full member of the community. If local voting by noncitizens is allowed, state and federal voting could be next. Either there is a policy basis for noncitizens to vote, or there is not. If we open the door, it cannot be closed halfway.[11]

Similarly, the Federation for American Immigration Reform (FAIR), a Washington-based organization that lobbies to restrict immigration, spoke out against the proposal: "We see Takoma Park setting a bad precedent and we don't want it spreading throughout the country," said Robert J. Callahan, president of Prince George's County Civic Federation, which passed a resolution opposing any county municipality giving aliens the vote.[12] Similarly, Cameron Whitman, a representative of FAIR in Washington, D.C., said, "Many of those who [would be] given the vote are those who have broken the law of the country getting here."[13] Moreover, FAIR organized a postcard mailing to congressional representatives opposing the extension of voting rights to noncitizens. They reported sending preprinted postcards to their 100,000 members urging them to send the cards to their congresspeople.[14]

Alternatively, Takoma Park spurred advocates in other jurisdictions to seek voting rights for immigrants. According to Jamin Raskin, one of the leading advocates and scholars of the contemporary movement for immigrant voting rights, Takoma Park "was widely seen as heralding a new movement for local alien suffrage and immediately triggered similar efforts in Washington, D.C., Los Angeles, and New York City."[15] For example, a Washington D.C. councilman, Frank Smith Jr., who represents a large immigrant population (Ward 1), said he might introduce legislation that would grant noncitizens the vote in D.C. elections.[16]

Proponents of the measure presented several arguments in support. They cited democratic principals and historical precedent; emphasized that the measure was aimed at local elections, not state or federal elections; and brought attention to the large number and variety of foreign-born individuals who live in Takoma Park who would benefit from the legislation, and who also make myriad contributions to the community. The community as a whole would benefit from all members participating in local decision making. Advocates also pointed to neighboring towns in Maryland that allow noncitizen voting, including "Somerset, Barnesville, Chevy Chase Sections 3 and 5, and Martin's Additions—have for decades extended the franchise in *all* local elections to inhabitants who are not U.S. citizens."[17]

For example, Brian Hughes, a Canadian-born immigrant who said he has been a taxpaying home owner since 1975, supported the proposal.[18] Larry Drake wondered where Dr. Martin Luther King Jr. would stand on this issue, concluding he believed that "Dr. King would have supported this." Lael Parish, director of CASA de Maryland, a nonprofit organization in Takoma Park that serves the Salvadorian and Guatemalan communities, said the proposed charter change would well serve these communities just as the city's sanctuary law had. Henry Quintero of the Hispanic Alliance of Montgomery County said the Hispanic community has been criticized for not participating in the life of the city and that this law would provide an opportunity to establish civic education programs and therefore would help to make Hispanics an integral part of the political process.[19]

Colin Norman, an immigrant from the United Kingdom who came to Takoma Park in 1976 and is a writer for a science magazine, argued that he may be more a part of the city than other U.S.-born citizens who are more recent arrivals to Takoma Park. "I have as much interest in the community as anyone. We're not asking for a voice at the national level or in foreign policy. But in local matters, we're no different than somebody who has moved to Takoma Park from California."[20] George Leventhal, one of the organizers of advocates' Share the Vote Campaign, said he thought the referendum helped shatter stereotypes about noncitizens and instead showed them in their true light—hardworking neighbors who participated in their community.[21]

During the City Council debate, opponents simultaneously sought to block the law—and also to reverse similar laws in four other Maryland towns—by getting the state legislature to change the state law that allows localities to define citizenship and permit noncitizen voting. Opponents found a sympathetic legislator, Delegate John Morgan, who proposed a bill (HB 665) prior to the vote by the City Council of Takoma Park. But HB 665 was defeated. Similarly, opponents sought to reverse the charter change at the local level by trying to place a referendum on the ballot. But they failed to obtain the necessary number of petition signatures (468 out of the required 1,417).

Ultimately the City Council voted 5–1 to amend Takoma Park's charter to allow noncitizens (both documented and undocumented immigrants) to vote in local elections on February 10, 1992.[22] According to the minutes of the City Council meeting, one of the council members, Marc Elrich, said he supported noncitizen voting because citizenship is "not just a national phenomenon but a local one, and that the people who resided in this community were citizens of this community; they pay taxes, they send their kids to school and get involved in the community, and they do this no differently than any other citizen of this community." Similarly, another council member, Bill Leary, said he supported the resolution and that "3/5ths of the voters in Ward One" also supported the change. He said the action taken was a "modest step and will have modest and positive consequences." If his prediction turned out to be inaccurate, the council could reverse its action. The sole council member who voted against the charter change, Lloyd Johnson, said he opposed the resolution "because it would discourage people from seeking citizenship" and the city council should instead be encouraging citizenship. He also said "an individual could only be loyal to one sovereign." Mr. Johnson's constituents voted, on balance, against the referendum.[23]

The Takoma Park law took effect on March 31, 1992, and became "the largest and most recent municipality in the United States to adopt complete noncitizen voting. The move was widely seen as heralding a new movement for local alien suffrage and immediately triggered similar efforts in Washington, D.C., Los Angeles, and New York City."[24] Capturing the spirit of the day, Francine Hayward, president of the Takoma Foundation that serves Takoma-area neighborhoods, said,

> As a resident of Takoma Park, I've always been proud of—if at times bemused by—my city's efforts to implement its unofficial motto of "Think Globally, Act Locally." Here in the nuclear-free zone, we don't just worry about the big issues, we address them. For instance, in pursuit of voter equity, the city council approved a controversial measure to extend the voting franchise in municipal elections to noncitizens. Underlying this and other progressive stances by the city is an all-encompassing definition of "community." People in Takoma Park seek to include, not

exclude. And when it comes to inclusion, actions speak louder than words.[25]

Similarly, Raskin argued,

the people who have joined us on our land are generally here to stay, and the question today is whether they will be democratically integrated and assimilated into our political culture or kept apart as a disenfranchised and increasingly disaffected population. . . . The virtue of extending the vote in local elections to noncitizens is that it invites noncitizens to participate in, and learn about, American political culture and practices without immediately requiring the greater psychic break of surrendering one's given nationality. Presumably the taste of democratic citizenship that some aliens get from local voting will make them hunger for a greater role in our politics. If so, the practice of alien suffrage, sometimes derided as a threat to the naturalization process, can become once again, as it was in the last two centuries, a pathway to naturalized citizenship.[26]

How It Works: Voter Turnout   In practice, Takoma Park's noncitizens have exercised their voting rights in local elections. In general, immigrants register and vote at lower rates than citizens and comprise a much smaller portion of the total population: several hundred noncitizens are registered to vote but fewer actually vote, compared with U.S. citizen voters who comprise several thousand of the registered population, with around one to two thousand actually turning out to vote.[27] Over four municipal elections (1995, 1997, 1999, and 2001), noncitizen immigrants tended to vote at lower rates than U.S. citizens on average. Variation, however, exists between certain wards. In some wards, immigrants and citizens vote at comparable rates. For example, in 2001 in Ward 2, 22 percent of the registered U.S. citizens turned out to vote compared with 21 percent of the registered noncitizen voters in municipal elections. In the 1997 elections, noncitizen immigrants cast more votes than registered citizen voters in three wards: Ward 6, 38 to 22 percent respectively; Ward 5, 21 to 18 percent, respectively; and Ward 3, 31 to 29 percent, respectively. However, in 1999 and in 2003 immigrants voted at lower rates in all six wards.

There are several factors that contribute to voter turnout, including the level of competition in a race, the appeal of candidates (and whether a noncitizen candidate is running for office, which will draw a greater number of noncitizen voters), and various other activities that encourage voter turnout. No doubt September 11, 2001, and the passage of the USA PATRIOT Act affected voter turnout, particularly by undocumented immigrants. As one observer noted, ongoing education and mobilization are critical to immigrant voter participation. Importantly, immigrants can—and have—helped determine electoral outcomes, particularly in close contests.[28]

Election Administration

Administratively, Maryland's election administrators keep two separate lists: one for both citizens and noncitizen voters who can vote in local elections, and a separate list for citizens to vote in state and national elections. Election administrators have developed two types of voter registration forms and use them to draw up the two different lists. For local elections—where both citizens and noncitizens vote—the clerks merge the two lists. In this way, the only people who know citizens from noncitizen voters are the election clerks. From the vantage point of an observer, all voters look the same. After a local election, however, noncitizen voter cards are removed from the voter lists and kept separately. Only citizens will appear on the voter lists for elections of state and federal offices. Similar systems are in place for the other five jurisdictions that allow noncitizens to vote in local elections in Maryland.

Barnesville   Since 1912, Barnesville's charter allows noncitizens to vote for the three town commissioners if they have resided in the town for "six months previous to any town election and [are] eighteen years of age."[29]

Martin's Additions   Since 1985, a "qualified voter" is "any person who owns property or any resident of Martin's Additions who is eighteen years of age or older" and "who presently lives in Martin's Additions and has done so for the previous six months."[30] Noncitizens can vote for the five members of the Village Council.

Somerset   Somerset, a historic district of Chevy Chase, has allowed noncitizens to vote for over three decades, according to Mayor Walter Behr, who stated, "I'm delighted that we have it. It's the right thing to do. Aliens are just as interested in our parkland, our streets and our municipal swimming pool."[31] Somerset is an upscale community that is home to diplomats and other international personnel.

Chevy Chase Section 3   The charter states explicitly that noncitizens can vote: a qualified voter is "any person who is a resident of Chevy Chase

Section 3, without regard to citizenship, and is at least eighteen years of age. The Council may maintain registration lists of residents of Section 3 for use in local elections."[32]

Garrett Park   Garrett Park, a municipality that more recently voted to allow noncitizens to vote, provides another window into debates over the issue. In 1999, Garrett Park passed a resolution to allow noncitizens to vote in town elections. This led to a change in the city's charter that granted noncitizens voting rights.[33]

Prior to passage of the charter change, an advisory committee was formed to explore the idea of extending the right to vote in local elections to noncitizens. In July 1998, the committee sent out a "limited-circulation questionnaire" to solicit feedback. It also held a public hearing on February 4, 1999, and received written and oral comments about this proposal. On June 10, 1999, the eight-member committee voted to recommend to the Town Council to amend the charter to permit noncitizen voting.[34] The charter states that residents are required to meet the following requirements:

> (1) pledges to respect the Charter and the laws of the Town of Garrett and affirms a basic understanding of the English language; (2) is at least eighteen years of age; (3) legally resides within the corporate limits of the town . . ; (4) satisfies those substantive qualifications required by the state of Maryland which do not conflict with the qualifications specified in this Charter;[35] and (5) is registered to vote in accordance with the provisions of the Charter [essentially, a thirty-day residency requirement].[36]

No committee member was opposed in principle to allowing noncitizens to vote in Garrett Park, and discussion focused on proposals to amend the town's voter qualifications for both noncitizens and citizens.[37] Some committee members argued to include a pledge to "support and respect the Constitutions, Charter and laws of the U.S., the State of Maryland, and the Town of Garrett Park," but this position was not supported by other members and was not ultimately included. Some committee members argued that noncitizens be required to "defend the Constitution of the United States against all enemies" and to "bear arms or perform non-combatant services for the U.S. when required to do so." But committee members "agreed unanimously that these requirements would impose obligations out of proportion to the benefit granted." Another suggestion by some committee members was to require voters to affirm "a basic understanding of fundamentals of government in the United States and the Town of Garrett Park." But this was voted down because "it would be undesirable to prepare a civics-knowledge test and administer it to prospective voters."[38]

Advisory Committee member Jim Agenbroad suggested extending the thirty-day residency requirement, arguing that "30 days is insufficient time for new residents to familiarize themselves with the town and its electoral issues and candidates." When the chairman, Stan Benjamin, pointed out that an extended residency requirement beyond thirty days might be unconstitutional in light of U.S. Supreme Court rulings,[39] Agenbroad responded that this court decision might not apply to noncitizens. Nancy Floreen agreed with Agenbroad, but the other members of the committee did not and voted to omit the recommendation to extend the residency requirement.

The committee also considered how inclusive the law should be: that is, to include only permanent resident aliens (green card holders), a larger list of visa-permitted individuals, or all legal noncitizen residents. There was no support among the committee members to analyze the various visa categories and develop a criterion. Chairman Stan Benjamin suggested, as an alternative to ensure that tourists, business representatives, and other temporary residents could not vote, to require noncitizen voters to reside in Garrett Park legally for a specified minimum time (one year) following any town election in which they vote. However, several other committee members noted that such a provision "would not guarantee any voter's 'stake' in the community beyond an election," and that all residents are equally entitled to depart at any time. In addition, some argued that noncitizens with renewable visas might be unfairly denied a legitimate vote. The town could also withdraw the vote of long-term resident noncitizens whose time to leave eventually approached. Again, these committee members objected to adding what amounted to additional burdens to noncitizens. Most importantly, some members noted that the "legal residency" requirement would exclude short-term residents who could not or would not transfer their legal residency. In the end, the majority of the committee voted to "permit voting by all otherwise-qualified noncitizen legal residents, regardless of specific federal visa-permit, or immigrant category."

Rockville   Rockville provides a cautionary tale for advocates. According to Tom Perez, Montgomery County councilman, this is a "good case study of how not to move forward."[40] Soon after being elected in November 2001, Mayor Larry Giammo introduced the topic for consideration by the town council as part of a broader discussion about charter revision.[41] Opposition on the Charter Review Commission, however, was swift and strong, and opponents ultimately blocked his effort. Nevertheless, members of the Charter Review Commission initially agreed to look into the issue.[42]

Two factors appear to have been decisive in stopping the noncitizen voting initiative. One was that the proposal came soon after September 11. Indeed, the post–September 11 context cannot be understated. Everywhere immigrants were under greater scrutiny and attack, and elected officials were few who spoke out in their defense. The second factor was that Mayor Giammo did not do sufficient groundwork, particularly in reaching out to community groups who would be affected and provide support. "The advocacy side was nonexistent," noted Perez. "Larry is a good guy and well-intentioned," but he did not involve advocates early on. For example, Perez explained, "Latino organizations were not consulted." When opponents raised objections, advocates were not organized or prepared, and Mayor Giammo was left out on a limb.

At a September 2002 public meeting of the commission, for example, fourteen out of the twenty people who testified opposed noncitizen voting (six supported it). For some, it would be "one more nail in the coffin of citizenship," and is the "only privilege aliens don't have."[43] Some who spoke in favor of allowing noncitizens to vote argued that the citizenship process is unduly lengthy. For example, Ana Sol Gutierrez, the first Latino American in Montgomery County ever nominated as a state delegate, said, "People are not sitting back not wanting to be citizens. They're eagerly waiting for it. The process is extremely long. If you've never had to deal with INS, you have no idea how cumbersome and difficult it is."[44] Andrew Martin of East Rockville argued that noncitizen voting would "help create socially responsible people." Another supporter, Henry Quintero of the Latino Civil Rights Center, told the commission that aliens are "not 9/11 terrorists. These are hardworking people who are making roots here . . . and they're not going to go anyplace else."[45] But in the end, most of the commissioners remained silent on the issue or opposed extending voting rights to noncitizens.

Prince George's County   Partly spurred by the success of campaigns and practices in Montgomery County, advocates have more recently launched an effort to extend voting rights to noncitizens in all twenty-seven municipalities in Prince George's County, a county that possesses a greater number and proportion of immigrants and noncitizens than does Montgomery County. Nine towns have noncitizen populations that exceed 10 percent of the total population (over eighteen years of age): Riverdale Park (33.2 percent, or 1,593 out of 4,799), Brentwood (23.7 percent, or 491 out of 2,071), Edmonston (21.6 percent, or 146 out of 677), Colmar Manor (18.3 percent, or 165 out of 901), Bladensburg (17.4 percent, or 961 out of 5,529), Cheverly (14.2 percent, or 654 our of 4,612), Landover

Hills (14.2 percent, or 146 out of 1,027), Cottage City (13.3 percent, or 116 out of 870), and Berwyn Heights (10.1 percent, or 235 out of 2,336). Additionally, there are even larger numbers of noncitizens—and proportions in relation to citizens—in other parts of Prince George's County. The U.S. Census shows many of these individuals live in unincorporated areas (or CDPs). For example, the Langley Park CDP has 65.5 percent noncitizens (or 7,697 out of 11,754) and three other CDPs—Adelphi, Chillum, and East Riverdale—have 30 percent or more noncitizens (with over 14,000 out of 46,000 people over the age of 18).

A concerted push for this ambitious goal began at the end of 2003 by a group of diverse advocates—ranging from immigrant rights organizations to civic organizations, academic institutes, and other groups—and they have gotten favorable responses from many elected officials.[46] Among the leaders of this push is Daniel Jones, president of the Young Latino Leadership Council of Hyattsville, and the Democratic Collaborative, an international consortium of academic centers and civil society organizations based at the University of Maryland, College Park, as well as other organizations. Jones said, "Our goal is to get the immigrant population more involved and more civic-minded."[47] Similarly, Margaret Morgan-Hubbard, associate director of Democracy Collaborative, said, "Immigrants are homeowners and taxpayers, but they are not visible. Voting is a way of showing their voices and showing they have a stake in the community."[48] Advocates contend that noncitizen voting is seen as a means toward these ends. It has worked, they argue, in other nearby communities to the betterment of all.

Advocates have received favorable responses from a number of elected officials, including mayors. Edmonston's mayor, Paulette Horan, said she supports extending voting rights to noncitizens in local elections: "The people have a stake in the community and they should have a voice in municipal elections."[49] 21.6 percent of Edmonston's population is noncitizens (146 out of 677). Similarly, Colmar Manor Mayor Diana Fennell said that giving noncitizens the vote in local elections would allow government to better serve their interests because it is "a way for us to know who's there. How can we help someone if we don't know their needs?"[50] Of Colmar Manor's population, 18.3 percent is noncitizens (165 out of 901). Advocates are working with these and other officials to amend city charters to allow noncitizens to vote.

But other town mayors have been more equivocal or not supportive of the idea. Riverdale Park Mayor Guy Tiberio said that he thought a detailed study of the issue is necessary before he would support any change in their charter. Thirty-three percent of Riverdale Park's population is noncitizens (1,593 out of 4,799). Hyattsville Mayor Bill Gardiner said, "Expanding the franchise of municipal elections isn't as critical as increasing participation of all citizens in both electoral processes and community events."[51]

Jones acknowledges that this campaign faces challenges and will require extensive education and organizing. "It is a very long process. We know some people aren't crazy about the idea of having noncitizens vote."[52] For example, Hyattsville resident Stephen J. Noel Sr. spoke out against the initiative: "It's just ridiculous. Let them go out and get citizenship and become part of our system before voting. Some don't understand the system or the language."[53] In addition, organizers acknowledge that immigrants themselves might be reticent to participate, given the post–9/11 climate of fear as well as the mistrust of government that many immigrants bring with them due to the oppressive nature of some regimes in their home countries. For example, Benito Vazquez, an organizer who works in the Montgomery County Public School system (as a pupil personnel worker), said, "This mistrust is an issue across the board and it is not going to go away."[54] But he noted that "this initiative is not new and other communities have done it to better themselves."[55] More importantly, Vazquez continued, "This is a way for noncitizens to feel they can be full-fledged members of the community instead of just taxpayers."[56]

To address such challenges, Morgan-Hubbard said advocates would tap student groups and other college-related resources. Advocates have held community meetings, and have launched informational and educational campaigns on radio and television and through the distribution of various materials.

Jones also is leading a related effort to have Langley Park incorporated. Currently, Langley Park is an unincorporated area that contains a high number of immigrants. The U.S. Census shows that noncitizens comprise 65.5 percent of an area of Langley Park (the CDP), or 7,697 people are noncitizens out of a total of 11,754 individuals over the age of eighteen. Maria Cristina Chinchilla, the executive director of the Langley Park Hispanic Parents Committee, is organizing on both fronts: "It is important to note that the number of Hispanics has grown considerably. We have to really educate the community on these matters."[57]

At the time of this writing, no changes have been enacted but advocates continue to press for noncitizen voting rights in these jurisdictions.

Does It Matter?

Given the proportion of the adult population that noncitizens comprise, they have the potential to affect the outcomes of elections— particularly close and contested races—and apparently have. An astute analyst described one recent election where noncitizens could have made the difference: "In the recent Board of Education election, Valerie Ervin won the District Four seat by 12,260 votes. There are roughly 148,000 non-citizens in Montgomery County, enough to have changed the results. Under most U.S. laws, legal non-citizens, or documented immigrants with permanent residence in the U.S., are not allowed to vote. Some want to extend suffrage to resident aliens, while others still believe that only citizens should have the right to vote."[58]

We now turn to examine two large cities where noncitizens vote (or have voted) in school elections.

New York City

The establishment of immigrant voting rights in New York City has been part of the broader civil rights movement. As aforementioned, today's immigrants owe a great debt to civil rights and black power activists of a generation ago, who helped open U.S. doors to immigrants from all across the globe and in struggles for equal rights and social justice. In New York in the 1960s, efforts by civil rights activists to attain greater community control led to the decentralization of some governmental operations, which included the creation of community school boards in New York City. Not only could noncitizen immigrants vote in community school board elections, but they could also hold office.

In some neighborhoods immigrant voters helped elect—or block the election of—certain candidates. For example, in Washington Heights, a predominantly Dominican section of Manhattan, an active registration drive in 1986 brought in 10,000 parent voters—most of them immigrants—which contributed to improvements in the schools and in reshaping community politics.[59] Ultimately, this political mobilization led to the first Dominican ever elected in the United States, Guillermo Linares.

New York City Community School Board Elections, 1969–2003

During the civil rights movement and social unrest of the 1960s, New York passed legislation to allow noncitizens vote in school board elections. As part of demands for greater decentralized community control, New York City created thirty-two community school boards, each with powers to hire superintendents and principals, and with funding for programs (such as after-school programs). Noncitizen parents of children in the pubic school system—regardless of citizenship status (i.e., both "documented," or "legal," and "undocumented," or "illegal")—were granted the right to vote in school board elections. In addition, all citizen voters who were registered, regardless of whether or not they had children in the school system, also could vote in school board elections. Noncitizens were also eligible to run for and hold office on the community school boards.

New York City also extended voting in Community Development Agency (agencies that determine the distribution of millions of antipoverty funds) elections to noncitizens. These changes required changes to New York State law, allowing the city to implement the local legislation. Community school board elections were held every three years in May at a separate time from all other elections (held in the fall), and were jointly administered by the New York City Board of Education and Board of Elections.[60]

Voter participation in community school board elections ranged from a high of 14 percent of the total eligible voters (i.e., registered voters) in 1970 (or 427,110 voters out of 2,971,707 registrants), which was the first school board election year; to a low of 3.3 percent in 1999 (or 112,610 voters out of 3,342,168 total registrants), the last year when school board elections were held.[61] Turnout hovered at about 10 percent in seven out of the ten elections held, mostly in the first decade and a half. Although in general voter turnout declined over time, the 1993 election posted a 12.5 percent turnout rate that deserves analysis and interpretation. In addition, the subsequent decline in turnout—to 5.3 percent in 1996 and 3.3 percent in 1999—warrants explanation.

The 1993 elections were characterized by sharp debate about the introduction of a Rainbow Curriculum, to which social conservatives objected.[62] Both proponents and opponents mobilized constituents to participate in the elections, garnering some media attention. In addition, Mayor David Dinkins made $600,000 available to the New York City Voter Assistance Commission, a nonpartisan charter agency mandated to facilitate voter participation, to send a notification to all registered voters notifying them of their eligibility to vote, the location of their polling place, and the times the polls were open, and encouraging them to vote in the community school board elections. This was unprecedented and contributed to the spike in turnout in 1993.

By contrast, in 1996 and 1999, no voter notification or guides were mailed or distributed, and media coverage was virtually nonexistent. Still, overall voter turnout in New York City's community school board elections was comparable to that of other jurisdictions nationally.[63] Voter turnout also ranged widely among school districts. For example, in 1996, which posted a low 5.3 percent turnout (174,539 voters out of the 3,238,796 eligible registered voters), turnout ranged from 1,456 in District 7 to 12,245 in District 2.[64]

Noncitizen parent voters comprised a smaller but significant share of all votes cast in community school board elections. Parent voters could be citizens or noncitizens, though most parent voters were noncitizens. Regular (or "standard") voters were citizens registered with the New York City Board of Elections, who could vote in federal, state, and local elections (including school board elections). Noncitizen parent voters were only permitted to vote in school board elections. In 1999, which posted the lowest turnout of 3.3 percent (or 112,610 voters of the 3,342,168 eligible registered voters), parent voter turnout was 42,121 of the total votes cast (37 percent); in 1996, 73,024 parent voters cast ballots out of 174,539 total votes (41 percent); and in 1993, there were 65,716 parent voters out of 425,849 total votes cast (15 percent).[65]

No doubt, noncitizen parent voters helped determine the outcome of some community school board races. For example, parents elected slates of progressive candidates in the Lower East Side and in the Washington Heights sections of Manhattan that supported multicultural curriculum. Noncitizen parent voters would likely have been an even greater force if it were not for the registration and voting system failures of the New York City Board of Elections and New York City Board of Education, which resulted in voter disenfranchisement.[66]

In 1997, there were over 1 million children enrolled in New York City public schools with 469,680 parents. Of these parents, 29 percent were foreign-born noncitizens and another 11 percent were foreign-born naturalized U.S. citizens.[67] In 2005, there were over 1.1 million students in the New York City public school system (K–12, not counting public higher education). Currently, an even greater number of the parents are estimated to be foreign-born noncitizens.[68]

Mayors as different as Dinkins (D), Rudolph Giuliani (R), and Michael Bloomberg (R) expressed a desire to reorganize the school board system to give themselves greater control over the schools. After all, voters often held mayors accountable for school conditions and educational quality despite the fact that the control of the education system was in the hands of a Board of Education, which was composed of appointees made by each of the five borough presidents, and the community school boards. Eventually, Mayor Bloomberg prevailed on the New York State Legislature and Governor George Pataki in 2002 to reorganize the governance structure of the New York City school system, creating a Department of Education under mayoral control and eliminating the thirty-two community school boards. Thus, voting by noncitizens was eliminated in 2003.

In an effort to appease parent voters who were disenfranchised and community school board members who were stripped of their powers, Community Education Councils, better known as "parent councils," were established by the New York State Legislature. The eleven-member parent councils, however, have few formal powers, such as input over changes to school zoning lines. Members of the parent councils, who could be noncitizens, are selected by Parent-Teacher Associations or the presidents or officers of PTAs, and two members are appointed by the borough presidents. (One nonvoting member is a high school senior who is appointed by the superintendent.) Leaders of the parent councils became dissatisfied with the new structure, which they say is a highly centralized system in which Mayor Bloomberg and Chancellor Joel Klein "hold all the cards." Some council members complained that they have been denied access to schools, not been given access to schools' budgets or ID cards, and not been permitted to distribute surveys to parents, principals, and teachers. In response, council leaders formed an association to make parents and communities a credible force in running schools.[69]

Even before the demise of noncitizen voting in the community school board elections, advocates and some legislators in New York City and State considered extending voting rights to noncitizens in local elections (and, in one case, to state and federal elections), first in the early 1990s and again in the mid-2000s.

We return to these efforts in the next chapter, but first we examine noncitizen voting as it is practiced in Chicago.

Chicago

Similar to New York City school reform, Chicago school reform—and with it noncitizen voting rights—was spearheaded by civil and immigrant rights leaders. Reform of the school system began under the mayoral administration of Harold Washington in the 1980s, and noncitizen voting in school council elections was inaugurated in 1989.[70] Chicago public schools were a flash point of dissatisfaction for critics of the school system and the old regime. Numerous strikes over two decades rocked the school system. In 1987, a strike lasting nineteen days pressed Mayor Washington, the teachers union, and the state into action.[71]

Following the 1987 strike, an Education Summit was held—a mass meeting of about 1,000 stakeholders, including parents, teachers, children, academics, community and business leaders, and elected officials—that led to the creation of the Parent and Community Council, a fifty-four-member body charged with drafting proposals for reform. Latino leaders in particular pressed for the inclusion of all residents—not merely citizens—who would be eligible to vote and serve in the reformed school system. Essentially, they called for giving the Local School Improvement Councils, which allowed noncitizens to participate in an advisory capacity, greater input in real policy making.

Thus, the impetus to grant noncitizens voting rights in school site council elections came, in part, as a response to the growing immigrant population and immigrant mobilization, particularly by Latinos. In addition, there was recognition by officials that parental involvement helps improve educational outcomes. Illinois has a large immigrant population: 1.2 million are naturalized citizens and there are 1.9 million noncitizens, according to the U.S. Bureau of the Census. In Chicago, 16.4 percent of adults were noncitizens in 2000 (21.7 percent were foreign-born).

This coalition of parents, teachers, academics, business leaders, members of Harold Washington's administration, and other elected officials (including Mayor Eugene Sawyer, who succeeded Mayor Washington) successfully lobbied the Illinois Legislature to pass the Chicago School Reform Act of 1988. The act gave every school in the city a local school council—an elected body of parents, teachers, and neighbors—with control over principals' contracts and part of the school budget. The law changed the Chicago school code to allow all community residents and parents of children in schools, regardless of citizenship, to vote in school site council elections.[72]

Like New York City, Chicago's Board of Education has power to make general policy and budgetary decisions, and it also decentralizes control to local school districts. Chicago shifted down power further than in New York, to the school site level where nearly 500 Local School Councils govern (instead of thirty-two community school boards). "Local School Councils are the site-based management team of each school. Their primary responsibility is to select the school's principal, renew the principals' contract, approve the School Improvement Plan for Advancing Academic Achievement, and approve the school's budget for the school year."[73]

The Illinois school code defines eligible voters for each school center as "parents and community residents for that attendance center." Noncitizens are also eligible to serve on school site councils. Parents and community representatives are elected for two-year terms.[74] In fact, the new structure of representation gave parents and community members a majority. Teacher and student representatives are appointed by the Chicago Board of Education.[75]

Chicago's school council elections take place on "report card pickup day" in April every two years on even-numbered years. The elections are held at a designated attendance center. There is no preregistration required. Utility bills, bank statements, and pay stubs are acceptable forms of identification to establish residency and to qualify to vote. In addition, school officials keep track of guardianship through "alpha records" and can identify each child's parents through these records. Election judges verify residency within a school site by using a detailed map of school site boundaries. Community residents and parents serve as election judges and are trained by school election officials before the election. Both noncitizen community residents and parents are allowed to serve on the councils.

Voter turnout varies by year and local school. For example, in 2000, 143,466 voters chose among 7,288 candidates citywide. The average per school was 89 parents, 53 community members, 43 teachers, and 570 students (with about 13 candidates per school).[76] In some schools, parent voter turnout can reach several hundred voters. For example, according to Reverend Walter Colman, "over 900 mostly Mexicans came out to vote at Rudolfo Lozano School in one election." Colman contends that Latinos—including undocumented Mexicans—vote at higher rates than other groups. Why? "It is the only elections they can vote in." This was especially true from 1991 to 1995, when many undocumented immigrants became eligible to apply for U.S. citizenship following the 1986 Immigration Control and Reform Act. In other words, immigrants felt safer to come out and vote because they were no longer illegal. In addition, turnout has been higher in elementary school elections than in high school elections.[77]

What impact do noncitizens have in Chicago school elections? According to James Deanes, school site elections are driven by local issues, which are not necessarily immigrant issues per se. "If crime is an issue in a community, folks may mobilize around candidates who say they will address crime. If there is a need for a new school, then candidates who say they will press the Board of Education for a new school will generate attention. If a principal comes under criticism, then that issue may drive turnout" and election dynamics in that district.[78] However, these issues are important to all voters, including immigrants, and therefore can be viewed as immigrant issues along with questions of language access, bilingual education, and so on. Moreover, in close and contested races immigrant votes can be decisive in determining election outcomes and school policy.[79]

In 2004, when advocates in San Francisco were promoting an initiative that would have permitted noncitizens to vote in school board elections, opponents there raised the specter of noncitizens controlling school funds and setting policy by citing the example of Chicago. "According to a [Chicago] Board of Education spokesperson . . . it is possible that some school councils in a few Chicago districts may be completely controlled by non-citizens and foreigners."[80]

The Urban Institute estimated that there were about 340,000 legal immigrants in Illinois in 2002 that were eligible for citizenship but had not yet attained it. What if these individuals had voted? A recent state level initiative to promote citizenship drew attention to the political and partisan ramifications of this question. Many wonder about the political motivations of encouraging noncitizens to pursue citizenship or to advocate for extending the right to vote. As I have argued elsewhere, these two are not mutually exclusive but are rather complementary. Regardless, the struggle for noncitizen voting appears to be here to stay.

We now turn to examine this question as it applies to other cities and towns across the county, specifically by focusing on campaigns to restore immigrant voting rights in several large and medium-sized cities from coast to coast.

CHAPTER 6

Campaigns to Restore Immigrant Voting Rights: California, New York, Washington, D.C., and Massachusetts

Immigrant advocates in more than a dozen cities and towns from coast to coast are currently waging campaigns—or have recently waged campaigns—to extend voting rights to noncitizens in local elections, including in California, particularly San Francisco, Los Angeles, San Bernardino, and San Diego; New York; Washington, D.C.; several cities and towns in Massachusetts; Portland, Maine; Minnesota; Connecticut; Madison, Wisconsin; Texas; Denver, Colorado; and New Jersey. This growing movement to win universal suffrage is gaining momentum and garnering increasing attention. Moreover, the movement to expand voting rights is a global phenomenon. Today, more than twenty countries on nearly every continent allow resident noncitizens to vote at various levels in the host countries' elections.

I begin by chronicling the campaigns in California, then those in New York, Washington, D.C., and Massachusetts. I conclude with a brief description of other locales in the United States where noncitizen voting initiatives are underway or have recently taken place, and a list of the countries around the world that allow nonnationals to vote in their elections.

California

California is the most populated state in America and has the largest proportion and absolute number of noncitizens in the United States. According to a study by Law Professor Joaquin Avila for the University of California, Los Angeles (UCLA), Center for Chicano Studies Research Center, California had 4.6 million voting-age noncitizen adults, according to the 2000 census. That means that 19 percent of California's adult population, nearly one out of five, is a noncitizen.[1] Of course, the number of foreign-born individuals is even higher. But the staggering number of immigrants who are not eligible to participate in elections poses daunting challenges to questions about how the newcomers will be incorporated, socially and politically, and raises serious questions about the nature of democracy in California. How can a polity call itself democratic if one-fifth of the population is formally excluded from political participation?

Advocates of democratic reform, led by immigrant and civil rights activists, have repeatedly raised the issue of noncitizen voting rights in California. Over the past decade and a half, nearly a dozen proposals have been discussed, debated, and acted upon in San Francisco, Los Angeles, San Bernardino, and San Diego, among other jurisdictions in California. In this section we examine these initiatives, focusing on San Francisco's, the most recent and highly visible campaign. Although no noncitizen currently votes in California, these campaigns suggest that it may only be a matter of time before they do.

San Francisco

Known for its "left coast politics,"[2] San Francisco has been at the center of several progressive political movements. From historic labor struggles to the free speech and antiwar movements and 1960s counterculture, to struggles for civil rights and gay rights, San Franciscans have championed these and other honorable causes. The struggle for immigrants' rights is a more recent cause, which is part of all these efforts to, more broadly, achieve greater human rights and social justice. Of course, not all San Franciscans are united in these causes. Moreover, California has been the home to some reactionary politics—from the historic taking of Mexicans' homeland to the repression of the Chinese and internment of the Japanese, to giving rise to Richard Nixon and Ronald Reagan, to the virulent strains of racism and anti-immigrant agitation that mark the contemporary period.

One of the most visible and contentious examples of anti-immigrant initiatives was Proposition 187, a 1994 ballot initiative that denied undocumented immigrants access to health care and education.[3] Although it was never implemented because of a court challenge, Proposition 187 contributed to an intense national debate on immigration and led to the passage of subsequent anti-immigrant legislation by Congress. Three such bills were passed in 1996 and signed by President Clinton: the Illegal Immigration Reform and Immigrant Responsibility Act of 1996 (IIRIRA), the Anti-Terrorist and Effective Death Penalty Act, and the Personal Responsibility and Work Opportunity Reconciliation Act (welfare reform).

To immigrant advocates, this legislative onslaught revealed their lack of political power. But the controversy about the newcomers led immigrants and their allies to seek ways to fight back and increase their capacity to influence politics. Mass voter registration and mobilization drives—coupled with efforts to help facilitate naturalization—have been conducted on a yearly basis in an effort to elect sympathetic representatives and to make elected officials more responsive to their needs. In seven years after Prop 187 in California alone, more than 1.6 million immigrants became citizens. Civil and immigrant rights advocates, such as Maria Blanco, executive director of the Lawyer's Committee for Civil Rights of the Bay Area, observed that immigrants "saw the legislative process and initiative process as impacting their lives" and got involved.[4] Indeed, then-Governor of California Pete Wilson and other anti-immigrant Republicans suffered losses at the polls at the hands of these new citizens who "were forged in that moment."[5]

Noncitizen Voting Rights Campaigns Emboldened by these victories, immigrants sought to expand their political power further and launched initiatives to extend the franchise to noncitizens in local elections. In the early 1990s, San Francisco School Board President Tom Ammiano floated a proposal to allow noncitizens to vote for school board supervisors. Similarly, Eric Mar, a school board member, also raised the issue. Although the idea generated some discussion and debate, it did not lead to formal legislative action.

In 1996, the Immigrant Voting Rights Initiative proposed allowing documented (i.e., legal) noncitizen parents to vote in school board elections and for noncitizen community college students to vote for City College trustees. Spearheaded by then–City Supervisor Mabel Teng (later city assessor-recorder), Teng's rationale for the proposal produced compelling themes that would appear in subsequent efforts to enfranchise noncitizens.

> This proposal is intended to initiate a serious dialogue among all segments of our diverse community on the issue of voter participation and parent involvement, and to explore new options for increasing broader involvement in our electoral process. The

proposal deals with permanent legal residents. They should not be confused with undocumented aliens, temporary visitors or temporary workers. Permanent residents are just that: permanent and legal. They pay income, sales and property taxes. They have the same obligation as citizens to serve in the military, should the need arise. By enfranchising permanent legal residents, the education system will be more accountable to those families whose children attend school. It will benefit the school system, the children and our city. For our schools and community colleges to serve our city effectively, students and parents, citizen and noncitizen alike, must have a voice in the design and administration of public education. Immigrants value education for themselves and their children. Allowing them a voice in school board elections will only improve the quality of education. The right to vote has evolved since the founding of the United States. Once denied to African Americans, other minorities, women and those without property, the eventual extension of voting rights to these groups came only through the long process of Reconstruction and the civil rights and women's suffrage movements. Voting rights have become increasingly inclusive of the true diversity of our nation. San Franciscans should be proud to move voting rights into the 21st century.[6]

Teng's proposal, however, quickly drew criticism in the anti-immigrant post–Proposition 187 climate in California. For example, State Senator Quentin Kopp called the proposal "lunacy" and Secretary of State Bill Jones was quoted as saying the courts would likely strike it down as unconstitutional.[7] Teng countered that the proposal should be allowed to go forward to foster debate and discussion of the issue. She noted the proposal would enfranchise an estimated 50,000 noncitizens and was projected to increase the pool of registered voters by at least 10 percent. "These people work and pay taxes, and just because they have not passed the legal requirements for citizenship, we should not disenfranchise them. I think if these people start voting in school elections because of this legislation, they would also be motivated to become citizens so they could vote in other elections."[8] However, the city attorney's office, headed by Louise Renne, who opposed the idea, said it would conduct research about the legality of the proposal; but ultimately nothing was reported, and other issues—including legislation to protect immigrants from the 1996 welfare reform act and the city's moving to district elections from at-large elections—dwarfed Teng's proposal.[9]

The issue of immigrant voting rights, however, did not just go quietly into the night as Teng's idea seemed to be headed. Two months after Teng announced her proposal, the immigrant rights movement called for a broader initiative that would have allowed both documented and undocumented immigrants to vote in all San Francisco elections. Led by Carlos Petroni, the editor of the leftist newspaper *Frontlines*, the immigrant rights movement was formed in 1994 to fight anti-immigrant initiatives such as Proposition 187. The group's far-reaching proposal, however, met with even harsher and swifter opposition than did Teng's. The immigrant rights movement submitted text to the Registrar of Voters for a ballot proposal it planned to put forward. City Attorney Louise Renne challenged the measure in court even before supporters could gather enough signatures for the measure to qualify for the ballot, essentially to avoid even drafting a ballot summary for the proposed measure that advocates planned to use for a signature petition to put the proposal on the ballot.[10] Petroni responded by saying, "This is a violation of equal treatment of the law,"[11] stating that this was the first time in San Francisco's history an initiative was blocked at such an early stage. Julie Moll, then deputy city attorney, replied to the accusation that blocking Petroni's initiative was politically motivated, saying, "If a person doesn't satisfy any of these requirements [being 18 years of age, a resident of California, and a United States citizen], that person simply cannot vote," arguing these are constitutional requirements for voting.[12]

In addition, San Francisco Registrar of Voters Germaine Wong estimated that Teng's proposal would be too costly and would have no significance on regular election processes. Wong projected that it would cost an additional $125,000 per election if Teng's proposal had become law. Furthermore, Wong opposed Petroni's proposal because its cost, even if unknown, would be high, and argued that the money should be spent for education, not for noncitizen voting.[13] In short order, San Francisco Superior Court Judge William Cahill ruled that both proposals would violate the state constitution.[14] Thus, both initiatives were blocked and never reached the ballot.

Some observes believed that the immigrant rights movement's broader and bolder proposal came too soon and instead served opponents who worked to undermine the legitimacy of the notion of immigrant voting. Worse still, it may have burnt some of the political capital that advocates had cultivated around immigrant rights and civil rights issues. Regardless, the proposals were widely regarded as essentially dead and receded into the background.

The 2000s But immigrant representation was back on the political agenda in 2002 with Proposition C, which would have given noncitizens the right to be appointed to certain public offices (boards, commissions, and advisory bodies). Nevertheless, the measure was soundly defeated by the voters at the polls by a margin of 68.24 to 31.76 percent. This was due in large measure to a technical error in drafting the proposition. Prop C as drafted would have allowed nonresident noncitizens to be appointed to public office in San Francisco, which is illegal. This error became apparent to the League of Women Voters and some labor unions who opposed the proposition, pointing out that the proposition would likely be found illegal. Soon after other organizations, elected officials, and progressives of various stripes took a hands-off approach to Prop C. As a result, there was little organizing done to support Prop C. Indeed, postelection analyses led some advocates to conclude that another kind of campaign might have a chance of winning. For example, advocates took heart by noting that in 2002, the insufficient grassroots organizing and mobilizing for Proposition C led to its defeat. In fact, only a small proportion of all voters actually cast ballots on this measure (about 21,000 total votes out of over 225,000 total voters). Advocates believed they could reverse these flaws in a future campaign. Finally, Prop C came close in time to September 11, when anti-immigrant sentiment was running high, which also fueled Prop C's defeat.

In 2003, Matt Gonzalez, president of the San Francisco Board of Supervisors and a member of the Green Party, ran for mayor and proposed permitting noncitizens to vote in school board elections. Gonzalez's proposal, which was one of the planks of his mayoral campaign, specifically called for allowing parents who have children in the San Francisco Unified School District (SFUSD) to vote for representatives in school board elections. "Noncitizens with children have a vested interest in the state of our City's schools. They need to have a voice in how the schools are run and in how policy is set. As Mayor, I will push for legislation allowing noncitizens with children to vote in San Francisco School Board elections."[15]

Gonzalez, who was born to a Mexican-born mother and Texas-born father,[16] first heard about noncitizen voting in the 1990s from a fellow Green Party member, Rod O'Donnell, who said Americans can vote in municipal elections in his country (New Zealand). Since that time, Gonzalez was intrigued by this electoral reform possibility, which held potential power to transform electoral dynamics, and when he first got into office he endorsed noncitizen voting.[17]

During the 2003 mayoral election, the San Francisco Immigrant Voters Coalition, a nonpartisan group with over thirty community-based and immigrant rights organizations,[18] sponsored a forum where Gonzalez and other mayoral candidates—Supervisors Tom Ammiano and now-Mayor Gavin Newsom—expressed support for the measure.[19] At the mayoral forum, Gonzalez stated,

I think one of the most important things is to try to create an environment in this city that is different than what is happening in the state and certainly from what is happening in the nation. I've been a supporter of the minimum-wage effort, to raise the minimum wage, which would help immigrant workers. And I have been talking about expanding the right to vote to non-citizens in municipal races, specifically school board elections where folks in our community have children in the public schools and I think that would further democratize our society and would only benefit our entire community.[20]

Other mayoral hopefuls also supported the idea: "We have to allow noncitizen parents to vote for their elected officials in the school district," said candidate and City Attorney Angela Alioto. Tom Ammiano also expressed support—he had floated this idea in previous years when he was on the School Board—although at the forum he focused on a separate proposal that would allow immigrants to hold appointed positions on the city's boards and commissions (i.e., reviving Prop C, which lost in 2002).

Given the large and growing immigrant population in San Francisco, candidates for mayor could hardly ignore immigrant concerns. Still, in the post–September 11 environment, when immigrants were increasing under scrutiny and attack, championing immigrant causes was not automatic. Fortunately, a simultaneous mobilization by immigrants and their advocates for protection and advancement—partly in response to the anti-immigrant onslaught—provided cover and impetus for progressives to advance such initiatives. Immigrant activism took many forms in San Francisco. For example, several hotels and restaurants were accused of taking advantage of immigrant labor to manage their labor force, including using nonpayment as a tool to discourage union activities. Struggles around the minimum wage and day labor issues were also flash points for immigrant organizing. These and other struggles spurred on candidates like Gonzalez to champion immigrant causes and pointed to an opening to advance the notion of noncitizen voting rights.

Although Gonzalez would ultimately lose the closely contested runoff election for mayor to Gavin Newsom (by 52.6 to 47.4 percent), he and a coalition of advocates continued to work to advance legislation that would enfranchise noncitizens in local elections. They created another chance in early 2004.

Proposition F Initially, Gonzalez and the advocates focused on a legal strategy to pursue noncitizens' voting rights. After all, the last time the issue was raised, it was thwarted on legal grounds. They had to find a way to argue it was legally viable. Advocates consulted with a team of lawyers who developed a legal theory—and strategy—to move forward with a proposal. Legal advocates pointed to sections of the California constitution that give charter cities such as San Francisco authority to enfranchise non-citizens.[21]

Gonzalez and the advocates believed this relatively modest proposal—allowing only immigrant parents of children to vote in school board elections—was politically more palatable and feasible than the 1996 proposal put forth by the Immigrant Rights Coalition that would have allowed all immigrants to vote in all municipal elections. Moreover, the legislation contained additional provisions designed to mute potential opposition: the law would sunset in four years (after two school elections). In this way, advocates could argue that the city was embarking on an experiment, which, if deemed unsuccessful or undesirable, provided a mechanism to eliminate it.

Advocates believed the timing was right, or at least better, for this proposal. During the 2003 mayoral race, Matt Gonzalez gave immigrant voting rights greater public visibility and increased chances for informed debate. Coming off the heels of Gonzalez's near victory in the mayoral race, where the issue received generally favorable reviews and gained greater public attention, advocates saw the electoral coalition that Gonzalez forged as a potential vehicle to win immigrant voting. Legal advocates also believed they had strong arguments that would withstand any legal challenge and hoped the new city attorney, Dennis Herrera, would be more sympathetic to the measure. In addition, advocates calculated that the number of immigrants who naturalized had grown (approaching 25 percent of all foreign-born residents), comprising a greater proportion of the electorate, and that this larger number of eligible voters might vote in favor of the measure. Moreover, in early 2004, initiatives underway in Massachusetts, New York, and Washington, D.C., began to make national news, giving the issue greater visibility and credibility.[22]

Finally, the War in Iraq was souring and opposition to the Bush administration was on the rise, particularly in liberal cities such as San Francisco, and opposition to immigrants seemed to soften a bit, particularly in light of the mounting numbers of noncitizen soldier casualties in Iraq, which gave advocates further ammunition in the battle for immigrant voting rights. In sum, advocates felt they had a decent shot at victory.

The ballot proposal, if it had passed, would have made San Francisco the first city in California to allow noncitizens to vote in local elections. As proposed, the measure would not have taken effect until 2006 and also contained a sunset clause, which meant it would expire after four years (or two election cycles), unless the Board of Supervisors opted in 2010 (or after two elections) to continue the law.

Gonzalez said his concern about immigrant issues, particularly in the post–September 11 world (which put people in an ever greater defensive position), led him to gravitate to noncitizen voting as a proactive effort that could yield significant gains: "It's such a drag to be going to the ballot trying to stop another anti-immigrant measure. It's nice to get a foothold in California with this concept."[23] Gonzalez noted that although some expressed concern about the possibilities for a backlash against immigrants if San Francisco moved forward with noncitizen voting, he felt the measure posed few dangers and instead held the possibility for an important victory.[24]

On May 18, 2004, Gonzalez formally introduced a ballot initiative that would amend the San Francisco City Charter to allow noncitizen immigrant parents with children in the school system to vote in school board elections.[25] The political campaign then began in earnest. Gonzalez, other supporters on the Board of Supervisors, and a broad range of advocacy organizations held a press conference on the steps of City Hall to announce support for the proposal. The coalition of supporters stated,

> A significant portion of SFUSD's students come from immigrant households that currently cannot fully voice their concerns to the school district because they are not allowed to vote for board members. Gonzalez's proposal will remove this barrier and encourage greater parental participation, which studies have consistently shown is required for good schools. Allowing all parents to vote in school board elections will increase accountability and the responsiveness of the school district so that all parents will have an equal voice in addressing their children's educational needs. The proposal will also help integrate immigrant parents into our democratic culture, providing an entry point for greater civic participation.[26]

According to estimates derived from data from the U.S. Census and San Francisco Unified School District (SFUSD), about 37 percent of the San Francisco population is foreign-born and about 30 percent of all SFUSD students live in non–English speaking households. Moreover, a disproportionate number of children in the schools are immigrant children—though many of them are U.S. citizens—and their noncitizen immigrant parents are not able to vote for school board members, who are elected every two years. Advocates argued that allowing noncitizen parents to vote would give them a means to hold elected school board members accountable.

Mabel Teng, San Francisco's assessor-recorder who spearheaded the idea of noncitizen voting in school elections in 1996 and supported the 2004 proposal, said, "This initiative is about improving our city's educational system and educating immigrants in the democratic process."[27]

Alan Wong, a San Francisco student delegate to the Board of Education and a student at Lincoln High School, said, "While all children have the fundamental constitutional right to an education, immigrant students don't have a voice that advocates for their needs. By voting, our parents will become more invested in the educational and democratic process."

In addition, advocates argued the process to become a citizen is flawed and unduly burdensome. For example, Bertha Hernandez, an organizer of the Prop F campaign and an immigrant from Mexico working as a social worker who has two children in San Francisco public schools, argued, "Most immigrants are doing everything they can to attain citizenship, but face enormous and costly INS backlogs and bureaucratic red tape. It is unfair to ask parents to wait an average of 10 years to become citizens while their child goes through a school system."[28]

Eric Mar, a commissioner of the SFUSD, said providing immigrant parents the right to vote in school elections would make the school system more representative, responsive, and accountable to immigrant parents.[29]

Demographics   Demographic data of the city's population reveal a significant and growing immigrant population. In 2000, 37 percent (285,000) of San Francisco's total population (776,000) is foreign-born.[30] Of these individuals, about 16 percent—122,000—were noncitizens, with a majority being Asian (61 percent) followed by Latino (21 percent) and European (14 percent). Twenty-one percent—163,000—of foreign-born San Franciscans have naturalized. The latter group, which have the same general demographic characteristics as noncitizens, comprise a significant block of potential voters who all sides believed would play a significant role in deciding the fate of Gonzalez's proposal, should it reach the ballot. Whites still comprise a sizable group of the total population—about 43 percent—but San Francisco is a majority minority city in terms of race and ethnicity (see figure 6.1).

The immigrant population and racial and ethnic minorities make up an even greater proportion of the public school system, with whites comprising 9.6 percent of the total (see figure 6.2).

According to David Lee, executive director of the Chinese-American Voter Education Committee, Chinese Americans had mixed reviews of the

Ethnicity: City of San Francisco (2002)

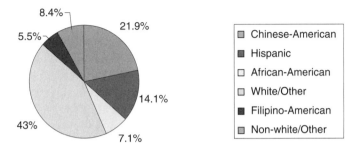

Fig. 6.1 Source: U.S. Census Bureau.

**Ethnicity of the San Francisco Unified
School District, 2003–2004 (%)**

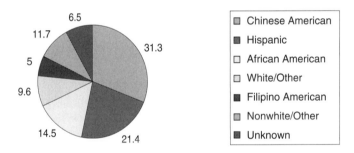

Fig. 6.2 Source: U.S. Census Bureau.

proposal.[31] Lee argued that Chinese American supporters of the measure are younger, are more liberal, and tend to be born in the United States. Lee claimed that opponents tended to be older, West Side homeowners who have gone through the naturalization process. Lee said that noncitizen voting might give more parents an outlet for protesting school assignments, even though many are already voters. There were, however, conflicting perspectives about how Chinese Americans would view the proposal. Although no hard data were available at the time, Latinos were generally believed to be more supportive of the proposal. As analysis of the vote later showed, a majority of both Asian Americans and Latinos supported Prop F, while only about 40 percent of whites did.

The Campaign   Advocates, who had been working in an ad hoc fashion, formerly convened a group in June called Parents United for Education, self-described as "a broad coalition of citizens, immigrants, community groups, labor, churches, elected officials and many others to pass Proposition F in the November 2004 election."[32] Eventually, they were able to assemble hundreds of supporters and dozens of endorsements.[33] As Matt Gonzalez put it, "Measures like this have to be won by broad-based coalitions, not just immigrants themselves."[34] But the process entailed many steps along the way, fraught with the potential to derail the campaign.

Indeed, even as news of the proposal spread, it was still not clear whether the proposal would actually reach the ballot. The proposal had to go through the Rules Committee of the Board of Supervisors, which held three public hearings, before it could get to the full Board of Supervisors for a final vote. The proposal needed to gain the support of at least six supervisors in order to place it on the November ballot, where the voters of San Francisco would ultimately decide whether to approve the measure or not. Initially, five supervisors—Matt Gonzalez, Tom Ammiano, Chris Daly, Sophia Maxwell, and Jake McGoldrick—sponsored the proposed charter change when it was introduced by Gonzalez on May 18, 2004. Thus, the quest for additional support was on and would be critical for its passage.

Public Debate: The Rules Committee   Public testimony before the Rules Committee of the Board of Supervisors was uniformly supportive. There were, however, a few concerns raised by some advocates that led to several amendments to the proposal. For example, Carlos Petroni, a leader of the 1996 immigrant rights movement initiative, argued that the definition of "parents" should be expanded to include "legal guardians" as defined by the SFUSD "to address [the] fact that often a relative—a brother, uncle, aunt, grandmother, sister, etc.—often take[s] care of kids and register[s] kids in schools."[35] Similarly, Renne Saucedo, director of the San Francisco Day Laborer Program, encouraged broadening the definition of "parent" to "caretakers," saying, "We just don't want to let anyone fall through the cracks."[36]

In addition, some advocates raised concerns about the sunset clause. Saucedo argued that advocates would have to fight the same "political battle again in 4 years." She contended,

> There will be sectors in the city who are going to find this very threatening because it not only is [the] first step in empowering

immigrant parents at [the] school board level, but this is the first step in granting voting rights to noncitizens in general elections in San Francisco. And there are going to be power groups who will not be happy with that. And I expect we will have a battle in 4 years. And who is to say we won't have [a] battle every 4 years as long as we have a sunset. I think the rationale behind the sunset clause makes sense; it's safer. However, we should promote legislation that does not have a sunset [clause] and can later review how it goes. If we have to negotiate it, fine. I just don't think it is necessary at this point.

She concluded, as did others who shared these concerns, by saying that "I can live with it, but I'm not crazy about it."[37]

Matt Gonzalez responded to this concern by saying, "Obviously I want to see this legislation pass. How do you put together a broad coalition and also win over communities that are on the fence; maybe with [the] sunset provision some might be more willing to vote for it. . . . I thought voters would be most likely to engage in what is essentially an experiment in our jurisdiction." If it is a successful experiment, Gonzalez assumed, "the Board of Supervisors would reaffirm legislation."[38]

Toward the end of the Rules Committee Hearing, Gonzalez moved that the proposal be amended by expanding the definition to include guardians (beyond just parents). In addition, Gonzalez asked the committee to amend the proposal's sunset clause so that the law, if enacted, would sunset after two elections or in 2010, in the event the measure was challenged in the courts and implementation was delayed,[39] something advocates anticipated opponents would try. Both amendments were approved and adopted by the committee.

Other people who testified at the public hearings spoke in favor of the proposed ballot measure, employing familiar arguments. For example, Elizabeth Milos, a U.S.-born child of Latino immigrants and a parent of a child in school, noted that in her years of experience she found that immigrant parents often hit brick walls when they try to advocate for their children. She said that immigrant parents must rely on other people's best intentions. But "the truth is they are not playing on a level playing field." Immigrant parents are subject to inequalities in education "from the dilapidated school structures to outdated books and a shortage of supplies," particularly in areas where a large number of immigrant children live. She noted that during

> every enrollment period disagreements emerge between different parents and different races and ethnic groups, many times pitting

immigrant communities against each other in a fight to get their children in more affluent west side schools. If immigrant parents pay taxes they should be afforded at least the basic right to vote for school board members to represent their interests and the interests of their children as well, and to be accountable to these parents where it really counts—at the ballot box. The reason I mentioned that I'm a U.S.-born citizen is I truly believe all children will benefit when all parents are involved.[40]

Wan Lin, a student who just graduated from Gateway Charter High School, noted that the population of students in San Francisco is about 51 percent Asian American and 21 percent Latino, and that many of these students come from families where English is not the primary language.

These parents should have input because different people and cultures have different needs, which includes different learning styles. So I think it is really important for our parents in San Francisco to have input; for us in San Francisco to increase democracy. An example: I have a friend in Galileo High School. A lot of times they send around notices about different issues, but only in English. He has to translate, but his English is not so good either so he has to have someone else translate. This just shows that a lot of parents are not being involved in child's education and don't know what's going on. In conclusion, though these parents are noncitizens they pay taxes, they fight in wars and they should have [the] basic right to vote for school board officials.[41]

David Chiu, a former immigrant rights attorney and one of the leading organizers of the coalition, argued,

There are numerous studies that show that parental involvement in schools improves the quality of education for everyone, and that is what this initiative is about. It's about bringing in those parents, the one out of three parents in S.F., bringing those parents into the process to help the system for everybody. Why has S.F. not seen the typical kind of anti-immigrant backlash seen in other parts of [the] country? Because S.F. is a city of immigrants. Immigrants come from all over [the] world and come from countries that allow immigrants to vote, such as Ireland, Israel, and the U.K. We are building a large coalition not just of immigrants, but of citizens; Green Party members and Democrats,

African Americans, and gays and lesbians, students, labor, and whites.[42]

In the end, the Rules Committee voted unanimously to support the proposal and sent it on to the whole Board of Supervisors for debate and discussion, and a final vote. News of the vote by the Rules Committee, which signaled the likely passage of the proposal by a majority of the Board of Supervisors (which ultimately voted on July 20 to support the measure), generated swift and fierce opposition.

Media Impacts: Media attention intensified during the days leading up to and following the July 20 vote by the Board of Supervisors to place the proposal on the ballot, fueling debate and shaping public perceptions. The views of proponents and opponents appeared in dozens of reports on a weekly and sometimes daily basis in print and on radio and television, garnering attention not only in San Francisco and the Bay Area, but also in many parts of California and across the nation. The themes highlighted in media reports framed debate and discussion over the ensuing months of the campaign and affected subsequent developments.

For example, ten days before the Board of Supervisors voted, Louise Renne, the former city attorney, claimed Gonzalez's proposal would violate the state's constitution, arguing it specifies that only U.S. citizens are eligible to vote.[43] As evidence, Renne pointed to a 1996 ruling by a San Francisco Superior Court and an opinion written by the city attorney's office when she was in office. Renne further argued that "citizenship is fundamental to voting" and created a stir by invoking the notion that terrorists would be able to vote: "If noncitizens can vote, can Osama bin Laden vote in a school election?"

Regarding the first charge—that the proposal was unconstitutional—lawyers for the advocates responded by pointing out that the home rule section of the state constitution grants special powers to charter cities (such as San Francisco) regarding elections. This reasoning was developed in legal briefs that advocates had prepared before the measure was introduced and the campaign began, according to David Chiu, a lawyer and lead organizer of the campaign. Other members of the legal team concurred, "We don't think it's clear cut. . . . Our sense is that if somebody were to look at this again in a school's context, this is not clearly unconstitutional," said Maria Blanco.[44]

Advocates also responded to Renne's charge that terrorists such as Osama bin Laden would be allowed to vote if the proposal was enacted. In a letter to Renne (and copied to all San Francisco Board of Supervisors and school board members), advocates said, "The comparison of law abiding school parents in San Francisco to Osama bin Laden was deeply offensive and disrespectful. Your statement substituted discussion of a genuine issue of civic participation with an appeal to base fears and prejudices."[45] This latter issue—inflaming anti-immigrant passions—which appeared over the course of the campaign in various forms was one that advocates repeatedly had to grapple with. Many opponents criticized the inclusion of "undocumented" or "illegal" immigrants. Advocates felt that the proposal should be broad and inclusive for moral and practical reasons, not wanting to create a two-tier status system within immigrant communities and society in general. They pointed to other jurisdictions, such as Maryland and New York City, where all noncitizens—regardless of status—were permitted to vote. Regarding concerns by immigrant advocates that undocumented persons might be exposed to scrutiny, detention, and deportation by the USCIS and Homeland Security by such legislation, Gonzalez said, "My thinking, and it sounds compelling from other jurisdictions, is that undocumented people generally don't come to city hall."[46] That is, they don't put themselves at risk and would not be put in jeopardy by enacting noncitizen voting that was inclusive of all immigrants. However, these views were not widely reported in the media.

More damaging news soon emerged on the legal front. A memo from the office of current City Attorney Dennis Herrera was leaked to the press that said the proposal would likely be struck down as unconstitutional if challenged in court. However, Herrera's memo noted there is precedent for supervisors to introduce questionable legislation or ballot measures that might overturn legal precedent. Furthermore, he said, "It is the prerogative of the city's elected policy makers to challenge the limits of the law . . . so long as there is a cognizable legal argument in support of their challenge."[47] Herrera did not take a position on the proposal, legally or politically; Renne continued to oppose the proposal on both grounds, despite being out of office.

The same day, Supervisor Fiona Ma announced her opposition to Gonzalez's proposal to allow immigrants to vote in SFUSD elections. "My position is one of principle. We should not be making special rules for certain segments of society. This would open up a Pandora's box of issues. Will we allow noncitizens who ride the BART [the Bay Area Rapid Transit system] to vote in BART board elections or noncitizen homeowners to vote in bond measures?" Ma also expressed concern that the measure was unconstitutional, saying it "completely oversteps the current democratic process."[48]

The next day, Leland Yee, a state assemblyman who represents part of San Francisco, said he would introduce a measure in the state legislature to change California's constitution so that noncitizens could vote, if the measure passed and was challenged in the courts. Yee cited his mother who spent nearly fifty years living in San Francisco working as a seamstress, paying taxes, and sending all five of her children to public schools, but did not have a say in school board elections because she never became a citizen.[49] Yee's proposal to change the state's constitution would be a longshot, requiring a vote of approval of a statewide ballot by the state's voters after a signature drive or two-thirds vote of both houses of the legislature.

Interestingly, Yee was a political rival of Ma. When Ma came out in opposition of the measure—Ma represents part of the same district as Yee and reportedly planned to run for state office and thus oppose Yee—the assemblyman took the opposite position. This appeared to be a case where, in part, taking opposite positions on the issue may have been bound up with having contending political interests. (Ma might later seek Yee's seat, and Yee might seek a Senate seat.) Moreover, Fiona Ma represents a district that has conservative elements. Some Chinese constituents, for example, believe people should become citizens in order to vote.

As the measure advanced, proponents and opponents strove to shape issues and perceptions in an effort to influence the outcome of the campaign. For example, a National Public Radio (NPR) program featured advocates and critics of Prop F. The first segment profiled Berta Hernandez. Hernandez said she is actively involved in her children's school, but she is often stymied: "Every time I have a question, have a complaint, have an opinion about it, I was treated with disrespect, even in San Francisco which is a liberal city. If I go and say something in regards to the classroom, it is like I don't exist. And I think that is because we have no political power, no political representation."[50] Also on the program was Matt Gonzalez, who argued, "Voting is about whether or not you allow people who reside in your community and who pay taxes to decision-make. We got this idea to try to empower parents of children in the school district to be able to vote in these school board elections. Many of those children are citizens. The question is, because they are not of voting age, they don't get to weigh in on those decisions affecting them. Their parents ought to."[51]

But opponents countered by arguing that voting and citizenship go together and should not be separated. Mark Krikorian, the executive director of the Washington D.C.–based Center for Immigrant Studies (CIS), argued, "The point is not that people should not participate—they should and we want them to—but they need to earn the right to vote by formally buying into America, by getting married to America, if you will, by way of citizenship, rather than just living together, which is essentially what getting a green card holder is doing."[52] This is one of the main objections raised by opponents throughout the campaign: the claim that voting and citizenship are inextricably tied and that allowing immigrants to vote would cheapen the meaning of citizenship. Further, Krikorian and other opponents argued, immigrants can participate in public affairs through other forms than voting, such as PTAs, and if they want to vote they need to become citizens.

One of the primary opponents of Prop F was SFSOS, a business-backed group founded by former San Francisco Mayor and current U.S. Senator Dianne Feinstein.[53] The day before the San Francisco Board of Supervisors was to vote on the measure, SFSOS announced it would hold a press conference the next day (the same day the Board of Supervisors would vote) at the Masonic Auditorium, where about 1,000 immigrants were to be naturalized, and issued an attack on the noncitizen voting proposal. "SF SOS views this [proposed charter] Amendment as an unfair slap in the face of those immigrants who dedicate their time and effort to become legal citizens, thereby earning the right to vote." SFSOS called the proposal an "irresponsible extension of voting rights" and noted the measure was opposed by prominent citizens, including U.S. Senator Dianne Feinstein, who said, "There is a legal procedure for becoming a citizen and allowing non-citizens to vote undermines the core of our democracy and discourages people from the very important step of becoming citizens." SFSOS called on members and the broader public to contact their supervisor and urge them to oppose the noncitizen voting measure.[54]

SFSOS emphasized a distinction that would become a focal point in the ensuing campaign: pitting hardworking legal immigrants who earn the right to vote by naturalizing against "illegal" or undocumented immigrants. SFSOS—and other opponents—framed the issue as one between "deserving" and "undeserving" immigrants, strikingly reminiscent of earlier debates about public assistance recipients. "Giving non-citizens (including illegal and temporary ones) the right to vote marginalizes the effort of those immigrants who go through the complete naturalization process."[55]

Dianne Feinstein focused her attack on several critical themes that framed subsequent discussion: "Allowing noncitizens to vote is not only unconstitutional in California, it clearly dilutes the promise of citizenship."[56] Feinstein said that "under no circumstances" should noncitizens be allowed to vote.[57] Feinstein believed that the initiative to allow parents with children in schools to vote in San Francisco school elections is a way to "get the camel's nose under the tent," which would likely lead to a push for expanding noncitizen voting rights to other elections and into other jurisdictions, and she feared it would open a Pandora's box.[58] Other opponents also worried that such measures would spring up elsewhere, particularly if Prop F was enacted. Moreover, opponents raised concerns that noncitizen voting could affect electoral outcomes. For example, Steve Camerata of the Washington D.C.–based CIS argued the San Francisco measure could lead to similar proposals at the state level or in other municipalities, and that it has "partisan implications."[59] These are serious—and legitimate—charges.

Some analysts and advocates argued these concerns lurked behind other stated objections lodged by opponents, whether by national groups such as CIS and the Federation for American Immigration Reform (FAIR) or by state and locally based opponents. Advocates contend that conservatives—of all political stripes, not just Republicans—are really concerned about losing votes and political power, if noncitizens were enfranchised.[60] To be sure, noncitizen voting rights represent an opportunity to advance progressive politics and pose significant challenges to opponents. For example, Sheila Chung, executive director of the Bay Area Immigrant Rights Coalition, said, "This is an exciting opportunity for cities across the country to really build a movement that recognizes that immigrant parents should have a say in their children's education."[61]

In point of fact, some advocates explicitly supported voting rights for noncitizens beyond school board elections. For example, Chris Daly, a member of the San Francisco Board of Supervisors, said he—like Gonzalez—would support extending immigrant voting rights to all San Francisco municipal elections, if the school board measure passed and proved successful.[62] Gonzalez said that "ultimately, we'd like non-citizens voting in all municipal elections" and that Prop F was "a starting place."[63]

Such explicit statements confirmed opponents' suspicions and fears. Clearly, advocates' efforts to build immigrant political power by enfranchising noncitizens directly ran counter to the efforts of groups that work to restrict immigration and limit immigrant rights. For example, the California Republican Assembly, a statewide group that lobbied effectively to recall Governor Gray Davis (D) and reverse the state law that allowed undocumented immigrants to receive drivers' licenses, said it would campaign to defeat Prop F. Mike Spence, the president of the group, said, "It completely undermines the citizenship process and blurs the line between citizens and people who are here illegally. There's a concerted attempt by what I like to call 'the illegal alien lobby' to give protection and privileges to people who have broken the law."[64] Opponents of the proposal said it was an outrage and claimed it would corrupt the citizenship process. For example, Mark Krikorian, executive director of CIS, said, "That kind of learning process, assimilation if you will, is something that has to take place as part of getting ready for citizenship. Voting is the end point." Krikorian disputed "the idea that this is a harmless measure."[65]

Debate by the Board of Supervisors: The Birth of Proposition F In the end, nine of the eleven supervisors on the board voted in favor of the measure on July 20, 2004, which became Proposition F. Only two opposed it,

Supervisors Hall and Ma (Tony Hall is the only non-Democrat on the Board of Supervisors and is generally characterized as "conservative"). The rationale expressed by the members of the Board of Supervisors in explaining their vote also reflected themes that manifested in public debate over the course of the campaign.

For example, Supervisor Fiona Ma (District 4), who voted to oppose the proposal, said that although she believes that the SFUSD needs to be improved, "expanding voting rights to noncitizens does nothing to further those ends."[66] Ma said her position on the issue emanates from a place of "principle."

> I think that when we make special exceptions for certain segments of the society in terms of voting we are going down a slippery slope . . . [can] noncitizens who own homes can vote for bond measures because those are issues that affect them; or noncitizens who attend one of our community colleges, they should be allowed to vote for Community College Board? I think when we make exceptions it opens up a slippery slope.[67]

In addition, Ma made an argument that advocates again and again came up against (and in every jurisdiction in the country): "I believe that voting should be an honor and privilege of citizenship. I value that highly and I think many other people do as well."[68]

Ma also expressed concern about the constitutionality of the proposal, another theme that arose throughout the campaign. While advocates claimed the proposal would stand a legal challenge, Ma and others believe that the "state constitution is very clear"[69] in limiting voting to U.S. citizens.

Other supervisors spoke in favor of the measure. Supervisor Bevan Dufty (District 8) highlighted America's immigrant past, recalling that his mother came to the U.S. "stateless," having no homeland to return to, but was eventually able to become a U.S. citizen. Dufty noted that although we are "a nation largely of immigrants, we're hypocritical." He said we "allow folks to come in but to work in low wage sectors. Now we want to close [the] door." He concluded by saying he feels that the proposal to extend voting rights to immigrant parents in school board elections "is fundamentally American."[70]

For Supervisor Michela Alioto-Pier (District 2), the proposal "would equal the playing field." She said the "main reason I'm supporting this measure" is because it would allow "our children (and parents) full representation," which is "a good thing." Moreover, she argued, it is feasible, and she pointed to other jurisdictions where immigrants vote, including Maryland, Illinois, and in New York City School Board elections (until 2003).

Sophie Maxwell (District 10) noted that "there was a time when there was another criterion for voting. It was race and gender." She asked rhetorically what this proposal could do for the San Francisco school system, and answered that it "can provide more parent participation." Maxwell observed that this has been a longtime mantra in education circles—get more parents involved, and the schools and education will improve. She argued that people need to be included and feel included, and that ultimately all of us will benefit.[71]

Jake McGoldrick (District 1), an early cosponsor of the proposal, said, "A friend from Shanghai gathering signatures for a petition said many new immigrants are fearful of signing something or giving their names. We have to open the door to trust. We have immigrants from Russia and Latin America where some have not had positive experience with government. We can offer opportunity to trust—that first step, government of people, by people, that their voice meant something."[72]

Toward the end of the meeting, Matt Gonzalez spoke in favor of the proposal, responding to objections raised at the meeting and in the media:

> It has been interesting to see this hit the public air waves and discourse in the city. . . . What is also confounding some of the opponents—they are not really sure who is going to benefit [from] it. And because it is a Green Party member bringing it forward their first instinct is that this must be empowering people to the left. But if you look at it carefully, one thing that we know about immigrants, first generation immigrants, is they tend to be very conservative. . . . I, nevertheless, am supportive of this measure because it further democratizes our society. It also takes into account that we are different from other cities. We have high number of immigrants. . . . And I think that immigrant parents should have a voice. . . . There was a time when the Irish and Italians were at the bottom [notwithstanding blacks, Native Americans, and Chinese]. I think we have to be mindful of that. This body has taken strong positions on controversial issues: gay marriage, domestic partnerships, ATM-fee-ban (which we lost) but that was the right fight to be in, and I don't think this is any different.[73]

In response, Supervisor Fiona Ma said that she agrees with Supervisor Gonzalez that new immigrants tend to be more conservative and I'm more moderate myself. My parents were immigrants from China and I was born a citizen so I can understand the arguments here, but I'm really looking at the big picture. There is a process and there is a procedure to become a naturalized citizen. This morning at Masonic Auditorium newly naturalized citizens came out and were registering to vote and were excited about registering to vote. So I do believe that voting is tied to citizenship and we should be encouraging everyone here to become naturalized to enjoy not only all the benefits but also to accept all the responsibilities that come with citizenship. And I still believe that voting is one of those sacred, inalienable rights of being a citizen.[74]

After the Board of Supervisors voted to approve the ballot proposal nine to two (the two "no" votes were, as aforementioned, from Supervisors Ma and Hall), both sides kicked into full campaign mode. Proponents and opponents sought funds and endorsements to sway voters for or against Prop F. News that the measure would be allowed to go before the voters on the November 2004 ballot generated further controversy and public debate.

Opponents: "Yes on Citizenship, No on F" Opponents garnered support from such divergent prominent figures as Bill Jones, the former Republican California secretary of state, and Barbara Boxer, the popular Democratic U.S. senator who he ran against (and lost). SFSOS, one of the major organized opponents, formed a "No on F" committee, funded by the group's political action committee. One prong of SFSOS's attack on Prof F was to focus on undocumented immigrants, which have been a hot topic and sore spot in California—and national politics—in debates over whether undocumented immigrants should be allowed drivers' licenses and have access to other public services and jobs, including controversy over President Bush's guest worker program. SFSOS President Wade Randell, for example, said that Prof F "is so cynical that the forces in favor of this included illegal residents. If you are here illegally, that you should be bestowed benefits is an affront to people who are here legally and playing by the rules." Editorial boards from some of the major papers, such as the *San Francisco Chronicle*, opposed Prop F and urged voters to reject the measure.[75] Donald Fisher, the founder of the Gap, contributed $50,000 to Yes on Citizenship, No on F, another group formed to defeat Prop F.

One of Fisher's group's related goals was to link its anti–Prop F campaign with efforts to defeat several incumbent supervisors and to elect other candidates for supervisor whom they supported. "Business and moderate groups took aim at the Board of Supervisors, using Prop F as a wedge issue to turn out their own votes in districts."[76] For example, in District 1 on the West Side, which is composed of mostly white and moderate voters, opponents attacked incumbent Supervisor Jake McGoldrick by using anti–Prop F campaign literature that said McGoldrick supports "allowing illegal immigrants to take over our schools" and pointed to a list of other candidates (backed by opponents) who don't. Similarly, in Supervisor Gerardo Sandoval's district, which is composed of mostly Asians and Latinos and is heavily immigrant, the opposition flooded the district with anti–Prop F campaign literature including a four-page mailer produced by Yes on Citizenship, No on F that showed Republican U.S. Attorney General John Ashcroft under the words "Thanks Gerardo." The literature presented Gerardo Sandoval's support of Prop F as a scheme for the federal government to get a list of illegal immigrants to deport them. Sandoval said the mailing falsely depicted him as anti-immigrant and sued to find out who was funding such misleading campaign material. It turned out that Don Fisher funded that anti–Prop F literature.[77] In fact, business-backed groups and opponents spent more than $200,000—much of it anonymously—to unseat Sandoval, who, despite this onslaught, ended up defeating the seven candidates that challenged him.[78]

Proponents: It's about Education and Kids Proponents, working under the banner of Parents United for Education, a coalition of immigrants, community groups, labor, churches, elected officials, and citizens, organized a grassroots campaign of community-based meetings, rallies, press events, and old-fashioned door knocking, leafleting, and phone banking. The coalition handed out 40,000 pieces of mail and mailed another 20,000 pieces for a total of 60,000 voter contacts. According to Chiu, Parents United for Education was a "totally volunteer effort. About 10 key people ran the campaign and we had about 100 volunteers. It was very energetic with many new people who participated into the campaign; not as many of the usual suspects."[79] The campaign was unique in that it brought so many people across divides—racial, class, and neighborhoods—including blacks, labor, Greens, Democrats, gays, and lesbians, who could recognize denial of legal status. Even in the business community, there was a split; some businesses supported Prop F, seeing the value of educating children who work in businesses.[80]

The campaign garnered a long list of endorsers, including the San Francisco Democratic Party; the Labor Council; lesbian, gay, bisexual, and transgender (LGBT) organizations; advocacy organizations for children; youth groups; the unanimous support of the SFUSD board; and notables including the Reverend Jesse Jackson. The pro–Prop F campaign focused on three primary messages: (1) it's about education and kids; studies show that the more involved parents are in their children's education, the better kids do; and one out of three kids in the SFUSD system come from homes where parents are noncitizens; (2) it is done elsewhere, pointing to the history and recent successful experience in other jurisdictions; and (3) the U.S. Supreme Court says noncitizen voting is legal and San Francisco can do this under provisions of the California State Constitution for charter cities.

"The more we got these messages out, the more people were persuaded." David Chiu provided a revealing example that exemplified this dynamic: one night he presented the case for noncitizen voting rights to a group of sixty San Franciscan Democrats who were skeptical at best of the idea. Following his presentation, the audience was separated into groups for discussion. Each group that received copies of the campaign's literature to read in their group discussions all supported the idea; the groups that only heard David's presentation but did not get the campaign literature had mixed support—about half and half; and groups that were composed of people who came in late and did not hear David's presentation or receive campaign literature by and large opposed the idea. "In other words, the more information about the issue and the greater the chance to hear the arguments for the initiative, the greater the support the campaign garnered." It is for such reasons that Chiu and others believe that if the campaign had more time and resources to get the message out, it would have made the difference and Prop F may have won.[81]

The Vote The official final vote tally, according to the San Francisco Department of Elections, was as follows:

NO: 164,924 votes = 51.45 percent

YES: 155,643 votes = 48.55 percent

Analysis of the data shows that less than a majority of whites supported Prop F, while more than a majority of Asians and Latinos supported Prop F.[82]

Although the outcome was disappointing to advocates, some took solace in the fact that they nearly won. Many advocates "thought it would be an uphill battle" from the beginning and viewed getting within 1.5 percent as a victory of sorts, or at least "not exactly a loss."[83] Given the campaign took place over only about six months and advocates were significantly outspent—by about $15,000 to about $100,000—getting as close as they did to winning was remarkable. "It took 100 years for African-Americans to get the right to vote after the Civil War; 50 years for women to get the vote after Seneca Falls; we had six months and did pretty well, getting within 1.5%."[84]

Advocates point to several factors that contributed to the loss. One was the fact that Prop F got caught up in the battle for control of the Board of Supervisors. Progressives had controlled the board for the last four years, and business-backed opponents spent some $500,000 to oust progressive incumbents and install candidates of their choice.[85] For example, Prop F was used as a wedge issue to oust Supervisors McGoldrick and Sandoval, albeit in a failed attempt. Still, opponents turned out enough anti–Prop F votes to win the day. According to David Chiu, "Prop F got caught in the cross-fire for control of the Board of Supervisors. If it were not for this, Prop F probably would have won."

In addition, the limited resources of the pro–Prop F forces relative to the anti–Prop F forces had a significant impact on voters: "If Parents United for Education could have raised more money, then they could have done more and may have won."[86] Others also concluded the role of money played a key role in the outcome. Eric Mar, for example, commissioner of the SFUSD, said, "The role of big business groups under the guise of 'SFSOS' and individuals like Don Fisher kicked in lots of $$$ to defeat Prop F," which proved decisive.[87]

Moreover, opponents were able to capitalize on anti-immigrant senti-ments in the post–9/11 world, particularly by latching on to controversy surrounding undocumented immigrants that prevailed in California and nationally, including access to drivers licenses, jobs, border issues, and so on. "The campaign made a tactical decision to include undocumented immigrants. Within [the] immigrant rights community it is seen as a mor-ally and legally arbitrary distinction. It may have cost us some votes, but we felt it was the right thing to do."[88] The pro–Prop F campaign tried to link Governor Arnold Schwarzenegger's immigrant past to the issue, but it did not seem to prove effective. Eric Mar said, "I honestly didn't expect it [Prop F] to pass given how close we still are to 9/11. . . . Sen. Dianne Feinstein and others were also central in creating an anti-immigrant climate to mislead voters about Prop F's impact as well."[89]

The context of the campaign was another factor: "The fact that with 12 school board candidates, 6 community college candidates, about 75 super-visor candidates, the presidential race, U.S. senate race, state assembly and senate races, 15 city initiatives, and 14 state initiatives, San Francisco was bled dry of volunteers, campaign consultants and field staff that typically would have come on board a campaign like this. It was a bit of a perfect storm of political overdosing."[90]

Mar pointed to weaknesses in the pro–Prop F's "field campaign," arguing that "we probably could easily have won with more deeper buy-in by white liberal community leaders and a little more money to get the message out to those constituencies. I think if we had a better run field campaign and raised a little more money to counter the opposition we would have won."[91]

In the end, nevertheless, progressives maintained their control of the Board of Supervisors. None of the targeted incumbents got knocked off. Matt Gonzalez, who voluntarily stepped down, was replaced by another Green Party member Ross Mirkarimi. Essentially, it was business as usual. Even Tony Hall was replaced by his aide Sean Elsebernd. In addition, other progressive ballot initiatives did not fare well either. For example, Proposition A, which dealt with affordable housing, lost, and two tax measures designed to help plug the deficit also lost.[92]

On the positive side, many advocates believed the campaign was successful by fostering

> a local and nationwide dialogue about educating our children of immigrants, immigrant voting, and democracy; . . . convincing 49% of San Franciscans within 6 months is a true victory.... We DID make a difference. Even if we don't get to 50%, the time will come on another day when our immigrant parents will have a real voice in our children's education. . . . I know it's a cliché, but of all of the political campaigns I have worked on, Prop F makes me think about Margaret Mead more than any other: "A small group of thoughtful people could change the world. Indeed, it's the only thing that ever has."[93]

Stephanie Ong, cofounder with Johanna Silva of Hope Road Consulting, a political consulting firm that worked pro bono for Prop F, said that forging this diverse and vibrant coalition—composed of Asians, Latinos, GLBT, Democrats, Greens, tenants' groups, labor, elected officials, and progressive whites, all in the same room, talking and strategizing—not only was inspiring but also will be critical to winning other victories in the future. Ong, an immigrant herself, believes keeping the coalition together and keeping the momentum going are critical to future successes for immigrant rights and progressive causes.[94]

Echoing the sentiments of other advocates, Chiu said, "Given the 1-percent margin, we will certainly be back. It depends when (whether next year, or in two years, or in three years), and also on who is willing to lead [the] campaign, and politically who will lead [the] campaign in [the] Board of Supervisors. They need to find a champion. There are some likely suspects, since most of the Supervisors are still the same."[95] Indeed, Eric Mar was made president of the SFUSD and Aaron Peskin was made president of the Board of Supervisors, both of whom are strong supporters of noncitizen voting.

Lessons Learned San Franciscan advocates made several recommendations for activists in other jurisdictions:

> Raise money early and often; coordinate a media strategy—get prominent folks to say supportive things early and often; identify immigrants and citizens who can be spokespeople; find families who have been trying to become citizens for years, for example; people of all walks whose stories exemplify the struggle, and give it a human face; expect the hard hits from opponents, and respond to them directly and hard. For example, call a xenophobe a xenophobe. It works. Work as hard and as fast to line up endorsements; develop a speakers bureau; come up with core messages and repeat them often; believe in the power of idea; that it can make a difference in people's lives and politics.[96]

The Prop F campaign in 2004 garnered significant media attention, helped popularize the idea of noncitizen voting—locally and nationally—and spurred on advocates and nascent campaigns in other jurisdictions, including in San Bernardino, Los Angeles, and San Diego, California; Washington, D.C.; Massachusetts; and New York City, where simultaneous campaigns were being waged. It also inspired advocates in Maine, Minnesota, New Jersey, North Carolina, and Wisconsin to explore similar efforts. Equally importantly, Prop F helped advance the cause of immigrants as human rights. At least indirectly, Prop F thus lent support to immigrant rights advocates engaged in struggles around a broad range of issues from maintaining access to drivers' licenses, health care, affordable housing, quality education, and language access services, to fighting bias crimes, improper detention, and deportation proceedings, to speeding up and improving naturalization processes.

We now turn to other jurisdictions in California that have and/or are considering restoring immigrant voting rights.

Los Angeles

Los Angeles also has a long history of struggles for immigrant rights, including immigrant voting rights. Home to more than 10 million people, about one-third of its adult residents are noncitizens. This fact has fueled efforts to enfranchise this vital but marginalized portion of its people.

As early as 1991, Hugo Morales, the founder and director of Radio Biling, proposed a law to give noncitizen parents the right to vote in school board elections. Morales argued that school board elections would engage parents more in their children's education and that parents would be better informed about rules and regulations of their children's schools.[97] The following year, Leticia Quezada, the first Latina president of the Los Angeles School Board, proposed granting voting rights for parents in school board elections. Her proposal was opposed, however, by other members of the community, particularly by African American parents. Vocal opponents threatened to take their children out of school. Because of this, Quezada responded by stating that the proposed change clearly could not be approved immediately, but she hoped that over time this idea might gain support and momentum. She made it clear that she would continue to struggle for noncitizen parent voting rights. Quezada said she was optimistic and was not disappointed by the response of opponents, saying she was sure that such changes may take a decade to achieve.[98]

In 1993, two Los Angeles City Council members, Josefina Macias and Rodolfo Garcia of the Bell Gardens section of Los Angeles, suggested the council consider a resolution requesting the state legislature to allow noncitizens the right to vote in local elections. In 2000, 56.5 percent of all residents over eighteen years old were noncitizens. In 1993, Bell Gardens' Mayor Frank B. Duran and Councilman George T. Deitch supported the resolution. During the mid-1990s, a candidate who ran for mayor of Los Angeles proposed extending voting rights to noncitizens.[99]

Following the publication of Avila's 2003 study, Los Angeles County Supervisor Michael D. Antonovich announced his opposition to noncitizen voting. Antonovich argued that this proposal would destabilize the ability of universities to get public support. Antonovich views this proposal as disrespectful to the law and a breach of political power.[100] One day later, Erwin Chemerinsky, a constitutional law professor at University of Southern California (USC), stated that Los Angeles's charter does not permit noncitizen voting: "The commission learned it didn't have the power to allow noncitizens to vote, although some members wanted noncitizens to participate in electing neighborhood councils."[101] Governor Arnold Schwarzenegger said he is opposed to voting rights for noncitizens, according to one of his spokeswomen.[102] According to a news survey, a majority of Los Angeles voters did not favor noncitizen voting.[103] Although there were voices in support, a number of editorials and op-ed pieces were published in the wake of Avila's piece that opposed the idea of noncitizen voting. It thus appeared that, on balance, opponents of immigrant voting had the upper hand, legally and politically.

However, San Francisco's 2004 campaign changed things. As legal analysts argued, charter cities could enact voting rights for noncitizens without a state constitutional amendment (though this may ultimately have to be determined in the courts). As David Chiu has argued, article 2 of the state constitution allows school boards and cities to give voting rights to immigrants: "We believe that [the] language is broad enough to allow local jurisdictions to pass legislation allowing immigrants to vote."[104] In addition, because of the strong campaign waged by advocates, who won over a near majority of the voters in support of their ballot referendum, Proposition F, the idea of granting voting rights to noncitizens has taken on greater credibility and a new life. This has reinvigorated activists in Los Angeles and other jurisdictions in California who continue to work for noncitizen voting rights.

San Bernardino

In early August 2004, immigrant advocates asked the San Bernardino City Unified School District to consider supporting a ballot initiative that would allow any parent who has a child in the district to vote in a local school board election.[105] Advocates asked the seven-member school board to formally consider the issue at a future meeting. Although no hard figures exist about how many noncitizen parents and children would be affected, it is estimated that about one out of four of the 57,000 students in the San Bernardino school system are "English-language learners." In most cases, it is estimated, their parents' primary language is Spanish and they are not citizens.

The effort in San Bernardino, which has a population of almost 2 million, came only weeks after the San Francisco Board of Supervisors passed a ballot proposal that would allow noncitizen voting in school board elections. Not coincidentally, the measures were quite similar. The arguments marshaled for and against the proposal were also strikingly similar. For example, school board President Elsa Valdez said, "These are parents of children who we are mandated by law to educate. We don't have a problem accepting the school attendance money the state gives us to teach them. How do you justify taking money from the government but not allowing the parents to participate by voting? That seems contradictory."[106] Gil Navarro, chairman of the San Bernardino and Highland chapter of the Mexican-American Political Association, who presented the proposal to the school board, said, "It's not going to be an easy thing to accept for some people. A lot of people are set in their ways. They've got this archaic mentality and don't want to bend with the changing times in this community." He argued that noncitizens are the same as citizens in so many ways, including by working and contributing economically, paying taxes, and even dying for the United States. The problem with a double standard, Navarro continued, is that "[t]hese parents are cheated out of the full educational process because they're looked at as second-class citizens."

But opponents also marshaled similar objections. One member of the San Bernardino school board, Danny Tillman, said, "I think that [voting rights] has to remain something that's reserved for citizens of the United States." Another school board member, Marlin Brown, objected, arguing that the proposal was "a typical power play by a group that wants to wield more power in government. Here, it would certainly be an attempt to get Hispanic folks elected. If they are really excited about voting for the school board, become a citizen and then vote."

Other school board members were somewhere in between. For example, Teresa Parra said that although she generally supports the concept, she has questions about how it would actually work. On the positive side, Parra said, "They should have a voice in who runs their school district. Their kids are our kids. We need parents to get more involved. Maybe that would help them gain some ownership of their communities and their schools." In the end, the proposal was discussed but it did not receive sufficient support to put it on the ballot that would have gone before the voters. At least not yet.

San Diego

Similarly, advocates in San Diego urged serious consideration of noncitizen voting rights during the summer of 2004, as San Francisco was in the midst of considering its initiative.[107] With a sizable immigrant population in a county of almost 3 million residents, San Diego sits close to the border of Mexico and feels the heat of contentious immigrant politics.

One of San Diego's leading advocates of noncitizen voting rights, Christian Ramirez of the American Friends Service Committee, who wants to launch a campaign in the next two years, argued, "Civic participation is of primary importance. If migrants are contributing economically, socially and culturally to a society, we feel that constitutes a premise of citizenship." Ramirez said that the right to consider oneself—and be considered—an American should be measured by actions and not by the accident of birth.[108] Although Ramirez and other supporters of these initiatives to restore voting rights to noncitizens argue that they have history on their side, it remains to be seen whether they can muster enough clout to change the law, if not the hearts and minds of their fellow community members.

New York

Manuel Medina left the Dominican Republic in 1972 and came to New York City with the hope of returning to his home country soon. Twenty years later, he was still a resident of Washington Heights, a largely Dominican area of Manhattan, working as a doorman. Even though he felt emotionally connected to his homeland, which held him back from renouncing his Dominican citizenship, he said he paid less and less attention to Dominican politics and more and more attention to the local politics and needs of Dominicans in New York City. Eventually, Manuel felt he had a right to have a say in how his taxes were spent: "I've been working here for more than 20 years. I've never been on unemployment. I've never been to [sic] welfare. I participate in every aspect of American life. So why shouldn't I have the right to vote?"[109]

Diana Salas left Ecuador and came to New York in 1989 as an immigrant. Sixteen years later, Diana now speaks fluent English, holds a master's degree in public administration, pays taxes, and considers herself raised in the United States. As another election approaches, Diana sadly reflects on something that makes her different from the rest of her family, all of whom have become U.S. citizens—Diana is prohibited from voting. Unlike other immigrants, Diana has not been threatened with deportation; she "speaks English and can defend" herself. As an advocate for immigrants—including noncitizen voting rights—Diana knows all too well that "not everyone is so lucky."[110]

Manuel's and Diana's stories are not uncommon. In fact, the over 1 million adult noncitizen immigrants from all over the world who live in New York City share common circumstances and express similar themes.[111] Like Manuel's political awakening and Diana's advocacy, contemporary efforts to expand noncitizen voting rights to all New York City municipal elections—beyond school board elections—began in the early 1990s and continue today.

Partly in response to protests and rioting during 1992 in Washington Heights, activists agitated for the expansion of voting rights to allow noncitizens to participate in elections. Perhaps not coincidentally, a New York State Task Force on New Americans housed in the Democrat-controlled State Assembly soon after announced plans to promote legislation that would allow local governments in the state to grant voting rights to noncitizen residents of their municipality.[112] As discussed in the previous chapter, Takoma Park, Maryland, concurrently made national news by extending the right to vote to noncitizens in their local elections in 1992. Given these developments, it was not out of the blue that several New York State legislators in both the Republican-controlled State Senate and the Democrat-controlled State Assembly introduced legislation that would have granted noncitizens voting rights in local and state elections. In fact, one state legislator, Vito Lopez (D), proposed allowing noncitizens to vote in all elections—local, state, and federal.[113] All the legislators were

Democrats and all from districts in New York City. Thus, it was not surprising that these bills did not get very far in the state legislature, particularly in the Republican-controlled State Senate.

Nevertheless, more recent efforts to expand voting rights to noncitizen residents have percolated in New York City that could bypass action by the state legislature. Advocates like Diana—and their allies in elected office—have forged a coalition among immigrant rights groups, civic and civil rights organizations, labor unions, and public officials to popularize the idea. Together, they crafted legislation that was introduced into the New York City Council in 2005. If passed, it would grant the vote in city elections to all "lawfully present" noncitizen residents who have resided in New York City for at least six months prior to a municipal election. Because this legislation came during a year when municipal offices were up for election, and because the proposed law has the potential to radically alter present and future election outcomes and public policy in the city, it has caused intense debate in New York and nationally.

Before we examine these developments, we begin with a review of demographic changes to the state and city of New York, which sets the context and has propelled advocates forward to pursue this avenue to attain greater political power. As is the case with other jurisdictions, the out-migration of white ethnics and the in-migration of new immigrants of color provide valuable insight into ensuing tensions between groups and the push for immigrant rights, which include municipal voting rights for local residents.

Demographic Change in the State and City

New York experienced significant change in its population during the past three decades. The state's population growth declined slightly, relative to the growth of the U.S. as a whole, and the out-migration was offset by an influx of new immigrants. In fact, within the past decade the state's total population grew by about a million, from 17,990,455 in 1990 to 18,976,457 in 2000 (see table 6.1).[114] Moreover, as the proportion of the population that was foreign-born grew, an increasing proportion of the new immigrants remained noncitizens in part because of the increase in the average time it takes to naturalize. In fact, the proportion of those who naturalized went from nearly 80 percent of all foreign-born persons in 1980 to less than half—46 percent—in 2000. By 2000, 12.8 percent of the state's adult population was noncitizens.

Within the state, population also shifted. For example, New York City witnessed the out-migration of nearly a million older-stock white ethnics and the in-migration of mostly people of color in each decade, and many

TABLE 6.1 New York State Population by Nativity, Citizenship Status, and Year of Entry

Population by Nativity, Citizenship Status, and Year of Entry	Population	Percent
Total population in 2000	18,976,457	100.0
Native-born	15,108,324	79.6
Foreign-born	3,868,133	20.4
Naturalized citizen	1,783,744	46.1
Not a citizen	2,084,389	53.9
Entered 1990 to March 2000	1,561,609	40.4
Naturalized citizen	267,516	17.1
Not a citizen	1,294,093	82.9
Entered 1980 to 1989	1,073,186	27.7
Naturalized citizen	539,443	50.3
Not a citizen	533,743	49.7
Entered before 1980	1,233,338	31.9
Naturalized citizen	976,785	79.2
Not a citizen	256,553	20.8

Source: U.S. Bureau of the Census, 2000. Summary File 3 (SF 3).

of the newcomers were immigrants.[115] While some suburbs are also rapidly diversifying and are increasingly the first destination of immigrants who arrive in New York,[116] the lion's share of the newest New Yorkers is still concentrated in New York City. By 2000, several areas of the state's population were more than 15 percent adult noncitizens (see table 6.2).

In New York City in 2000, over 1.3 million adults were noncitizens, comprising more than the entire population of the Bronx and more than the total population of eleven of the fifty states. Moreover, the city's adult noncitizen population was highly diverse, composed mostly of Latinos, some whom identify as "black" (37 percent); Asian Americans (22 percent); whites (20 percent); and blacks (18 percent; this proportion would be higher if Latinos who identify as black were included). Table 6.3 presents a breakdown by race and citizenship.

Moreover, in some neighborhoods—and city council districts—noncitizens make up a quarter or more of the total population, and in some cases noncitizens comprised a third or more of the total (see table 6.4). For example, more than 35 percent of the total population in four districts in Queens is noncitizens, and 25 percent of the total population in four districts in Brooklyn and 25 percent in three districts in Manhattan are noncitizens.

TABLE 6.2 Noncitizens in New York State, 2000

	Geography	Population Eighteen Years and Over	Population Eighteen Years and Over; Not a Citizen (Foreign-born, Not Naturalized)	% Non-citizen Eighteen Years Old and Over
1	New York City	6,078,005	1,394,508	22.9
2	White Plains, Westchester County	41,825	8,852	21.2
3	Newburgh, Orange County	18,864	3,886	20.6
4	New Rochelle, Westchester County	54,977	10,612	19.3
5	Mount Vernon, Westchester County	51,101	9,681	18.9
6	Glen Cove, Nassau County	20,990	3,859	18.4
7	Yonkers, Westchester County	148,640	25,822	17.4
8	Peekskill, Westchester County	16,940	2,941	17.4
9	Rye, Westchester County	10,532	1,595	15.1
10	Ithaca, Tompkins County	26,464	3,314	12.5
11	Poughkeepsie, Dutchess County	22,170	2,449	11.0
12	Middletown, Orange County	18,258	1,904	10.4

Source: U.S. Bureau of the Census. "Citizenship Status for the Population 18 years and over," (GCT-P.16), 2000.

Representation and Immigrants

Immigrant political representation has lagged behind their growing numbers. Consequently, immigrant concerns go often unheeded. Although minorities comprise 40 percent of the governing bodies in New York City, minorities comprise over 60 percent of the total population (see figure 6.3). Moreover, the number of Latino and Asian representatives lags far behind their numbers in neighborhoods, outflanked by both African Americans and whites.[118] For example, although Asian Americans comprise over 10 percent of the total population of New York City, there is one city council member who is Asian American (John Liu)

TABLE 6.3 Race and Citizenship Status of the Voting-Age Population in New York City, 2000

	Non-citizens	Citizens	Total
White	268,203	2,117,184	2,385,387
	19.7%	45.3%	39.5%
African American	40,578	904,798	945,376
	3.0%	19.4%	15.7%
Afro-Caribbean	168,426	268,587	437,013
	12.4%	5.7%	7.2%
African	36,299	38,431	74,730
	2.7%	0.8%	1.2%
Mexican	99,951	29,886	129,837
	7.3%	0.6%	2.2%
Puerto Rican	6,635	535,394	542,029
	0.5%	11.5%	9.0%
Cuban	6,317	30,400	36,717
	0.5%	0.7%	0.6%
Dominican	164,375	130,223	294,598
	12.1%	2.8%	4.9%
Colombian, Ecuadorian, and Peruvian	88,060	65,818	153,878
	6.5%	1.4%	2.6%
Salvadoran	9,983	5,789	15,772
	0.7%	0.1%	0.3%
Other Latino	128,725	179,899	308,624
	9.5%	3.9%	5.1%
Chinese	126,877	153,513	280,390
	9.3%	3.3%	4.6%
Indian	63,929	56,740	120,669
	4.7%	1.2%	2.0%
Filipino	17,104	29,417	46,521
	1.3%	0.6%	0.8%
Japanese	16,752	3,110	19,862
	1.2%	0.1%	0.3%
Korean	37,221	27,541	64,762
	2.7%	0.6%	1.1%

(*Continued*)

TABLE 6.3 Race and Citizenship Status of the Voting-Age Population in New York City, 2000(*Continued*)

	Non-citizens	Citizens	Total
Other Asian	34,321	28,455	62,776
	2.5%	0.6%	1.0%
Native American	11,067	14,190	25,257
	0.8%	0.3%	0.4%
Other Multiple	36,184	51,957	88,141
	2.7%	1.1%	1.5%
TOTAL	1,361,007	4,671,332	6,032,339
	100.0%	100.0%	100.0%

Source: John Mollenkopf. 2003 Census 1% Public Use Microdata Sample (PUMS), cited in "Citizenship and Voting," by Michael Huang. *Gotham Gazette*. August 25, 2003.[117]

and one state assembly person (Jimmy Meng), and both were recently elected—Liu in 2001 and Meng in 2004. These two districts were crafted specifically to allow Asian Americans to more easily select an Asian American representative if they chose. And although there are several Latino representatives, there is only one Dominican American (Hiram Monseratte).

Although immigrants comprise a large and growing proportion of the electorate in New York City—nearly one in three eligible voters in 2004 were foreign-born individuals who had naturalized—they remain a minority of all voters, especially in proportion to the total number of adult immigrants. The New York Immigration Coalition (NYIC), which is made up of roughly 150 groups, commissioned and helped organize three surveys of voters in the 2000, 2002, and 2004 elections. The surveys showed that "hundreds of thousands of new immigrant voters have registered and turned out to vote" over the past several elections, according to Margie McHugh, the executive director of the Coalition. McHugh pointed to the political significance of this development: "This means that as a group they now have the power to swing the outcome of key local and citywide races, and because of that they can put issues important to the City's working families—like good schools, affordable health care and living-wage jobs—at the center of key political races." This holds important implications for elections and politics in the city. However, because immigrant voters comprise a subgroup of all immigrants in the city and immigrant voters are an even smaller minority of all voters, the participation and representation gaps remain wide.[119]

TABLE 6.4 Noncitizen Population in New York City Council Districts, 2000

District	Council Member and Borough	Total Population	Noncitizen Population	% Non-citizen
15	Joel Rivera, Bronx	159,632	32,041	20.1
43	Vincent J. Gentile, Brooklyn	163,863	33,374	20.4
16	Helen D. Foster, Bronx	163,333	33,359	20.4
44	Lewis Felder, Brooklyn	161,056	34,922	21.7
47	Domenic M. Recchia, Jr, Brooklyn	160,127	34,799	21.7
37	Erik Marin Dilan, Brooklyn	149,341	33,379	22.4
45	Kendall Stewart, Brooklyn	152,383	34,476	22.6
24	James Gennaro, Queens	162,604	38,622	23.8
34	Diana Reyna, Brooklyn	150,085	36,820	24.5
7	Robert Jackson, Manhattan	161,873	40,111	24.8
29	Melinda Katz, Queens	149,702	37,807	25.3
1	Alan Gerson, Manhattan	149,355	38,437	25.7
22	Peter Vallone, Jr., Queens	162,594	42,099	25.9
14	Maria Baez, Bronx	157,915	42,295	26.8
48	Michael Nelson, Brooklyn	159,480	43,922	27.5
40	Yvette Clarke, Brooklyn	153,833	44,319	28.8
38	Sara Gonzalez, Brooklyn	149,420	45,037	30.1
26	Eric Gioia, Queens	161,803	57,297	35.4
20	John Liu, Queens	157,483	56,326	35.8
10	Miguel Martinez, Manhattan	150,147	54,531	36.3
25	Helen Sears, Queens	164,655	68,011	41.3
21	Hiram Monserrate, Queens	163,877	71,958	43.9

Source: "2003 New York City Council Districts—Total Population by Citizenship Status." 2000 Census Table SF3 P21. February, 2004 (The Council District numbers are for 2003, after redistricting).

Moreover, although the concerns of newly naturalized immigrant voters and native-born voters tend to be similar in many areas—most notably jobs and the economy, the War in Iraq, and access to health care, education, and housing—immigrant concerns have not always been well represented in public policy and debate. For example, a survey of New Yorkers in the 2004 elections revealed that newly naturalized citizens were more concerned with immigration issues than native-born residents, respectively 21.4 and 5.6 percent.[120] "Immigrant voters were four times more likely than native-born voters to list immigration policy as one of the issues that mattered most to them when they cast their vote."[121]

Similarly, the minimum wage was reported by first-time immigrant voters to be a significant issue by a larger margin than for native-born residents, respectively 16.6 and 7 percent. On one hot button immigrant issue—drivers' licenses—immigrant voters are more supportive than native born residents of noncitizens obtaining drivers' licenses, respectively 67 to 51 percent.[122] As a result of this underrepresentation, other issues important to immigrant communities go unheard, such as funding for English classes and translation services.

Ana Maria Archila, executive director of the Latin American Integration Center, a community organization that has helped over 10,000 immigrants to become U.S. citizens, summed it up: "Not surprisingly, these results tell us that while immigrants share many of the same concerns as other working families in New York, some issues hit closer to home for them because of our broken down immigration system and the backlash immigrants have suffered, particularly since September 11th."[123]

Advocates emphasize that new Americans face many obstacles to participating in the political process, particularly in elections, including a "lack of adequate translation and interpretation services and translated materials, frequent disenfranchisement at the hands of poll workers, and . . . discrimination."[124] All of these issues reflect immigrant political marginalization and exclusion.

The effort to restore voting rights for noncitizens is a proactive attempt to address immigrant political marginalization. The prospect of enfranchising a million mostly working-class people of color has profound political implications. Indeed, the campaign for noncitizen voting lays bare the self-interests of the political players involved: political allies of immigrants would likely gain additional votes, and immigrant advocates and noncitizen communities would gain more influence. Opponents fear that immigrant voters would vote against them.

Although many assume that new immigrant voters will benefit Democrats, the partisan implications of enfranchising noncitizens are not entirely clear. Immigrants are not monolithic and vary widely in their political preferences and party allegiances. But no one really knows what noncitizens really think and how they would affect electoral politics in New York City, if they were enfranchised in local elections. The closest proxy indicators of their potential impact are surveys on newly naturalized immigrant voters. Lorraine Minnite, a professor of political science at Barnard College, directed a study of voters in the 2000, 2002, and 2004 elections. Interestingly, the surveys show that naturalized foreign-born voters tend to register and vote Democratic as a whole, like most other New Yorkers.[125]

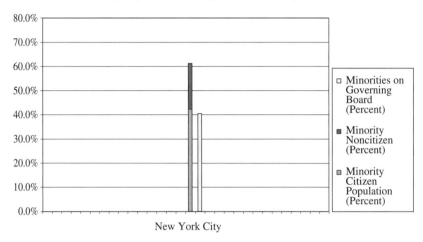

Fig. 6.3 Census 2000 Summary File 1, Table GCT-P6, Race or Hispanic or Latino—2000; Major City Website Sources; National Association of Latin Elected Officials, 2004; National Directory of Latino Elected Officials, Passim (2004); Data compiled by Joaquin Avila.

However, the surveys also showed that some immigrant groups have been trending toward Republicans, albeit slightly. For example, in 2004 about 18 percent of immigrant voters chose Bush compared with 15 percent of native-born voters; similarly immigrants registered as Republicans by about 2 percentage points more than did native-born New York City voters, respectively 12 and 10 percent.[126] (See figures 6.4 and 6.5).

Similarly, John Mollenkopf, who directs the Center for Urban Research at the City University of New York, reported that both Mayor Bloomberg (R) and Governor Pataki (R) got more than a third of Latino votes in New York City in recent elections, producing more Republican votes than usual. Surveys show that Asian voters are even more likely than Latinos to vote Republican.[127] Nevertheless, in 2004 almost 80 percent of New York City's immigrant voters chose John Kerry over George Bush.[128]

While some advocates of noncitizen voting hope it will help minority and progressive candidates gain victories, other advocates emphasize potential benefits to immigrants if elected officials and candidates for public office had to take their concerns seriously as potential voters. For example, according to Bryan Pu-Folkes, executive director of New Immigrant Community Empowerment (NICE), "I would relish seeing candidates seeking public office vying for immigrant hearts and minds. It would certainly make government more responsive to the needs and wishes of immigrants. And it would benefit all New Yorkers by invigorating public

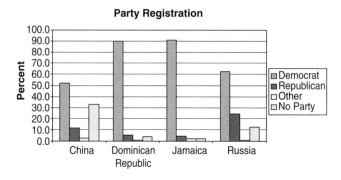

Fig. 6.4 Lorraine Minnite, principal investigator, "The New Americans Exit Poll Project: Results from the 2000, 2002 and 2004 New York City Exit Polls," New York Immigration Coalition, February 2005, http://www.thenyic.org/images/uploads/NAEP%202004%20Results.pdf.

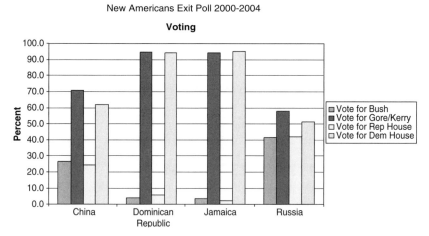

Fig. 6.5 Lorraine Minnite, principal investigator, "The New Americans Exit Poll Project: Results from the 2000, 2002 and 2004 New York City Exit Polls," New York Immigration Coalition, February 2005, http://www.thenyic.org/images/uploads/NAEP%202004%20Results.pdf.

debate."[129] Regardless, both kinds of considerations have been at the center of efforts to boost immigrant political clout in New York over time.

Campaigns for Immigrant Voting Rights in New York State: The 1990s

As a response to the growing numbers of immigrants and lack of representation and political power, a twenty-four-member Task Force on New Americans was set up by the New York State Assembly in 1986 to explore what could be done to address the needs of the newest New Yorkers. The Task Force, led by Executive Director Howard Jordan convened a series of meetings and held public hearings, recommending noncitizen voting in the early 1990s.[130] Jordan contended that noncitizen suffrage "would make the legislature more responsive to immigrant demands for a greater share of government resources." Jordan than argued noncitizen voting would "empower immigrant communities to participate in local decision-making . . . [and] serve as a catalyst and training ground for fuller participation," including as a "pathway to eventual citizenship." Further, he noted, the "fires of frustration and discord" that manifest in immigrant communities, such as among Dominicans in Washington Heights and Central Americans in Washington, D.C., might be put out by granting noncitizens voting rights, or at least conflict might be better worked out at the polling booth. Citing an anti-immigrant climate that was on the rise in the U.S., Jordan argued that noncitizen voting would give immigrants "a political weapon" to defend themselves against "legislative and physical assaults." Jordan noted America's long history of allowing noncitizens to vote—and New York's then-current practice of noncitizen voting in community school board elections and in Community Development Agency elections, which affect the distribution of millions of antipoverty funds—and the growing contemporary movement in several jurisdictions around the country.[131] Several immigrant and civil rights advocates also supported noncitizen voting, calculating that people of color and minority candidates might stand a better shot at the polls if their numbers were increased. They met with members of the Black and Latino Caucus at the state and city levels and with various organizations to promote the idea and organize support.[132]

The prevailing assumption among task force members and other advocates was that New York State election law, which currently requires voters to be U.S. citizens, would have to be changed in order to implement noncitizen voting.[133] Eventually, they were successful at urging several representatives to introduce legislation. On March 30, 1993, Assemblyman Vito Lopez introduced such legislation to permit noncitizens to vote in elections (A-6547) and Assemblyman Nick Perry also introduced a bill with related but different provisions (A-6828). Lopez's bill would have extended "the right to vote in Federal, state and local elections conducted in New York State to aliens lawfully admitted for permanent residence in the United States."[134] Perry's bill limited noncitizen voting to only local elections in New York City. Moreover, Perry's bill required legal permanent residents to live in the U.S. for three years, live in New York State for three years, and have applied for U.S. citizenship; it would thus apply to a much smaller number of immigrants. In the State Senate, David Patterson introduced legislation (#4857) that was the same as Perry's bill.

The bills were publicly supported by immigrant and civil rights advocates and by many elected officials. Privately, however, some worried that the legislation would have the effect of dividing groups. African Americans saw the bills as Latino bills, Puerto Ricans saw the legislation as Dominican legislation, and the citizenship movement saw the proposed law as a threat to efforts to win amnesty.[135] Legislators who supported the legislation perceived it would help them get elected or stay elected by expanding support among key constituents. Conversely, other legislators opposed the bill because they thought the enfranchisement of new immigrants might hurt their electoral fortunes. Howard Jordan put it bluntly: "The task force's advocacy ignited anxiety and an unspoken fear that giving noncitizens the right to vote could cost many politicians their seats and provoke a radical reorganization of politics in New York. This phobia contributed to the task force's elimination."[136] For these and other reasons, the bills languished in committees and were not enacted.[137]

New York City: The 1990s

As news of legislative efforts at the state level and other efforts—and victories—in other parts of the country spread, advocates in New York City called for extending voting rights from community school board elections to all municipal elections. Given the rapidly changing demographics of the city—action at the state level and the political implications, particularly for Democrats and certain factions within Democratic ranks—minority and immigrant rights advocates began to exert greater influence and their concerns were having greater traction. A report published by the Center for Immigrant Rights, which laid out political arguments and legal parameters for pursuing legislation to re-enfranchise noncitizens in New York, gave advocates further ammunition.[138]

City Councilwoman Una Clarke, herself a Jamaican immigrant, spearheaded a resolution introduced in 1993 that called for holding hearings about extending noncitizen voting from school board elections to include all municipal elections in New York City.[139] The resolution, which was cosponsored by eleven other council members, called on the council to "investigate the economic importance of legal permanent residents to the City of New York and convene a hearing to assess the impact on the City of New York of extending local voting rights in city-level elections to this group."[140] The resolution, however, languished in a committee and died.

New York City: The 2000s

Over the past decade, various immigrant rights and civil rights organizations, labor unions, and elected officials expressed interest in expanding noncitizen voting rights to local elections. It is hard to underestimate the effects of September 11, particularly the rise in anti-immigrant racially motivated crimes, massive detentions, and skyrocketing deportation of immigrants in New York City that emanated from the federal government. Immigrant advocates, looking for ways they could make positive impacts at the local level, saw municipal government as a place that might be able to fend off the anti-immigrant onslaught, such as through the public advocate's office, the City Council, and the mayor's office. For some, noncitizen voting was seen as a way to wage a proactive fight instead of merely a defensive one.

One of the earliest public proponents of exploring the idea of extending noncitizen voting to municipal elections was Fernando Ferrer, the former Bronx Borough president and a candidate for mayor of New York City in the 2001 and 2005 elections. As president of the Drum Major Institute for Public Policy, Ferrer published a report I wrote on the subject in October 2002.[141]

The issue, however, did not gain much visibility until August 2003 when the New York City Charter Revision Commission, an eleven-member panel appointed by Mayor Michael Bloomberg to study ways of increasing voter participation (particularly the question of introducing nonpartisan elections in the city), debated a draft resolution that would grant green card holders the right to vote in local elections. "If they can go to war, if they can pay taxes, and if they're here legally, they should be able to vote in municipal elections," said Bill Lynch, a member of the Charter Revision Commission and a Democratic political consultant.[142]

Lynch's proposal sparked public discussion and debate, and garnered media attention. Supporters rallied behind the idea. For example, Roberto Ramirez, the former Bronx Democratic Party chairman and an advisor to Fernando Ferrer, said, "When you are a taxpaying legal resident, you have a stake in the future of this city, and it makes sense for you to vote. . . . It is an idea whose time has come."[143]

Others disagreed. Councilwoman Maria Baez, for example, who represents the Kingsbridge and Fordham sections of the Bronx, said, "I don't think it should happen. The vote should be only for citizens, for people who have unequivocally made a commitment to abide by U.S. laws." Instead, Baez said that the city should help immigrants become citizens: "The real issue that we have to take care of is the backlog in citizenship applications."[144] Similarly, City Council Member James Oddo, the Republican minority leader from Staten Island, argued, "Voting is a fundamental right of being an American citizen and I don't think we should throw around that right ad hoc."[145] Stanley Renshon, a professor at the Graduate Center of the City University of New York, said, "If you allow non-citizens to vote you are removing the incentive to take the naturalization test and become a citizen. You'll take out, if not the heart, perhaps the soul, of citizenship."[146]

Lynch's proposal was ultimately sidelined by the Charter Revision Commission when its lawyers believed it could not be done unilaterally by the city. Nevertheless, Paul Elliott, a spokesman for the commission, said, "The commission thinks indeed that voting by noncitizens would go to the heart of the objectives of the commission, which is to increase access and participation with local government across the board for all New Yorkers."[147] Moreover, the idea of local voting rights for noncitizens was again the stuff of news articles and public discussion and debate.

In September 2003, Fernando Ferrer sent a letter to New York elected officials—including Mayor Bloomberg—urging them to "consider this proposal and its implications for your constituents."[148] In the letter, Ferrer included a report by John Mollenkopf and John Logan that detailed the changing demographics in New York and Los Angeles, highlighting a "representation gap" and recommendations that included exploring avenues to increase political participation by immigrants, including non-citizen voting.[149] The letter also included a copy of my report, which argued for restoring noncitizen voting rights.[150] A few days later, Ferrer said of the issue, "It is a matter of fairness. If a citizen were barred for some reason or another from participating in the franchise some might say 'Wait a minute, we pay taxes, what are we talking about here?'"[151]

Media attention to Lynch's proposal—and renewed interest in state legislation (discussed below)—contributed to activity by several immigrant rights organizations and civic groups, labor unions, activists, and elected officials who began to explore the possibility of mounting a campaign to extend voting rights to noncitizens.

In September 2003, NICE held a public forum on the subject in Flushing, Queens, a heavily immigrant community, which garnered additional media attention. It also spurred on advocates to form a working group to further explore the idea. Led by NICE, these and other groups formed the New York Coalition to Expand Voting Rights in early 2004 as a vehicle to advance a campaign to enfranchise noncitizens in local elections.

> It was Bill Lynch's resolution which led to the formation of the New York Coalition to Expand Voting Rights. Mr. Lynch's resolution received significant attention in the ethnic and local media in Queens and prompted NICE to host a community education

forum in Flushing in September of 2003. After that forum a number of advocates, academics, lawyers, and community members decided to create a formal coalition to address this issue here in New York City.[152]

Forum participants included Guillermo Linares, the first Dominican ever elected to office in the United States—initially as a community school board member before he gained his U.S. citizenship, and then after as a New York City Council member—who described how noncitizen voting opened the door not only for him but also for tens of thousands of immigrants who clamored for better schools in Washington Heights.[153] As aforementioned, a mobilization of parent voters in the mid-1980s led to his election and to the building of new schools.[154] Another forum participant, Ramon Peguero, a legislative assistant to Assemblyman Vito Lopez, said Lopez intended to reintroduce legislation that would allow noncitizen voting in New York State. Peguero said, "I believe it is time for noncitizen legal residents to have a bigger say in their community." Peguero noted that two common arguments against noncitizen voting are an ignorance of American values and uncertain loyalties, but countered, "I don't think that argument will fly with the legal residents fighting in Iraq and Afghanistan."[155] Luciano Coloma, a Filipino green card holder for five years who attended the forum, said, "We have jobs, pay taxes to support state services, send our children to school, and can even serve in the U.S. military, but we are not allowed to exercise our rights to vote. I want to become a U.S. citizen in order for me to vote, but the naturalization process takes forever."[156]

Advocates organized another forum in March 2004 sponsored by Demos, a nonpartisan public policy organization,[157] which brought together representatives from New York City and other states to discuss the prospects and politics of noncitizen voting rights campaigns, including individuals from Maryland, Massachusetts, Connecticut, and Washington, D.C, where noncitizen voting was a reality, where legislation had been passed on the local level, or where campaigns to enact such legislation was underway. The focus, however, was on New York City. Councilman Bill Perkins, who represents Harlem, participated in the forum and expressed interest in crafting legislation that would enfranchise noncitizens in local elections in New York City. The prospect of a real legislative initiative garnered increased attention. Indeed, advocates and analysts believed a noncitizen voting rights bill had a better shot at passage than in previous years because of several changes, including greater support from black elected officials, who see this cause as an extension of the civil rights movement, and analysis by lawyers at the City Council, the Brennan Center for Justice, and the New York City Bar Association, who all concluded that change in state law would not be necessary to enfranchise voters in local elections.[158]

Shortly after the forum, an article appeared on the front page of the *New York Times* announcing that an effort was underway, led by several immigrant and civil rights advocacy organizations and a few labor unions, and with the support of some elected officials, to give noncitizens the right to vote in New York City elections. The article explored the potential political impact of such a change that would enfranchise up to 1 million legal immigrants who are not U.S. citizens, most of whom are Latino and Asian: "This would be seismic in its impact. Both parties would have to develop a different mindset to address policy issues for those residents who have historically not been part of the political process," claimed Roberto Ramirez, the former state assemblyman and chairman of the Bronx Democratic Party and later a political consultant and advisor to mayoral candidate Fernando Ferrer. Advocates argued that granting these residents, one in five voting-age New Yorkers, municipal voting rights would affect the electoral calculus of candidates for public office at every level from city council to borough president to mayor. Not only would such a change affect political outcomes, including likely increasing the number of minority representatives, but it would probably also be felt in public policy terms from ballot questions and spending priorities on programs such as access to language classes, affordable housing and health care, and naturalization and deportation proceedings.[159] In short, advocates argued that enfranchising noncitizens in local elections would make New York City government more representative, responsive, and accountable to all its community members.

One of the leading advocates, Bryan Pu-Folkes, said, "In the past two years New York has passed strong laws that protect immigrants and give them better access to government, and we are confident New Yorkers will support voting rights once they fully understand the issue."[160] Pu-Folkes maintained that noncitizens are not adequately represented and treated fairly and equally, and that this legislation would go a long way to help address these problems. Advocates also emphasized other benefits the legislation would bring. "In many ways, this prepares people," said Gouri Sadhwani, the executive director of the New York Civic Participation Project, one of the groups that endorsed the issue. "They start local, and then they become citizens and vote in national elections."[161]

But opponents, such as Mark Krikorian, the executive director of the Center for Immigration Studies, a Washington group that favors greater restrictions on immigration, countered, "Extending voting rights to noncitizens eliminates the last distinction between people who have accepted permanent membership in the American people and those who have not. That distinction is important to maintain."[162]

Advocates disagreed. For example, Chung-Wha-Hong, advocacy director for the New York Immigration Coalition, said, "Giving legal immigrants the right to vote locally doesn't take away from the concept of citizenship. They would be deciding what happens to their communities; these are not national elections where foreign policy decisions are made. It is legitimate to ask for representation at this level for these people who work, pay taxes and contribute so much to the city."[163]

The article in the New York Times generated swift negative responses from opponents. For example, Mayor Michael Bloomberg said, "The essence of citizenship is the right to vote, and you should go about becoming a citizen before you get the right to vote."[164] Responding to statements of proponents of noncitizen voting, Mayor Bloomberg said, "I'm sympathetic that people say, 'Well, I pay my taxes. Why don't I have a say?' Well, my answer is: Go through the process and become a citizen."[165] Michael Long, the chairman of the New York State Conservative Party, agreed with Mayor Bloomberg: "The Mayor couldn't have said it any better. I think he's right on target. Citizenship is something you have to earn, and work for."[166]

Mayor Bloomberg also addressed the argument put forth by advocates that invoked the civil rights movement: "There's been an awful lot of people over the years that have fought and died for the right to vote—for giving you and I the right to vote—and I don't think that we should walk away from that concept. If you want to have full rights, and voting is a very big part of full rights, become a citizen."[167] Even Gifford Miller, the Democratic speaker of the City Council and a mayoral candidate, was cool to the idea, according to his press secretary, David K. Chai: "The Speaker believes that encouraging citizenship is the best way to increase participation in the voting process."[168]

Advocates responded by stating that they would forge ahead with plans to enfranchise noncitizens, arguing, "Taxation without representation is tyranny, not democracy," in the words of City Council Deputy Majority Leader Bill Perkins. "Restoring immigrant voting rights is as American as apple pie," he added, referring to the history of noncitizen voting in the U.S. and to historic struggles to realize the promise of democracy for all: "The tradition of expanding the franchise is one that has been seen over and over again in this country."[169] Bertha Lewis, the executive director of the New York office of the Association of Community Organizations for Reform Now (ACORN), challenged Bloomberg's opposition by claiming it was rooted in a fear that immigrants would not vote for him. Furthermore, she said, "We don't want political lip service to immigrants—we want real action. This is a campaign that we intend to wage over the next year."[170]

Short-Term Impacts: The Naturalization Backlog

Interestingly, shortly after these developments there were several changes to city policy. One change had to do with the long backlog of citizenship applications. A series of news articles detailed the backlog problem, and several editorials called for improvements in the citizenship process. For example, the *Daily News* helped establish a Citizenship Now phone bank with the assistance of the City University of New York (CUNY) and the office of the mayor. Over the course of five days at the end of April 2004, the phone bank received thousands of calls from immigrants who complained about long delays on pending citizenship applications, the USCIS losing documents, and the denial of immigrants' applications over minor infractions. The backlog and litany of problems prompted Sayu Bhojwani, Mayor Bloomberg's commissioner of immigrant affairs, to vow to address such complaints: "We can find ways to bucket [bundle] the concerns and advocate with, say, CIS, that this is a common concern and is there something we can do about it." CUNY Chancellor Matthew Goldstein said, "There are people who are desperate to know how to become citizens and all of the quagmire that they have to go through, but they don't know who to call, who to speak to, even what the right questions are."[171] Allan Wernick, chair of CUNY's Citizenship and Immigration Project who is also an immigration lawyer and a columnist for the *Daily News*, said the backlog "deprives immigrants of very fundamental rights, such as voting and fully participating in American democracy."[172]

Citizenship delays and the backlog became issues as the 2004 elections approached. In New York State, about 60,000 newcomers, who had been approved for U.S. citizenship but were caught in a persistent and significant backlog at the USCIS and the Department of Homeland Security, were prevented from voting in the 2004 elections, according to a study by the New York Immigration Coalition.[173] The president of the Russian-American Voters Educational League, Vladimir Epshteyn, described one situation that involved a man and his wife who had applied for naturalization on the same day almost two years ago, but the man's application was delayed for more than a year and a half after hers was approved. (The man did not know the reasons why his application was delayed.) The man's application was finally approved and he came to Epshteyn seeking assistance in filling out a voter registration form so he could vote, but was told the registration deadline had passed and he would not be able to vote. Epshteyn said, "I had to tell him it was too late. He was so disappointed—even, I would say, depressed." Margaret McHugh said that many "citizens-in-waiting" were disappointed and bitter: "They feel their voices have been silenced and their votes have been robbed, even though it could well determine the outcome of the election. They all take it seriously that they now live in a democracy. Unfortunately the government has not taken seriously the obligation to include them."[174] The study showed that New York—although among the worst—was not alone, and that there were thousands of immigrants who similarly had been approved for naturalization but whose applications were delayed in many of the 2004 battleground states. The NYIC released a report and held a press conference detailing the delays and the kinds of consequences such delays had on individuals. In 2005, a study commissioned by ACORN showed that New York City had one of the longest backlogs in the country.[175]

Members of the New York Coalition to Expand Voting Rights have long supported efforts to reduce the backlog but saw no conflict in continuing to make the case for municipal voting rights for noncitizens at the same time. In fact, the problem of the backlog, some contended, helped buttress their case. The longer immigrants had to wait for citizenship, the more the notion of local voting rights made sense. Moreover, advocates contended that pressing for speedier naturalization and citizenship did not conflict with the idea of having local voting rights. Many immigrants may not be eligible for citizenship or not choose to naturalize but still have a legitimate stake in their local communities. The idea that immigrants should have a say in local affairs, advocates argued, is based on fundamental democratic principles. Naturalization grants new citizens the right to vote in state and federal elections, which local voters would still be precluded from participating in. Some advocates also argued that voting in local elections would better prepare immigrants for eventual citizenship and give them a taste of democracy and schooling in election processes. Essentially, these advocates argued the two issues were not mutually exclusive but rather were compatible and mutually reinforced each other.

State Activity: The 2000s

At the state level, several legislators continued to press forward with bills that would grant noncitizens voting rights. State Assemblyman Vito Lopez reintroduced his legislation, which would grant voting rights to legal permanent residents in local, state, and federal elections, in 1997 and again in 2003. Nick Perry also reintroduced his bill in 1999 and again in 2003. But the outcome did not change—the bills went nowhere. Still, as the issue gained greater visibility, these legislators considered making changes to their bills, and along with other state legislators—including Senate Democratic Leader David Paterson and Senator Martin Dilan—expressed interest in reintroducing their bills in the 2005–2006 legislative cycle. Also, partly in response to the lack of movement of state legislation, ACORN planned to initiate a campaign to change state law that would allow local governments the option of extending voting rights to noncitizens in local elections.

Meanwhile, State Senator David Patterson, the Democratic leader who represents Harlem, revived the New York State Task Force on New Americans. In April 2004, the task force held a public hearing on immigrant rights and access to services in East Harlem, including electoral access, educational access, health care access, and workers' rights. The event, which was chaired by Senator Kevin Parker and cosponsored by several civic groups, community-based organizations, and unions, included testimony in support of noncitizen voting rights from several advocacy organizations and an elected official—City Councilman Bill Perkins, who represents Harlem.[176] Councilman Bill Perkins, who is the chair of the Government Operations Committee and deputy majority leader of the New York City Council, testified in favor of restoring voting rights to immigrants, or "resident immigrant voting in local elections." Perkins listed a series of items to make his case. Because Perkins reiterated many of these points throughout the campaign in many different venues, I quote him at length:

> Over 1 million New York City residents of voting age cannot vote. Immigrants pay over $18.2 billion in taxes to New York State (about 15% of all taxes collected). From [the] 1770 to 1920s, 22 states and federal territories allowed noncitizens to vote in local, state and federal elections. The average current wait time for citizenship is ten years or longer; several domestic and foreign communities allow or are in [the] process of allowing noncitizens to vote, including five towns in Maryland, Amherst and Cambridge Mass., San Francisco, Washington D.C., Denver, Connecticut, Barbados, Belize, Venezuela, Chile, Iceland, Sweden and [the] European Union. New York had noncitizen voting as recently as last year [i.e., 2003] in school board elections. Immigrants pay income taxes and sales taxes just like everyone else; we take voting as a right, not a privilege. People have a right to voice their local issues. Citizenship is not equal to voting. Immigrants don't get citizenship to vote; they do so for a variety of other reasons, including employment opportunities, educational opportunities,

and housing opportunities. I won't dismiss voting as being on that list, but nevertheless it is not the reason people travel to this country just to vote. The federal process presently takes too long and is only getting longer.

For many of us, this is another step in the struggle for voting rights and civil rights. In the African-American community it is our legacy to stand on the principle of taking down the barriers to voting and opening up democracy to be as inclusive as possible. And those barriers have not always [been] on the basis of citizenship. We know that at one point in time all you had to be was a white man with land to be able [to] vote. At another point in time women who might have been citizens could not vote. We know that African-Americans could go fight for democracy overseas and came home and were not able to vote. So voting and citizenship have not always been one and the same. We have a history of allowing people to vote . . . without necessarily being citizens and we are trying to return New York City back to that history. And frankly, it seems to me . . .common sense that we would allow people to vote especially on issues that affect their daily life. Immigrants pay taxes and on the basis of that, we should allow them to vote. Immigrants also serve in the armed forces but can't vote. There is something wrong with that.[177]

New York City in the 2000s: Coalition Building   From late 2003 to early 2005, the New York Coalition to Expand Voting Rights—which grew to more than fifty organizations including immigrant groups, civil rights and voting rights organizations, community-based organizations, labor unions, faith-based groups, and several public officials—engaged in a wide array of activities to promote the idea, including developing literature and materials; holding dozens of meetings with hundreds of groups; organizing public forums and actions in various communities; meeting with most of the fifty-one city council members, members of Mayor Bloomberg's office, several candidates running for mayor in 2005, and state representatives; and organizing press briefings and events. To further ties to activists in New York—and build greater public visibility—the coalition forged ties to the Immigrant Voting Project, which housed some of its materials on their website. The Immigrant Voting Project, codirected by Michele Wucker of the World Policy Institute and myself, established a Listserv and website in early 2004 that has served as a clearinghouse for advocates, researchers, journalists, and the general public interested in immigrant voting. In addition, the Immigrant Voting Project linked the New York City initiative to other campaigns and advocates around the country.[178]

Who Would Be Enfranchised?   One of the biggest issues the New York Coalition to Expand Voting Rights faced was the question about whether to include all immigrants or only documented (legal) noncitizens in the proposed legislation. Early on, the coalition embraced the idea that all immigrants should be included. However, over time it became clear to advocates, through conversations with legislators, members of the media, and other advocates, that it would be more prudent and feasible to only include "lawful residents." Still, "lawful residents" would include a much larger group of immigrants than merely legal permanent residents (green card holders). "Lawful residents" includes individuals who holds any kind of visa, such as student and work visas, but many such visas do not carry with them the possibility of obtaining U.S. citizenship. (There are many different kinds of visa holders, starting with the letter "A" and going to "V.") Coalition members also thought it wise to require a period of residency so as to keep tourists from being able to vote. A six-month residency requirement was settled upon. Advocates hoped this would allow the campaign to get beyond the "You can't mean you want to give the vote to 'illegal' immigrants naysayers, and other opponents."

Another concern arose from advocates themselves, who worried that if the legislation included all immigrants, it might put undocumented people at risk of scrutiny and possible federal prosecution and deportation. The question advocates came to grapple with was how to best protect immigrants from such risks and at the same time craft legislation that would be as inclusive as possible. Some advocates argued that undocumented folks would stay away from government and not register or vote so as not to put themselves at risk. This seems to be what is happening in Maryland, at least in part, where immigrant voter registration and turnout have dropped in recent years. Of course, the potential response by opponents is "Why, then, include illegal immigrants at all?" These concerns led advocates to conclude that it was not worth putting people at risk in the current anti-immigrant climate and that the political price would be too high anyway. Thus, they settled on a strategy that would enfranchise "lawful residents" who lived in New York City for at least six months prior to a municipal election.

To Pursue Legislation or Not to Pursue Legislation, and When   Despite obtaining a substantial number of endorsements and achieving greater visibility, some advocates urged the coalition and Councilman Perkins to wait until after the 2004 municipal elections to move forward with the introduction of legislation. These groups, which included several unions and immigrant and civil rights organizations, raised concerns that such an initiative might create confusion among immigrants, causing some noncitizens to register to vote (which is illegal), and could result in their deportation. In addition, the groups said they had already committed resources to getting out the vote for 2004 and other activities. Although these groups supported local voting rights for immigrants, the issue was timing. The coalition discussed these concerns and decided to not go forward with legislation in 2004, as requested. Members of the coalition agreed that significant education of community members would be needed to prevent ineligible immigrants from inadvertently registering to vote, and understood that valuable resources would be scarce given election year commitments.

Nevertheless, members of the coalition decided to continue their educational work, recruit support, and continue to plan a campaign. For example, member groups of the coalition held several community meetings and public forums, and made presentations to various organizations. In addition, members of NICE made a presentation to the Black, Latino and Asian Caucus of the New York City Council in June 2004 about the work of the coalition and the campaign for resident voting rights, seeking their support. Coalition members also met with council members individually. In fact, over the course of the summer months, members of the coalition met with at least thirty of the fifty-one council members and/or their staff in one-on-one sessions to inform them of the proposal and inquire if they would be supportive of any such legislative initiative. About twelve members indicated their support for resident voting rights in municipal elections. Another ten were open to such a proposal but wanted to know more about the actual legislation. The remainder were noncommittal in either direction. By the year's end, advocates had held a series of meetings among themselves and with Councilman Perkins and his staff to iron out details of the legislation and make plans for efforts in 2005. In February, a draft of the legislation was completed and a tentative date was set to introduce the legislation into the city council in March.

Again, however, several representatives of unions and immigrant and civil rights organizations reached out to leaders of the coalition and to Councilman Perkins to express their concerns about moving forward. Essentially, the unions and other organizations thought it would be best to delay the introduction of legislation until next year and to mount a multi-year campaign. Their concerns included wanting more time to conduct base building within their institutions, because not all their members—including immigrants—understood and/or supported noncitizen voting. To mount a successful campaign, they argued, more time would be needed to educate and mobilize members. A related issue was the concern about what impact the introduction of legislation would have on the mayor's race and other elections. Some candidates might shy away from the issue, or the issue might put candidates in an awkward spot and possibly hurt their chances, especially in the case of Democrats. In addition, the organizations wanted to build a campaign around this issue in a way that fit with their other ongoing work and other related issue campaigns. Another concern was about where to put organizational resources: how much staff time and funding—and political capital—would be feasible and wise to expend at this time versus another later time. The organizations also expressed concern about what they perceived was a lack of a well-developed plan and sufficient support among more significant players with sufficient resources to win this campaign. Finally, they worried that if the coalition and Councilman Perkins moved forward without the full support of these partners, who have greater resources and capacity to move the issue forward successfully in the city council, it might jeopardize the overall campaign and the issue for a long time. What if the coalition moved forward and opponents fiercely attached advocates, which was likely? The issue could be soundly defeated, which might set back the issue for years to come. Was the councilman, who was running for borough president because he was term-limited out of office, merely looking for a way to garner more votes, particularly among Latinos? Were other coalition members advancing their own agendas at the expense of other immigrant-related issues?

As a compromise, the unions and other advocates who raised these concerns suggested that Councilman Perkins introduce a resolution instead of legislation. That way, they argued, organizations would be able to work to build support among their membership, elected officials, other potential partners, and the public more generally. They asked the coalition not only to consider these concerns and questions, but also to come up with a plan that might answer them.

The coalition took these questions and concerns seriously and considered them legitimate. In response, after a series of additional meetings among coalition members and union representatives and other key players, the coalition came up with an alternative plan and presented it to the groups that raised the concerns. The coalition's plan presented a strategy for moving forward, a timetable for various activities and events, an organizational structure that included three levels in which organizational members could participate, and so on—all with the aim of moving forward with the introduction of legislation in 2005. In short, the coalition believed there were good reasons to go forward, including that it had generated significant support, felt they could obtain tangible results in waging a legislative campaign, and believed an opportune political moment was available. Councilman Perkins, who had been pressing the coalition to move forward with legislation, also decided it would be best to do so in 2005. In the end, the union representatives and other groups who had raised concerns—and reiterated them—agreed to support the issue and legislation, but said they would not be able to devote resources to waging the campaign.

Intro 628   The New York Coalition to Expand Voting Rights and their allies formally launched a city legislative campaign on tax day, April 15, 2005. The coalition held a press conference and rally, attended by over 100 people, including elected officials, union members, community groups, and noncitizen immigrants who spoke about the injustice of taxation without representation. "'No taxation without representation' is our rallying cry, because on tax-filing day, more than 1 million hard-working New Yorkers will hand over their money to the government and get no direct political voice in return," said Cheryl Wertz, the director of the Government Access at NICE. Candy Mojica, a graduate of Hunter College's School of Social Work and a resident of Harlem, said, "I truly believe that if people are paying taxes they should be allowed to vote."[179]

The event garnered significant media attention, particularly in the multilingual media sources. The event also provoked responses by several of the candidates running for mayor. C. Virginia Fields, the Manhattan Borough president, supported the idea and legislation; Fernando Ferrer said he "believes we need a robust public debate" on the issue and quietly supported the idea; Gifford Miller and Anthony Weiner declined to support the idea and bill; and Mayor Bloomberg's representatives responded by claiming that the city council "does not have the power to act in this area alone without the voters" (meaning a city charter referendum) and reiterated that the city could assist immigrants who are eligible to become citizens as soon as possible.[180]

Five days later, on April 20, 2005, Bill Perkins introduced legislation (Intro 628) that would enfranchise approximately 1 million noncitizens who lawfully reside in New York City for at least six months prior to an election. In the next weeks and months, Councilman Perkins and members of the coalition sought the support of other council members. Perkins scheduled a public hearing on the bill in June. Coalition members organized community events, a lobbying campaign, and a press conference on the day of the city council hearing. The issue gained more attention—both supportive and in opposition—as the elections approached.

Conclusion

The campaign in New York City has huge implications. As a symbol of America around the globe and as the unofficial capital of the United States, raising the issue of noncitizen voting rights will have ramifications for other cities and states for years to come, regardless of the outcome. As two advocates of noncitizen voting have argued, "New York, home of the Statue of Liberty and Ellis Island, symbolizes America's past, present and future as an immigrant nation. How appropriate it would be to affirm this leadership role by restoring noncitizen voting in municipal elections, a policy that would reinforce our founding principles and update our democracy for global times."[181]

At the time of this writing, the outcome is not known. If nothing else, the legislation provided an opportunity for advocates to pose a question that another advocate and piece of proposed legislation asked a dozen years earlier: "Immigrants are here to stay. The urgent question is whether our citizenry will empower noncitizens as an integral part of 'we the people,' or continue our tortured history of abuse and exclusion?"[182]

Washington, D.C.

In the spring of 1991, rioting shook Washington, D.C. Three days of looting and burning were sparked by a police shooting of a Latino man in the predominantly Latino neighborhoods of Adams Morgan and Mount Pleasant. Following the riots, Latino activists developed a network of agencies to help residents and formed the Latino Civil Rights Task Force to examine the roots of the disturbances and make recommendations. They concluded that the community's frustration and anger were the result of years of "harassment and discrimination." The task force also monitored allegations of abuse, and it pressured city officials to hire more Latinos as police officers and for other government jobs and to fund social programs and improves services.[183] The U.S. Civil Rights Commission also looked into the riots and issued a report, which concluded that Latinos were routinely abused by police and denied "basic civil rights to an extent that is appalling." The Civil Rights Commission said a variety of governmental and institutional obstacles denied Latinos equality of opportunity in criminal justice, employment, education, and social services.[184]

A few months after the riots and one day after Takoma Park voters approved a nonbinding referendum calling for noncitizen voting in that city's elections, Latino community leaders announced plans to seek similar legislation in D.C. District advocates sought voting rights, however, only for legal immigrants—not all immigrants, as in Takoma

Park—recognizing that "Washington is not Takoma Park" and in anticipation of a more contentious political fight. Advocates deployed familiar democratic principles to rally support for such legislation. For example, Pedro Lujan, a member of the D.C. Latino Civil Rights Task Force, said, "These are people who already have permits to work in the United States... People who pay taxes, who send their children to school in the community." Lujan said they "want to work with the City Council" to introduce a bill, but that if that route "doesn't work, then we might have to go to a referendum."[185]

In response, City Councilman Frank Smith Jr., who represented Mount Pleasant, introduced a bill that would allow noncitizens to vote in municipal elections. "It's very important for everybody to feel that they are part of the system. . . . The ones who want to stay here, who pay taxes and send their children to school here . . . deserve to have something to say about who their leaders are," Smith said.[186] Smith, who is an African American, believed the perceptions by noncitizen members of his district that they were "locked out" of political processes contributed to their frustration, which led to the riots during the previous spring.[187] Smith, who had visited El Salvador, argued that his bill "would invite them into full partnership with us and [encourage them to] become full citizens."[188]

In an effort to gain support in what was expected to be an uphill fight, Smith crafted his bill more narrowly than Takoma Park's law, granting voting rights in local elections only to legal permanent residents. As expected, Smith's bill drew criticism from many quarters. In fact, because some community members—especially African Americans—objected to the bill, Councilman Smith amended his bill to apply only to immigrants who had formally applied for U.S. citizenship. "The Latino versus African-American issue is not an issue of political power at this point; it's an issue of economics. Some folks say I'm encouraging people to stay here and compete with us. But they're going to stay here anyway."[189]

The amendment, however, elicited criticism from immigrant advocates who worried that Smith's bill would now be too narrow; it would enfranchise only a few hundred immigrants who would be become citizens in six or so months anyway.[190] For example, Pedro Aviles, chairman of the Latino Task Force, said, "We should give the right to vote to anybody who pays taxes in this city. I don't see how this bill has any bite. At best, it is better than nothing."[191]

Of course, some opponents—from community leaders to national immigration control groups—objected to both versions of the bill, viewing any sign of a budding movement to expand the franchise to noncitizens as dangerous and threatening. For example, Lillian Cooper-Wiggins, a civic leader in Brightwood, argued against the bill, "I am very concerned about this bill . . . when you have residents who have fought long and hard to get the right to vote. People appreciate the right to vote when they had to struggle for it."[192] Ultimately, opponents on both sides prevailed and Smith's bill failed.

Demographic Change

During the next decade, however, demographic changes to the District of Columbia made the representation gap even sharper. Between 1990 and 2000, the District of Columbia's population declined by 5.7 percent but the immigrant population grew by 25 percent, according to the U.S. Bureau of the Census. In 1990 9.7 percent were foreign-born (58,887 out of 606,900), but by 2000, immigrants comprised 12.9 percent of the total population (73,561 out of 563,384). Moreover, more than 51,000 of the foreign-born individuals are not citizens. Of the voting-age population, noncitizens make up a total of 8 percent (46,683).[193]

Immigrants are dispersed in all of D.C.'s eight wards and are not highly concentrated. One exception is Ward 1, which includes the neighborhoods of Mt. Pleasant, Columbia Heights, Pleasant Plains, and Park View, where about 15,000 or approximately one-third of the population are foreign-born. In the Brightwood, Manor Park area in Ward 4, about one-fifth of the population are foreign-born (3,775). Smaller concentrations of immigrants also live in the DuPont Circle and K Street areas.[194]

Immigrants from Latin America comprise about half of the newcomers to D.C., with the remainder coming from Europe (18 percent), Asia (17 percent), Africa (13 percent), and the Caribbean (11 percent).[195] Importantly, a large proportion of D.C.'s noncitizens have lived in the U.S. for over a decade (34 percent), and more than one in ten have lived in the U.S. for over two decades (11 percent). Projections of population growth predict that immigrant growth will continue along these lines.[196] At the same time, the District witnessed a widening representation gap. Elected representatives do not reflect the changing demographics of the city. No Latino holds office in the council, nor do any other ethnic minority other than African American.

The 2000s

The issue remained relatively dormant until the early 2000s, when advocates revived efforts to enact noncitizen voting in Washington, D.C. Interestingly, efforts to enact a bill for noncitizen voting rights came shortly after a series of reports were released on the eleventh anniversary of the 1991 riots, which found that many of the "same problems . . . continue to plague the Latino community."[197] The reports, which were compiled by the Washington Lawyers' Committee for Civil Rights and Urban Affairs (composed of nine major D.C. law firms and a civil rights review panel of local and national Hispanic advocates), focused on police abuses, the criminal justice system, health care, education, employment, immigration, rental housing, and home ownership. Partly due to the national recession in the early 1990s, D.C. experienced a fiscal crisis in the mid-1990s that cut into services that affected Latinos. In addition, the Latino Civil Rights Task Force, which was established after the 1991 riots, was disbanded. Advocacy and litigation of civil rights issues declined. At the time of the 2002 reports, no Latino held elected office, even as the Latino population grew by 8 percent in the District. Although there have been strides forward in addressing problems that affect immigrants and Latinos, frustration accompanied the lag.

For example, a report entitled "The State of Latinos in the District of Columbia" noted the Latino population grew by 37 percent since the 1991 riots, and although "some important steps have been taken, particularly to address the unique problems faced by the immigrant members of this community, the rate of progress . . . has been uneven at best. Latinos in the District still experience lack of representation, discrimination, and a failing education system."[198] Similarly, Saul Slorzano, the cochair of the civil rights review panel and the executive director of the Central American Resource Center (CARECEN), argued, "We're at a point where we still need to deal with these concerns and issues with a task force—not in the community, but in the city council with the participation of the mayor's office. It needs to . . . come up with a set of solutions to make sure Latinos are included in the governance of the city."[199]

Their persistence began to pay off. In late September 2002, Mayor Anthony Williams announced his support for noncitizen voting rights only months following the release of these reports and accompanying media attention, and just weeks after officials in Rockville, Maryland, said they were considering extending the right to vote to noncitizens in local elections. Mayor Williams proclaimed his support on the day another report was released—this one by the Council of Latino Agencies that documented a lack of services to Latinos and access to local government. The Council of Latino Agencies, which represents dozens of organizations that provide health, legal, and others services to Latinos, reported that the group as a whole lacks health insurance, access to government jobs (only 1.8 percent of government workers were Latinos in 2002), and quality education and housing. The report suggested that a lack of political participation was at the root of these problems and recommended exploring ways to expand Latino registration and voting. Mayor Williams, who was running for reelection, pledged to work with government officials and experts to extend voting rights to noncitizens for the "mayor on down."[200] At a news conference sponsored by the Council of Latino Agencies, where Executive Director Eugenio Arene suggested that all local taxpayers should be allowed to cast ballots, Mayor Williams said that "sounds like a good standard to me." Mayor Williams stated, "I'm committed to expanding the franchise." He said the city needed to have a new standard for voting and proclaimed, "It isn't citizenship."[201]

As during the earlier period, opponents and supporters of the idea quickly emerged. Opponents raised familiar objections. For example, some argued, "The most important right of citizenship is the right to vote. It shouldn't be taken lightly or bestowed cheaply. Those who want to vote should earn the right by becoming citizens; they'll cherish it all the more."[202] Similarly, another opponent argued, "If people care enough to vote, is it really that hard for them to first apply for U.S. citizenship?"[203]

Advocates also marshaled familiar arguments: "With a five-year residency requirement and backlogs in processing naturalization applications, many immigrants have long waits to become citizens." Noting that tens of thousands of D.C. residents—many of whom are permanent residents, which is a "symbol of their commitment" to the U.S.—are noncitizens, some advocates argued that allowing such noncitizens to vote follows "the democratic principle that all people should have equal representation."[204] In an attempt to organize a base of support to push forward a noncitizen voting rights initiative—and shortly after bills were introduced into the House of Representatives and U.S. Senate that would have granted the District of Columbia representation in Congress—advocates formed the Voting Rights for All D.C. Coalition in March 2003.[205] The mission of the coalition "is to extend the right to vote in local elections to all residents of the District of Columbia including non-U.S. citizens." The coalition is comprised of a broad range of immigrant and civic groups, faith-based organizations, unions, individuals, and other entities.[206]

Members of the coalition successfully obtained endorsements and support from key political players. One of the first was the Mount Pleasant Advisory Neighborhood Commission (ANC-1D; ANCs are elected bodies representing residents at the local level that make recommendations regarding a range of issues to D.C. government agencies and the city council).[207] The Mount Pleasant ANC represents one of the largest concentrations of noncitizens in D.C., predominantly Latinos. Mario Cristaldo, the coordinator for the Voting Rights for All D.C. Coalition and a community organizer for the tenants' rights organization Manna Inc., and Eugenio Arene made a presentation to the ANC-1D in September 2003, urging their support of the voting rights initiative. Arene emphasized that about one-third of Mount Pleasant residents do not have access to political representation, including longtime residents who have been active in community life, and that the lack of political representation had a direct connection to the types of problems that face the Mount Pleasant community, including youth violence and gang activity.[208] Cristaldo said, "There are 50,000 District residents who would be enfranchised by such legislation—we are building a grass roots campaign from the ground up."[209] He said the coalition would use the ANC-1D's resolution as a tool to engage other ANCs and community organizations, and eventually work with supportive city council members to introduce legislation.[210] This strategy proved effective.

The Mount Pleasant ANC voted unanimously to support local voting rights for documented residents. ANC-1D Commissioner Barbara Bitondo, who sponsored the resolution and who also chairs the Latino Committee, said, "Thirty percent of Mount Pleasant residents are not citizens. Whenever we try to advocate for our neighborhood through the political process, it is as if we were flying on three engines out of four, because so many of our neighbors cannot stand with us at election time." ANC-1D Chair Dominic Sale stated there were many potential benefits to the community as a whole that would follow from such an expansion of the voting franchise: "This [initiative] opens up a whole new world to people who don't have a voice in the community. If we give people this opportunity, I believe they will come to feel a greater ownership of the community, they will take up greater responsibilities in the community, and the seeds will be sown for resolving some of the persistent problems that stem from lack of ownership in the community."[211]

Aside from holding meetings at other ANCs—and at other community-based venues—to educate residents about the voting rights initiative, advocates manufactured media attention to further make their case. Advocates organized press conferences in conjunction with their community forums to announce endorsements by labor unions and city council members. Flanked by community residents, advocates and their allies grew in number and strength.[212]

Much of the media coverage was favorable and helped advance arguments for the legislation. For example, Mario Cristaldo, who was born in Paraguay and has lived in D.C. since 1994 as a noncitizen, countered critics who argue that immigrants should become citizens before they get the vote: "I invite anyone who says we don't want to become citizens to navigate the [immigration] system. It is not easy." Cristaldo stated that foreign-born residents are "not going anywhere" and that "[w]e want to elect our council members, ANC commissioners, school board representatives and the mayor."[213] Advocates cited a report by the Catholic Legal Immigration Network, which showed that non–U.S. citizens who are eligible for naturalization "are consistently stymied by naturalization backlogs in the INS, unnecessary bureaucratic complexity, poor and non-existent instructions to applicants, increased fees, and a lack of preparation opportunities for the citizenship test."[214]

Perhaps most effective were compelling statements by advocates and affected individuals. For example, Mary Williams, a coalition member and civil rights advocate, said, "Immigrants are playing an increasingly vital role in the growth of the District but it takes immigrants an average of ten years to achieve their citizenship. That is too long for them not to have a say in the vital civic issues that affect their everyday life, such as the education of their children, the safety of their neighborhoods, the economic opportunities available to them. This bill would allow them to vote in local elections as they continue to work towards full U.S. citizenship."[215]

The coalition marshaled economic data to support their campaign. They cited a 1997 National Academy of Sciences publication that shows that immigrants contribute more in taxes than they receive in public benefits (by about $1,800), and a 1995 report by the Cato Institute that showed that immigrants put more money into the "pockets of natives" via taxes than they use in public expenditures ($2,500 in 1995 dollars).[216]

Advocates presented data showing that "immigrants don't take jobs from non-immigrants," dispelling the widely held myth that posits the opposite effect. Indeed, the Cato Institute study concludes, "Immigrants do not cause native unemployment, even among low-paid or minority groups." Moreover, newcomers also "make jobs" with new businesses they start that "are at least as numerous as the jobs which immigrants fill." Advocates also emphasize that immigrants have also repopulated areas where significant portions of the population previously fled, increased enrollments in public schools, renovated housing, and revitalized distressed neighborhoods and the city as a whole.

Equally important, advocates showed that noncitizen voting was feasible. They detailed ways in which such a law could be implemented with security measures, without excessive costs or logistical barriers. They explained that a noncitizen voter would have to show proof of immigration status, identification, and place of residence—all things required to receive a driver's license. Advocates noted that a 2002 Voter Registration Subcommittee of the D.C. Board of Elections and Ethics recommended the District "develop a voter registration application for non-U.S. citizens for the purpose of participating in local elections." Advocates say the cost will be "relatively small, but not insignificant." Pointing to neighboring

Takoma Park, Maryland, and other jurisdictions, they contend that noncitizen voting is doable.[217]

As political support—and clout—grew during 2003, the coalition gained the support of two city council members who drafted legislation.[218] By the summer of 2004, the coalition gained the support of five city council members out of thirteen (seven are needed to pass legislation). Already having Mayor Anthony Williams on record as supporting legislation, advocates' hope was not unrealistic.

On July 13, 2004, legislation was formally introduced in the D.C. council that would grant legal permanent residents the right to vote in municipal elections.[219] Councilmember Jim Graham (D–Ward 1), one of the prime sponsors of the legislation, said upon its introduction, "Approximately, one out of every four residents in Ward One is an immigrant. Immigrants pay taxes, their children attend our public schools, they serve in the military, contribute to our economy and enrich our cultural diversity. This bill would allow them to vote in local elections as they continue to work towards full U.S. citizenship." Another councilmember, Adrian Fenty (D–Ward 4), said, "Ward 4 has the largest growing immigrant population in the city. It is important to my constituents that this legislation move forward, in that it will provide a much needed franchise to thousands." At-Large Councilmember Harold Brazil (D) said, "Our immigrant communities have already proved their willingness to take on the full obligations of being a D.C. resident. They work to improve our neighborhoods, they help our economy with their labor and entrepreneurship, and they even serve in the military. So, it is only fair that we extend to them the right to vote in our local elections."[220] Having the support of these and two other council members—Sharon Ambrose (Ward 6) and Kevin Chavous (Ward 7)—advocates focused their lobbying efforts on obtaining support from two additional council members needed to pass the bill.[221]

Within days, however, members of Congress who call for greater restrictions on immigration moved to block the District's initiative, deflating advocates' hopes. Because Congress has ultimate constitutional authority over the District of Columbia, it can stop D.C. laws by intervening during a thirty-day review period and, more commonly, can intervene by including riders on the District's budget. In this case, opponents in the House of Representatives approved the District's 2005 budget only after Republican leaders pledged to stop the D.C. Council's immigrant voting rights initiative. Representative Tom Tancredo (R-CO) rallied members of Congress to oppose the D.C. initiative: "Passage would eliminate one of the few remaining distinctions between noncitizens and citizens, and I think, frankly, it's not too much to ask that being a U.S. citizen is required to vote in an American election."[222] Tancredo wrote a letter asking members of Congress to oppose the D.C. law, arguing, "One of the things that differentiates American citizenship from simple residency is the right to vote. The passage of this measure would not only blur that distinction, it would erase it—allowing as many as 40,000 aliens in the District of Columbia to vote."[223]

Thomas M. Davis III (R-VA.), who chaired the House Government Reform Committee that oversees the District, pledged Congress would not permit such a law.[224] Essentially, House Republicans used this tactic as a "preemptive strike" to deter the District from passing the legislation; it apparently worked. David Marin, a spokesperson for Representative Davis, said, "Every indication is that the council will not pass this bill, so the point is, a preemptive strike [by amendment] was unnecessary." Thus, Tancredo was persuaded to drop his amendment that would have blocked the D.C. immigrant voting bill.[225]

Advocates in the District viewed these tactics by opponents in Congress as heavy-handed. It also was indicative of partisan implications, particularly in an election year. District Councilman Jim Graham shot back, saying Tancredo's amendment "should send a very interesting message to Republicans in California, Texas, New Mexico, Florida—need I continue—about the Republican Party's views on immigrants and Latinos, specifically."[226]

These developments engendered greater sparring by advocates and opponents in the national media. For example, on a CNN show hosted by Lou Dobbs, D.C. Councilman Adrian Fenty argued, "This country is founded on taxation with representation, not taxation without representation. So you've got a group of residents out here who pay my salary, pay for the governments to work, but don't have any say in who runs the government." Peter Schuck, a professor at Yale Law School, disagreed: "I think immigrants should not be able to vote until they have naturalized and become American citizens, but, once they have committed themselves to American society by showing a mastery of English, at least a limited level, and some understanding of the political system. Then and only then should they be able to vote." Congressman Tancredo, another guest on the show, argued it is essential for immigrants to go through the citizenship process to earn the right to vote, contending that the difficulty of the naturalization process was a positive feature of our system: "This is one of the things that we provide people to go through a very laborious process. It's very difficult to do. It's also a mark of citizenship. We should not be simply casually handing this out because what we are doing is essentially destroying the whole concept of citizenship in this country." Dobbs concluded by noting that Tancredo exacted a promise from the chairman of the House Appropriations Committee and the Government Reform Committee to make sure Congress will override any local legislation that would give immigrants the right to vote in D.C.[227]

Although these developments cast a cloud on the prospects of immigrant voting rights in the nation's capital, it did not deter advocates and supportive council members. They continued to work for the bill's passage, even while they acknowledged Congress's threat. Councilman Graham said he believed the District bill would pass, recognizing that it may not be in 2004. He said supporters continued to lobby two more members of the council, who they needed to pass the bill, even if they had to reintroduce the bill in 2005: "This is not a 50-yard dash issue. This is an issue you just have to keep working on."[228] Similarly, Tamrat Medhin, a civic activist from Ethiopia living in D.C., said determinedly, "It will happen. Don't you believe that if people are working in the community and paying taxes, don't you agree that they deserve the opportunity to vote?" Another D.C. advocate, Sergio Luna from Guatemala, said he wants to improve his son's schools: "If we have the opportunity to vote for the school board, the Council and the mayor, we'll be making some changes."[229]

Massachusetts

Massachusetts provides advocates of immigrant voting with a crucial challenge: state action is needed to enact voting rights for noncitizens at the local level. Although community-based advocates have been successful at getting legislation enacted that would grant noncitizens voting rights in municipal elections, implementation of these local laws has been stymied by a lack of requisite state action.

Both Cambridge and Amherst passed legislation to permit noncitizens to vote in local elections in the mid-1990s and again in 2003. But these local laws have not been implemented because enabling legislation is required—passage of a home rule petition by the state legislature. Still, advocates remain hopeful and active. Advocates and supportive local and state legislators continue to work for the enactment of state law that would allow Cambridge and Amherst to move forward to implement noncitizen voting in their local elections. These two cities led the fight for noncitizen voting in Massachusetts. They would subsequently be joined in the struggle for immigrant voting rights by activists in several other cities and towns, some that have an even higher percentage of noncitizen residents among their total voting-age populations, including Somerville, Chelsea, Everett, Newton, and Boston. Together, they collectively have gained a greater presence and more political clout in their respective communities and in the state legislature.

In chapter 4, we explored the key players, arguments, and activities of the campaigns for noncitizen voting in both Cambridge and Amherst. In this section, we briefly outline the highlights of these campaigns. We begin by presenting some demographic information to set the context.

Demography

According to the U.S. Bureau of the Census in 2000, about 8 percent of the almost 5 million adult residents in Massachusetts are noncitizens: 381,751 out of 4,853,130, the eleventh highest in the nation. There are over 770,000 foreign-born individuals in the state. In some jurisdictions, however, the proportion rises to nearly one in ten or one in five.

In Cambridge, for example, immigrants comprise a sizable portion of the population. In 1990, the U.S. Census showed there were 21,350 foreign-born residents, 14,754 of whom were noncitizens (the total population was just under 100,000). That meant that almost 15 percent of Cambridge's residents were noncitizens and over 20 percent were foreign-born. The number of noncitizens rose even higher by 2000. In 2000, Cambridge's voting-age population had grown to 87,942 with 16,307 (18.5 percent) being noncitizens eighteen years of age or older.[230] In Amherst, 9.4 percent of their adult population is noncitizens.

Other cities where advocates are pursuing immigrant voting rights include Chelsea, in Suffolk County, where 8,788—or 34.4 percent—noncitizens of voting age reside out of 25,523 adult residents, the highest proportion of noncitizens of any city in Massachusetts; Somerville, which has a higher number of noncitizens of voting age, 14,191 (or 21.4 percent) out of 66,269; Everett, which has 4,821 adult noncitizens out of 29,872 voting-age residents, or 16.1 percent; Newton, which has 8.2 percent; and Boston, which has the largest number: 84,688 noncitizens of voting age out of 473,267 adults, or 17.9 percent (see table 6.5).[231]

Campaigns in Cambridge and Amherst

The campaign in Cambridge for noncitizen voting grew out of struggles to protect and defend housing and other basic services for immigrants. In 1991, Haitian tenant organizers raised the issue of local voting rights for immigrants. According to Kathleen Coll, a volunteer in the Campaign for Immigrant Voting Rights in Cambridge, tenant organizers realized that "we're not getting anyone to listen to us." These tenant organizers wondered, "What if we had the right to vote?" Surely, they reasoned, immi-

TABLE 6.5 Noncitizens of Voting Age in Massachusetts Cities

Geography	Population Eighteen Years and Over (Total)	Population Eighteen Years and Over, Not a Citizen (Foreign-born, Not Naturalized)	% Noncitizen Eighteen Years and Over
Chelsea, Suffolk County	25523	8788	34.4
Lawrence, Essex County	49066	13498	27.5
Somerville, Middlesex County	66269	14191	21.4
Cambridge, Middlesex County	87942	16307	18.5
Lowell, Middlesex County	76876	13922	18.1
Boston, Suffolk County	473267	84688	17.9
Lynn, Essex County	65219	11480	17.6
Malden, Middlesex County	45102	7929	17.6
Everett, Middlesex County	29872	4821	16.1
Revere, Suffolk County	37468	5445	14.5
Waltham, Middlesex County	50055	6783	13.6
Brockton, Plymouth County	67999	9145	13.4
Marlborough, Middlesex County	27884	3503	12.6
New Bedford, Bristol County	70623	7977	11.3
Fall River, Bristol County	69733	7695	11.0
Worcester, Worcester County	132040	13913	10.5
Quincy, Norfolk County	72633	7620	10.5
Watertown, Middlesex County	28304	2796	9.9
Medford, Middlesex County	45667	4238	9.3
Newton, Middlesex County	66067	5439	8.2

Source: "Citizenship Status for the Population 18 Years and over," Census Table GCT-P.11.

grant concerns such as housing and access to public services would move up higher on the political agenda. This novel idea—linking tenant's rights and the concerns of low-income residents to the institutional empowerment of immigrants—caught on and evolved into a campaign for immigrant voting rights.[232]

After these organizers forged ties to other immigrant rights and civil rights groups, forming the Campaign for Immigrant Voting Rights, they launched an initiative for noncitizen voting rights in 1993 that was spearheaded by and housed in the Eviction Free Zone, a nonprofit organization dedicated to protecting affordable housing for low-income residents. Over time, the coalition became "a very broad coalition of immigrant rights groups, religious organizations, and tenant rights organizations."[233] These efforts focused on gaining voting rights in local elections, initially for school committee. In Cambridge, the elected offices are school committee and city council.

Laura Booth, who led the effort in 1993, said the Eviction Free Zone "learned that a professor at a university in Takoma Park campaigned for a referendum to allow noncitizens to vote and succeeded."[234] Soon after the Cambridge campaign was launched, however, Natalie Smith, an immigrant from the United Kingdom, took over the leadership role and expanded the coalition.[235]

In 1995, a proposal to rescind rent control led tenant organizers to launch a statewide organizing effort to protect rent control. After a protracted struggle, that effort ultimately failed; rent control was rescinded, which was a blow to low-income and immigrant rights struggles.

In 1996, however, the idea of voting rights for noncitizens reemerged in a campaign in San Francisco, garnering national attention. This spurred activists to renew efforts first in Amherst, and then again in Cambridge.

In Amherst, Vladimir Morales, a native of Puerto Rico, a school committee member since 1985, and a member of the town assembly, led the fight for noncitizen voting rights in local elections. Morales built a cadre of activists and allies who together have persuaded the town to pass local legislation several times: in 1996, 1999, 2001, and 2003. Morales made several arguments which proved persuasive: "It's 'taxation without representation. . . . They should have a right to have a say on things that affect them. . . . If we want to look at the United States supporting democracy around the world, we should have more democracy inside the country."[236]

The Amherst effort successfully passed legislation at the local level in 1996 that also led to the introduction of a state bill in 1998, which in turn "re-inspired folks in Cambridge to take up the struggle for voting rights again."[237] Morales got a hold of a law review journal article by Jamie Raskin, which gave him critical information that prompted him to pursue the effort in Amherst. Kathy Coll noted, "It is an interesting thing that community activists are being empowered by legal scholarship."[238]

After much grassroots organizing to build support for the idea in both jurisdictions—and after meeting with key elected officials at the local and state levels—the Cambridge Coalition pressed forward. In 1998, the city council in Cambridge established a task force to address conflicts between different racial and ethnic groups, as well as class tensions. The task force sought to find ways to ameliorate tensions, including typical methods such as sensitivity training for city employees, examining the lack of diversity in government positions (including top managers), and even expanding affordable housing.

Natalie Smith recommended that the task force explore the idea of immigrant voting as a mechanism to address class and race tensions that divided the city. She found an ally in Denise Simmons, who headed the task force and was also a school board member: Simmons said, "People who use public schools, pay taxes, and participate in community activities should have a say not only in their children's education, but also in how their taxes are spent. We understand that some people feel the right to vote should be a privilege only for citizens, but you have to look at it from a participatory point of view." Expanding voting rights, Simmons argued, would give a larger number of people who have a stake in the city a greater voice in decision making "and, in turn, show city-government officials that all members of the Cambridge community have a vested interest in the future of the city and its schools."[239] Because of their work, the Cambridge City Council passed legislation in December 1999 allowing documented noncitizens to vote in school board elections, so long as they declare their intent to become citizens.[240]

The plan, if implemented, would provide for a voter registration form that includes a declaration signed by noncitizens that they are residents of Cambridge, and that their presence is known to the U.S. Immigration and Naturalization Service (now USCIS) and they intend "in good faith to become a U.S. citizen" or intend "to begin the process, if eligible."

The Cambridge measure allowed all immigrants to vote for school committee; the Amherst measure was for legal permanent residents in all local elections. The Cambridge legislation would enfranchise more immigrants by including any local resident who could prove residency in Cambridge, regardless of immigration status, so long as they declared themselves to the INS and stated that they intended to regularize their status and become a citizen. This legislation was crafted to build on an old tradition, the declarant aliens—people who declare their intent to become citizens as soon as they are able to do so, and who show that they are permanent residents of the town. But the legislation would have only allowed immigrants to vote for school committee. However, both the bills for Cambridge and Amherst were sent for "study" in the state legislature but were never reported out of committee, and no report or statement was ever issued.

The Cambridge Coalition redoubled its efforts. After intensive and sustained organizing and lobbying, the Cambridge City Council voted in 2003 to expand noncitizen voting to all municipal elections (i.e., both city council and school board elections). Moreover, Cambridge's legislation continued to make no distinction between documented (legal) and undocumented (illegal) noncitizen residents, though it did retain the provision that such voters must declare their intent to become citizens. "In a very hostile time, our City Council actually chose to expand its demand on the state. And even more significantly, Amherst and Cambridge are working together to lobby for both of our bills simultaneously."[241]

In fact, advocates in Cambridge began to work with activists in nearby towns that have large and growing working-class immigrant populations, including Somerville and Chelsea. These communities, which have close to majority minority populations, have a majority of white elected officials. "They are watching closely to see what happens to us [Cambridge and Amherst]," said Kathy Coll. As she put it, the campaign for immigrant voting is a "long term struggle that builds locally, but it is also building regionally. Over the last two years we have really begun to appreciate the importance of linking with other immigrant groups around the state. Only then will we get it through statehouse. When groups from other towns around the state call their legislators and say 'we think this is a good idea—let them try it.' It is particularly important to target legislators on the election law committee."[242]

When the bills from Cambridge and Amherst were refiled in 2003, they were crafted in a way so they were more similar. Though not identical, they helped their mutual cause. The Amherst bill was similar to its original version—granting legal permanent residents voting rights for all offices—and the Cambridge bill allowed for immigrants to vote for all local offices (not just for school committee).

Kathy Coll noted something that advocates in other campaigns across the country have also stated: "Our movement owes a tremendous debt to those who've struggled for the right to vote before us." Previous struggles laid the groundwork on which they could build. Moreover, prominent African Americans in Massachusetts currently support the Amherst and Cambridge bills, which has been important for the cause of immigrant voting rights. In 2001, for example, supporters of the Amherst measure included the State Legislature's Black Caucus and Mel King, who ran for mayor in Boston and who was a founder of the Rainbow Coalition.[243]

At the time, however, opponents countered that such a measure would discourage immigrants from becoming citizens. For example, an editorial by the *Boston Globe* argued, "If becoming a citizen seems too great a commitment, immigrants do not have to make it, but they should not expect to be full partners in the democratic process until they do."[244] Others objected for related reasons. A high school history and economics teacher, Gregg Anderson, said that paying taxes doesn't ensure a sense of responsibility and history that go along with the right to vote, adding, "There's something mystical about the vote." Anderson, who described himself as "pro-immigrant," said, "God love them, but if they really want to vote, they should become citizens."[245]

Coll reiterates an important justification for noncitizen voting:

> In addition to being surprised when they learn about the long history of noncitizen voting in the U.S., public officials are often most impressed when they learn about the terribly long timeline to naturalization for so many immigrants. Most non-immigrants don't realize that depending on your nationality and visa status upon entry, you can wait twenty years to become eligible to naturalize. This situation has gotten worse rather than better in the last ten years due to changes in federal immigration law. It's not "just" about backlogs, but about institutional barriers to even obtaining the legal permanent resident status, much less citizenship. How many people are disenfranchised and underrepresented during all those years? How many U.S.-born as well as immigrant children are without political representation through the exclusion of their parents from local elections? Immigrants who have or are themselves going through these long and complicated processes offer the most compelling personal testimonies about the importance of noncitizen voting in our meetings with elected officials.[246]

During the past several years, other towns in Massachusetts have launched similar campaigns, including Newton, Somerville, Chelsea, and Everett. Kathy Coll notes that how Cambridge and Amherst fare will have an impact on the campaigns in these other jurisdictions: "They are watching closely to see what happens to us."[247]

Several state legislators have championed the legislation (Alice Wolf and Jarrett Barrios for Cambridge, and Ellen Story for Amherst). In February 2004, a bill (HB 45400) was sponsored by Alice K. Wolf, Paul C. Demakis, Anne M. Paulsen, Jarrett T. Barrios, Byron Rushing, and others. In February 2005, legislators (Alice K. Wolf) refiled a home rule petition (specifically naming Cambridge) and an enabling act to allow adult noncitizen residents to vote in municipal elections. But at the time of this writing, the state legislature has not yet passed home rule petitions that would enable the localities to implement these local laws.

Many advocates have traveled to the capital, Springfield, to speak in favor of the bill (and/or have sent written testimony). For example, Ali Noorani, the executive director of the Massachusetts Immigrant and Refugee Advocacy Coalition (MIRA), a statewide membership organization that advocates for the rights and opportunities of immigrants and refugees across Massachusetts, presented testimony to the Election Law Committee of the state legislature at a public hearing, stating that immigrant communities "face discrimination and prejudice in our neighborhoods, workplaces and schools," and in the current period are "subject to surveillance, detention, deportation and a general erosion of civil liberties." He argued that granting immigrants the right to vote in local elections would "increase civic participation, make our democracy truly representative and improve the quality of life of all Massachusetts residents. Moreover, allowing immigrants to vote in local elections will better protect their rights as individuals, and create a constituency elected officials can work with for generations to come."[248]

The matter remains before the Massachusetts state legislature. Advocates continue to work at the local level and to collaborate regionally and at the state level. If they are successful at building sufficient power to persuade the state of Massachusetts to pass enabling legislation, which would be no small feat, these jurisdictions would join the six municipalities in Maryland, which already allow noncitizens to vote in local elections, and in Chicago, which permits noncitizen parents to vote in school board elections. Perhaps more importantly, it would signal to advocates everywhere that community-based organizing in collaboration with partners regionally and statewide can prevail.[249]

Portland, Maine

In September 2004, as the growing number of campaigns for immigrant voting rights was generating increasing media attention, advocates in Portland launched an initiative to grant legal permanent residents local voting rights. In this case, several progressive elected officials spearheaded the campaign, led by Stephen Spring, a school board member, in a largely immigrant population. As with other initiatives, information about past practices and the context of current campaigns spurred advocates to take action.

Following September 11, Portland experienced a number of hate crime attacks on members of the city's increasing Muslim population. In addition, immigration and law enforcement officials investigated suspected individuals, which "resulted in random searches, harassment, and about a dozen deportations. Families were scared and many children stayed out of school." Following these actions, the Portland City Council passed two resolutions in 2002 and 2003, denouncing the immigrant sweeps and the USA PATRIOT Act. On the heels of these events, immigrant activists also searched for ways to promote pro-immigration initiatives, one of which was a campaign for immigrant voting rights.[250]

As background, the U.S. Bureau of the Census reported that in 2000 Portland had 4,895 foreign-born residents or 7.6 percent of the total population. Moreover, since 1990, there was a significant increase—49.1 percent—of immigrants to Portland. More than half of the city's foreign-born population—57.8 percent—arrived since 1990. Of these new arrivals, more than a third, 34.2 percent, naturalized and became U.S. citizens. This came during a period when 2.8 percent of the native-born population left Portland.

The campaign for immigrant voting rights began with a course, Hate Crimes and Public Policy, that Stephen Spring took in the spring of 2004 at the Muskie Institute for Public Policy. While researching topics for his final paper, he came across web links detailing the campaigns for immigrant voting rights in nearby Cambridge and Amherst, Massachusetts. Subsequently, Spring learned about immigrant voting in Maryland, Chicago, and New York City. Spring decided to write his final paper on noncitizen voting in municipal elections. When Spring presented his work to his colleagues, they encouraged him to make the work public. Spring did that and more. Stephen Spring mailed copies of his paper to the nine Portland city councilors and to his eight colleagues on the school board. From there, he began to work in earnest with several members of both the school board and city council sympathetic to the cause, along with immigrant and civic groups. They would have discussions and strategize, seek endorsements, make presentations at community forums, and work to gain media attention.

Spring made many of the arguments we have seen in other campaigns for immigrant voting rights: "Immigrants coming to us need to be part of a community. We need to make them feel welcome and part of the process, more a part of society." Spring said that if noncitizen voting rights were granted, elected officials like himself could "do our job more accurately" because they would be more accountable and better "represent all of our constituents."251 One of Spring's allies, Tae Chong, a school committee member, is a citizen but his parents remain noncitizens. "My parents have been in Portland 28 years and paid taxes for 28 years. It's too bad my mom and dad couldn't vote for me to be on the School Committee." Chong said his parents, who took the citizenship test, failed to understand all of the questions and/or adequately deliver their responses in English.

Chong noted that Portland has long been a city of diversity with a history of progressive politics. He points out that in the public school system today, "over 60 languages [are] spoken in our school system" among "over 30 nationalities." Moreover, Chong argues, Portland has a long history of openness and progressive policy making, and granting voting rights to immigrants would be another step forward.

Portland has the first African-American bishop in the United States, it was one of the first cities to support the Abolition movement, it was the first city in the state to have an openly gay mayor, it was the first city in the state to pass the anti-discrimination ordinance and it was the [first] city in the state to pass the anti-harassment ordinance. In many ways, Portland has been the social conscience for the rest of the state as well as being its business and political leader. It is only fitting that Portland passes an ordinance allowing its permanent residents to vote in local nonpartisan elections—even the ancient Greeks allowed its slaves to have a voice in certain elections. Allowing all permanent residents be concerned about how their taxes are used to run our schools and all its city departments only makes the city more livable. We all know that being named as one of the most livable cities in the United States helps us to draw in more business and more potential jobs. Giving all permanent residents the right to vote in local elections makes sense. It respects our past, it encourages our present.[252]

Spring and his allies obtained support from other members of the school board, two state legislators, and groups such as the Portland Chapter of the Maine Green Independent Party, among others.

In Maine, a change in state law would be needed to enfranchise noncitizens in local elections (but no change to the state's constitution would be necessary). Spring obtained the support of two state legislators, Representative John Eder and State Senator Ethan Strimling, who said they would propose such legislation in 2005, granting permanent residents voting rights in city council and school board elections. At the local level, the lawyers for the city wrote a brief that claimed it would be possible to expand voting rights without a charter change. It is hoped this will garner greater support among city councilors.[253]

Spring noted in the course of the campaign that such divisions also represent tensions in Portland "between the Green Party and the Democratic Party." Spring also acknowledged that there was insufficient mobilization "within the immigrant communities" thus far.[254] Additional challenges have surfaced in this campaign.

Opponents included several city councilors, critical to the passage of any legislation, and other community members who similarly marshaled familiar objections. For example, Portland City Councilor Will Gorham said, "People should be legal citizens before they're allowed to vote." From another angle, City Councilor Jill Duson said, "I think it's OK for voting to be a privilege of citizenship." Interestingly, Duson also said that her son-in-law from Trinidad is a noncitizen who serves in the U.S. military services, noting, "It seems strange to me that (he) can volunteer to serve in Iraq, but he can't vote here until he attains citizenship. If he can die for us, he ought to able to vote." Duson, however, suggested as a solution that the citizenship process should be "sped up."[255]

In 2004, three city council seats were up for grabs, including two seats by opponents of noncitizen voting rights who were being challenged by supporters. At the state level, several supporters in state legislature were up for election. After the election, Spring said that advocates petitioned "the city council to expand the vote to noncitizens in school board elections (or possibly all municipal elections)." Advocates also hoped that media attention to the campaigns in San Francisco; Washington, D.C.; and New York City would provide "fuel" to the work needed to win the campaign in Portland. Spring predicted that the Portland School Board would have the votes to petition the city council.

Reflecting on what would help the cause of immigrant voting rights in Portland, Spring named the following: success in other cities with national media attention (such as Washington, D.C., or New York City); the ousting of conservative city councilors by supporters of noncitizen voting; the mobilization of immigrant groups, particularly Somali, Sudanese, Southeast Asian, Balkan, and Central Asian immigrants; and the formation of an effective broad-based coalition in Portland. Indeed, these ingredients have proven successful and/or helpful in every campaign for immigrant voting rights across the country.

Minnesota

For the past few years, the Minnesota Coalition for the Expansion of Voting Rights has been working with state representatives from St. Paul and Minneapolis, which led to the introduction of legislation to allow "permanent resident aliens" to vote in local elections. Interestingly, Minnesota's immigrant voting rights initiative began with a discussion on an e-democracy message board called Minneapolis Issues Forum, which included state legislators, neighborhood leaders, business leaders, arts leaders, and many people from the community at large.[256]

If enacted, the legislation would amend the state's constitution, which currently restricts voting to U.S. citizens. Two bills were introduced into the Minnesota House of Representatives, one in 2003 (HF 0071) and the other in 2005 (HF 818).[257] The current bill would put the following question on the 2006 ballot for the voters to decide: "Shall the Minnesota Constitution be amended to allow local units of government to authorize permanent resident noncitizens to vote in local government elections?" In January, 2003, five state legislators introduced a bill in the state House of Representatives to amend article VII, section 1, of the state constitution to give communities the authority to allow legal permanent residents to vote in its local elections. The bill would have placed the constitutional change on the November 2004 ballot for approval by Minnesotans. However, it never made it out of the Governmental Operations and Veterans Affairs Policy Committee.

The State Green Party put alien voting rights in their platform, but there has been little organizing done around the legislation and the media has more or less ignored it.[258]

Connecticut

During the past several years, immigrant and democracy advocates in Connecticut have worked to defend and advance the interest of immigrants. One form it took was a proposed state bill that would have allowed immigrants who own property and/or pay taxes equaling the value of $1,000 to vote in local elections. Initially, some immigrant advocates were interested in supporting the bill, given that it came in 2003 during an anti-immigrant period in Connecticut. However, others worried about the bill's connection to property ownership, which smacked of similar restrictions in history. In the end, the bill died. Nevertheless, it opened the door to more progressive legislation, which advocates have been working towards since.[259]

Madison, Wisconsin

Alderman Austin King, who represents the eighth district in Madison's Common Council, included a proposal for noncitizen voting when he campaigned and won in 2003.[260] Even though no formal legislation was introduced, other aldermen and their opponents campaigned against the idea of immigrants voting in local elections. One of King's first resolutions condemned John D. Wiley, chancellor of the University of Wisconsin–Madison, for supporting an additional fee of $125 that was applied to international students, in order to comply with then–Attorney General John Ashcroft's surveillance of student exchange programs. The resolution generated criticism of the chancellor, who later rescinded his order (the University of Wisconsin now covers the costs). It also generated condemnation of the resolution by some city council members, even "xenophobia," said Alderman King. This was King's "personal motivation" for supporting immigrant voting rights.[261]

Reelected in 2005, Alderman King and several of his colleagues plan to work toward introducing legislation within the next two years.[262]

Advocates are working in coalition with various groups, including a "major" Latino nonprofit organization and the National Lawyers Guild, who are providing legal support. One of the key elements to their success may be how the city attorney—and others—view this local initiative. If the city attorney or others don't believe that the city of Madison can enact such legislation without state approval, it will be an even harder and longer fight.[263]

North Carolina

In 2004, John Herrera, a member of the Carrboro Board of Aldermen, asked the board to request that the state legislature grant "Carrboro immigrants who are permanent residents and have applied for U.S. citizenship the right to vote in local municipal elections."[264]

Herrera, who formerly lived in Takoma Park, Maryland, was born in Costa Rica. Even though Herrera married a U.S. citizen, he had to wait ten years to naturalize because "the INS lost my papers, twice."[265]

Herrera said he wants to increase civic participation in the town: "I'm just looking as an elected official to strengthen the bureaucratic process and to get people involved early on. Communities could contribute more if they are allowed to."[266] Soon after Herrera raised the issue at the Board of Aldermen, the *Daily Tar Heel* wrote an editorial supporting Herrera's proposal. However, state representatives were cool to the idea and have not acted on it.

Texas

State Representative Robert Alonzo (D-Dallas) introduced legislation in 1995 that would have granted local governments the option to allow legal permanent residents voting rights in local elections. Although he did not generate sufficient support at that time to get the bill moving through the legislature, he said in 2004 that he thinks the idea is still worth pursuing.

> At the time, we were discussing school issues, talking about local control and that people locally should be involved in their community, definitely on school issues. In a lot of cities like Houston (with an estimated 587,000 non-citizen residents) there are parents who are legal residents, they're in line to become citizens, they pay taxes, they can go to PTA meetings, but they can't elect their local school board members. The biggest involvement they can have is to allow them to make decisions that affect their children.[267]

TABLE 6.6 International Voting Rights
(Items in Parentheses Indicate Rights That Either Have Been Proposed or Are No Longer Currently in Practice)

Country	Date Measure Passed or Defeated	Type of Voting Rights	Geographic Limitations	Nationality Limitations	Residency Requirements
Australia	Passed in 1947. Retracted in 1984 with a grandfather clause for those registered before 1984	National and local	None	British only	One month in municipality
Austria	Passed in 2002.	Local	Vienna only	None	Five years of legal residency
Barbados	Passed in 1990. Voided by Constitutional over 2004	National	N.A.	Commonwealth citizens only	Three years
Belgium	2004	Local	None	None	Legal residency for five years; sign declaration to respect Belgium laws and Constitution
Belize	N.A.	National and local	N.A.	None	Three years
Bolivia	Constitution changed in 1994 to allow noncitizens to vote. Has not been implemented.	Local	None	None	N.A.
Brazil	N.A.	National	N.A.	Portuguese only	N.A.

Country	Date Measure Passed or Defeated	Type of Voting Rights	Geographic Limitations	Nationality Limitations	Residency Requirements
Bulgaria	2005	Local	Local	EU Nationals	N.A.
Canada	N.A.	Provincial and local	n.a. / Provinces of Saskatchew and Nova Scotia	Commonwealth citizens / British only	N.A.
Chile	Passed in 1989.	National and local	n.a.	None	Five years
Colombia	Constitution changed in 1991 to allow noncitizens to vote. Has not been implemented.	Local	None	None	
Czech Republic	2001	Local	None	EU Nationals	N.A.
Denmark	Originally in 1977. Expanded to current level in 1981.	Local	None	None	Three year
Estonia	2004	Local only	None	Russian-speaking minority only—they are not Estonian citizens.	Must be "permanent residents"

(Continued)

TABLE 6.6 International Voting Rights
(Items in Parentheses Indicate Rights That Either Have Been Proposed or Are No Longer Currently in Practice) (*Continued*)

Country	Date Measure Passed or Defeated	Type of Voting Rights	Geographic Limitations	Nationality Limitations	Residency Requirements
Finland	Original law enacted in 1919. Expanded to current level in 1991.	Local	None	None	Four years
France	Failed in 1981 and 2000.				
Germany	Passed in 1989. Struck down by Constitutional Court in 1990.	Local	State of Schleswig-Holstein	Danish, Irish, Dutch, Norse, Swedish, and Swiss	Five years
	Passed in 1989. Struck down by Constitutional Court in 1990.	Local	State of Hamburg	None	Eight years
	Passed in 1989. Struck down by Constitutional Court in 1990.	Local	West Berlin		Five years
Hungary	1990	Local	None	None	"All permanent residents"
	2004 (Revised)	Local	None	Hungarians and EU Nationals	
Iceland	Passed 1986—grandfathered from 1920 Constitution.	Local	None	Nordic Countries	Three years
Ireland	Passed in 1963.	Local	None	None	Six months
	Passed in 1984.	National	n.a.	British citizens	

Country	Date Measure Passed or Defeated	Type of Voting Rights	Geographic Limitations	Nationality Limitations	Residency Requirements
Israel	Passed in 1950.	Local only	None	Based on Law of Return—Jewish residents only	N.A.
Italy	Passed in 2004.	Vote for four nonvoting members of city council (one from Africa, Asia, Latin American, and E Europe) and one nonvoting seat at each of nineteen district councils	Rome	None	N.A.
Japan	In 1995, Japan's Supreme Court ruled that noncitizens do not have the right to vote. In 2000 Japan considered legislation, but did not pass it.	N.A.	N.A.	N.A.	N.A.

(Continued)

TABLE 6.6 Table 6.6 International Voting Rights
(Items in Parentheses Indicate Rights That Either Have Been Proposed or Are No Longer Currently in Practice) (*Continued*)

Country	Date Measure Passed or Defeated	Type of Voting Rights	Geographic Limitations	Nationality Limitations	Residency Requirements
Latvia	Parliament considered it in 2000, but did not pass it.	Local	None	EU Nationals	N.A.
Lithuania	2002, in effect 2004	Local	None	EU Nationals	N.A.
Luxembourg	2003	Local	None	None	N.A.
Maha	1993	Local	None	EU Nationals	N.A.
Netherlands	1982	Local	None	None	Five years
	1982	Local	None	None	Five years
New Zealand	1975; earlier for British residents.	All national and local elections	n.a.	None	One year
Norway	Original 1978. Expanded in 1982.	Local	None	None	Three years
Portugal	1976	National	None	"Subject to reciprocity"; in practice—Brazilian citizens only	
	1982	Local	None	Cape Verde	Three years

Country	Date Measure Passed or Defeated	Type of Voting Rights	Geographic Limitations	Nationality Limitations	Residency Requirements
	1997	Local	None	Peru, Uruguay, Argentina	N.A.
Spain	Passed in 1985.	Local	None	None	N.A.
Sweden	Passed in 1975.	Local only (and some national referenda)	None	None	Three years
Slovakia	2002	Local	None	None	Three years (or permanent resident)
Slovenia	2002	Local	None	None	Eight years
Switzerland (six of 26 Cantons)	Original 1849; restored in the late nineteenth century.	Local only	Canton of Neuchatel	N.A.	N.A.
	1979	Local only	Canton of Jura	N.A.	N.A.
	Considered but rejected measures.		Seven additional cantons	N.A.	N.A.
United Kingdom	1948	National	None	Commonwealth and Irish citizens only	N.A.
	1972 (Local governments established)	Local			

(Continued)

TABLE 6.6 International Voting Rights
(Items in Parentheses Indicate Rights That Either Have Been Proposed or Are No Longer Currently in Practice) (*Continued*)

Country	Date Measure Passed or Defeated	Type of Voting Rights	Geographic Limitations	Nationality Limitations	Residency Requirements
Uruguay	1952	National	N.A.	None	Fifteen years
Venezuela	1983	State and local	None	None	Ten years

Sources: T. Alexander Aleinikoff and Douglas Klusmeyer, *Citizenship Policies for an Age of Migration* (Washington, D.C.: Carnegie Endowment for International Peace, 2002); David Earnest, "Noncitizen Voting Rights: A Survey of an Emerging Democratic Norm" (paper presented at the American Political Science Association meeting, August 28–31, Philadelphia); Rainer Bauböck, "Expansive Citizenship–Voting beyond Territory and Membership"; Waldrauch, Harald, "Electoral rights for foreign nationals: a comparative overview. Paper prepared for Exploratory Workshop. "Citizens, Non-citizens and voting rights in Europe," sponsored by the European Science Foundation, The Europa Institute and the School of Law, University of Edinburgh, Edinburgh, UK. June 2–4, 2005. And the Immigrant Voting Project, "Immigrant Voting Project: Democracy for All," http://www.immigrantvoting.org.

Others agree. For example, Victor Landa, regional director for the Southwest Voter Education Project in San Antonio, said, "We are a formidable force as it is, with just those citizens that are eligible to vote. If we could just tap into that, it would be outstanding. I'm not really sure if those residents awaiting citizenship would be more eager voters—who's to say?" Landa said he thinks that allowing noncitizens to vote on local issues makes sense. "But I don't know if Texas is ready for something like that. Hopefully we could debate it."[268]

Other States and Cities

Immigrant advocates in New Jersey, Virginia, Denver, and Vermont have explored the idea of noncitizen voting campaigns. Some are still pursuing it.[269]

For example, immigrant advocates in several counties in New Jersey recently discussed launching initiatives to expand voting to noncitizens in school board and possibly to other local elections.[270] In Burlington Vermont, immigrants explored the idea with legislators in 2005.[271] In Denver, members of several human rights groups—as well as former legislators and aspiring public officials—discussed the prospects of a campaign for noncitizen voting rights.[272] In Virginia in 1994, Arlingtonians for a Better County (ABC), a local nonpartisan political organization, allowed noncitizens to vote in its internal elections to recommend members to the local school board. ABC also advocated for allowing noncitizens to vote in local school boards elections.[273] More recently, immigrant voting advocates in some locales in Virginia have explored the prospects of expanding voting rights to noncitizens in school board and local elections.

Globally

As many as forty five countries grant voting rights to resident noncitizens.[274] New Zealand has the most inclusive policy: all noncitizens can vote in national and local elections after one year of residency. Similarly, Ireland, the Netherlands and Scandinavian states have allowed universal suffrage for all residents in local elections, regardless of their nationality. At the other end of the spectrum, voting rights are restricted to particular categories of individuals in certain local elections, and in some cases only after an extended residency period. In Canada, for example, only British citizens can vote in provincial elections in Nova Scotia and Saskatchewan, reflecting their past colonial ties. In Britain, citizens of Commonwealth countries can vote in United Kingdom national elections (and can also hold office). In Uruguay, the residency requirement for noncitizen voting is fifteen years. The European Union's Maastricht Treaty provides a middle ground. The 1993 Maastricht Treaty granted all members of the European Union (EU) the right to vote in the local elections of European Union countries. An Italian living and working in France, for example, can vote in local French elections and vice versa.

Europe provides a compelling case for noncitizen voting rights. The creation of the European Union, currently twenty-five member states, expanded upon well established practices of allowing noncitizens to vote in host countries elections. Again, while variation exists regarding which noncitizens can vote (only EU nationals or all third party nationals, meaning anyone from anywhere) in which elections (local and/or national), several European countries have provided some form of voting rights for noncitizens for thirty years or more, including Ireland (1963), Sweden (1975), Denmark (1977), and Norway (1978). In the 1980s, the Netherlands (1982), Venezuela (1983), Ireland (expanded to national elections in 1984), Spain (1985), Iceland (1986), and Hungary (1990, revised in 2004) enacted legislation enfranchising resident aliens. More recently, Lithuania (2002), Slovakia (2002), Slovenia (2002), Luxembourg (2003), Belgium (2004), and Estonia (2004) allow noncitizen voting at the local level. Several Swiss cantons (Neufchatel and Jura) have long permitted noncitizen voting, since 1849.

In fact, noncitizens vote on nearly every continents.[275] Clearly, the push for immigrant voting rights shows no sign of abatement. In general, the trend is going in the other direction—campaigns to extend voting rights to noncitizens are growing in number in recent years. The next chapter explores what the future might hold for these campaigns.

CHAPTER 7

The Future of Immigrant Voting

Immigrants are here to stay. Population projections indicate the foreign-born will grow in number and disperse further throughout the United States, given current family reunification policies, birth rates, domestic economic needs, and so on. Their large and growing numbers make them increasingly important political players. Although questions remain about the direction of U.S. immigration policy, there is little doubt that how immigrants will be incorporated—socially, politically, culturally, and economically—will remain a burning issue for years to come. In other words, it is not a question about whether the millions of immigrants in the United States will be incorporated, but *how* they will be incorporated.

Local voting rights offer a way to facilitate immigrant political incorporation and at the same time present a means to address a deficit in our democracy. Immigrants' taxation without representation not only challenges America's mantle of democratic governance but also provides a rationale and foundation on which to organize noncitizens and their allies around an agenda for civil rights and human rights. Immigrant voting rights can help build political power that could challenge the subordinate position that many noncitizens—and often people of color—are relegated to in the United States. The unequal distribution of social and economic opportunity for immigrants—not to mention the severe exploitation and harsh oppression that many noncitizens suffer—is a reflection, in part, of a lack of immigrant political power.

The representation gap that characterizes governments at every level—which is both a symptom and a cause of immigrants' lack of political power—is the result of several factors. John Mollenkopf and John Logan explore three possible factors that may contribute to the representation gap in urban settings: "barriers arising from the specific characteristics of . . . electoral systems; barriers arising from the potential for conflict and competition among native and minority groups; and barriers arising from the larger patterns of racial inequality." Their study finds evidence primarily of the first and the last factor as the major contributors of the representation gap. Specifically, they point to the low rate of citizenship among immigrants—and lack of eligibility to vote—that makes "it more difficult for them to become politically active and win office." Their lack of voting power contributes to political parties, candidates, and elected officials essentially ignoring newcomers. Incumbents of all kinds turn away from immigrants, and political party organizations rarely seek to advance new immigrant candidates. One remedy for the representation gap, they suggest, is to extend voting rights to noncitizens in municipal elections.[1]

What if noncitizens had the vote? While we can't be certain, places where noncitizens vote in local elections provide some evidence and insight. In addition, what we know about newly naturalized immigrant voting patterns and their effects on electoral outcomes and public policy can shed light on these questions. In many instances, evidence shows that immigrants can prove decisive in electoral outcomes where noncitizens have voted. Moreover, their votes and voices can affect which issues are considered by policy makers, and sometimes they can influence policy outcomes. These facts were captured in several slogans depicted on signs waved by immigrant advocates in New York City at a recent rally, proclaiming "votes = voice" and "participation = power."

For example, the successful mobilization of mostly Dominican noncitizen parent voters in the Washington Heights section of New York City during the 1980s and 1990s resulted in changes in school policy, including the building of new schools, the reduction of class size, funds for after-school programs, and the like. In fact, these improvements helped *all* parents and children—not merely Dominicans—and not just in this one neighborhood but in the many districts across the city because increased funding for schools extended beyond Washington Heights. In other words, many parents and children—both immigrant and native-born—benefited from the mobilization of noncitizen Dominicans. Although it would be an overstatement to suggest Dominicans helped produce these improvements alone, it would be an oversight not to acknowledge the decisive roll Dominicans played. In addition, the political mobilization of Dominican parent voters led to the first-ever elected Dominican in the United States, Guillermo Linares. The political coming of age of Dominicans, who comprise one of the largest immigrant groups in New York and one of the largest Latino groups, is hardly complete. It has been enhanced by supportive members of the New York City Council and by the mayoral administration of David Dinkins, the city's first African American mayor.[2] We found similar patterns for immigrant groups in some of the over 500 school site elections in Chicago, and in the dozens of races in Maryland's six towns where immigrants currently vote.

These examples suggest that the enfranchisement of noncitizens would encourage candidates, parties, and elected officials to turn toward immigrants and their neglected concerns, from access to language programs to workplace conditions and general well-being. Indeed, at several stages of American history when the electorate was expanded, government became more responsive to the needs and wishes of the new voters (or potential voters) and, thereby, more accountable to and more representative of their interests in these instances. Connections between government and the people are invigorated. Perhaps just as importantly, benefits would go beyond the realm of politics and reach into other dimensions of civil society.

In the face of resurgent nativism and xenophobia, immigrant voting rights could help advocates struggle for equal rights and social justice. The use of democratic and moral claims on the polity has often been an effective tool used by social justice advocates in struggles for equality. Indeed, what Jennifer Gordon calls "rights talk," the moral and political claims that empower people individually and collectively, have proven to help organize and win victories for some of the most disadvantaged and oppressed immigrants in America today. Some of the victories entailed gaining dignity and respect, as well as obtaining fair wages and equal treatment in the workplace.[3] Noncitizen voting rights could help improve access of immigrants—and others—to good jobs, affordable housing, quality education, health care, and a better overall quality of life.

The civil rights movement broke down barriers and opened doors, not only for African Americans but also across the board. Women benefited directly and also built their own movement against patriarchy, drawing upon similar demands for equality.[4] The fight for voting rights has been a vehicle for these movements to advance and achieve a more democratic, even progressive, political and social agenda. The story of immigrant voting rights is one of the latest chapters in the struggle for equal rights and justice for all.

Campaigns for immigrant voting rights, however, present a different set of challenges. As many have pointed out, new immigrants are transforming—"without erasing"—racial hierarchies that characterize social structures, workplaces, neighborhoods, public agencies, and legislative bodies. Similarly, new immigrant groups have modified competition for power from one that "pits native minorities against whites to one that pits new immigrants not only against whites, but also against native minorities."[5] No doubt, immigrant voting may create or exacerbate interethnic conflict and competition in some cases, especially in our winner-take-all elections.[6]

Thankfully, in many places there is greater evidence of cooperation than competition among and between immigrant and minority candidates and groups. In their study of New York and Los Angeles, which together hold almost 40 percent of all immigrants in the U.S., Mollenkopf and Logan found that some districts have been "greenhouses for growing new kinds of inter-group alliances." They note that in some instances, "cultural, geographic, and class differences exist among" groups, which make it "possible to activate political cleavages," but they also point out that "commonalities seem stronger than these differences" in some campaigns.[7] In fact, a black-Latino coalition emerged in the 2005 election in Los Angeles, which catapulted the first Latino into the mayor's office, Antonio Villaraigosa.[8]

As we have seen, immigrant voting rights can be won by multiracial coalitions forged along working-class lines. In many of the campaigns we examined, such coalitions created effective campaigns to win the franchise for immigrants, which ultimately advanced their mutual interests. Making common cause among immigrants—and with other people of color, particularly African Americans—has been crucial for democracy advocates to win immigrant voting rights, or at least to wage viable campaigns. Black and Latino alliances have been—and will continue to be— critical in places like New York; Latino and Asian alliances are especially crucial in places in California; and in other jurisdictions, the multiracial alliances reflect the particularities of each place.

Of course, invoking the need for working-class solidarity across racial and ethnic lines will not alone overcome the multiple and significant challenges that advocates face in forging and sustaining such alliances. Still, the advancement of one is predicated on the other. Progress by working people hinges on undoing racial hierarchy—especially white privilege—and the liberation of groups subordinated on the basis of race and ethnicity is intertwined with the progress of the working class. Immigration simultaneously complicates these processes. At the same time, the struggle for immigrant rights offers an opportunity to achieve greater strength through unity. Campaigns for immigrant voting rights put a human face on the millions of newcomers and can elevate other causes important to immigrants and all working people, including affordable housing and health care, access to good schools and jobs, and so on.

But the problem of persistent and "structural" racism complicates how immigrants will be incorporated.[9] Today, just as in the past, some immigrants are becoming "white" while others are becoming "black."

> Racial group status can change, but not easily. A group that is subordinated in one era can move closer to power and privilege in another era. In the past century, groups such as the Irish, Italians, and Jews in America started low on the socioeconomic and political ladder and "became white" over time. More recently, "model minority" status has been given to some Asian groups, allowing group members to gain access to some of the privileges associated with whiteness. It must be stressed that position and mobility within the racial hierarchy, which in some ways resembles a caste system, cannot be determined by the nonwhite or subordinated groups. How those who are at the lower end of the privilege scale perceive themselves, or how they behave, is less significant to their racial privilege status than broadly held perceptions about them. European immigrants to nineteenth-century America could not "become white" by simply adopting the mainstream habits and declaring themselves its members. They had to be allowed access into occupational, educational, residential, and other settings that had previously excluded them. In other words, racial and ethnic group position reflects the dominant group's exclusionary or inclusionary exercise of political, economic, and cultural power.[10]

On the one hand, campaigns for immigrant voting rights could further reinforce racial hierarchies by pitting newcomers against the native-born, particularly African Americans, both as voters and as candidates. This is evident in tensions between immigrants from the Caribbean and native-born African Americans, for example, or between Dominicans and Puerto Ricans.[11] Fear of the other, particularly by African Americans who witness their numbers dwindle compared with an increasing Latino population, is not unfounded. Just when African Americans have gained political power in electoral terms, they are watching their strength diminish. In addition, whites can use divide and conquer strategies to push and pull immigrants in different directions. These dynamics strain already fragile multiethnic coalitions.

On the other hand, new immigrants create challenges for incumbents across the board—especially whites—who need votes to win from a much more diverse electorate. As we have seen, some progressive whites may support immigrant voting for political reasons; other whites will oppose it for incumbency reasons. Multiracial alliances—particularly between blacks and Latinos—have the most to gain, but these kinds of alliances require concerted efforts to sustain themselves over time to be effective.

Although winning immigrant voting rights will be no easy task, particularly in some jurisdictions, we have seen several campaigns that won legislation or at least other victories for immigrants. Immigrant voting campaigns put a human face on millions of newcomers who all too often are being scapegoated by everyone from elected officials at the highest levels to neighborhood residents. Immigrant voting campaigns provide a proactive response to the current anti-immigrant backlash and passage of draconian legislation at every level of government aimed at limiting rights and access to services vital to immigrants, including an alarming rise in racially motivated bias assaults, random detention and deportations, and new laws such as the REAL ID Act. Noncitizen voting campaigns raise the level of immigrant voices, which have elevated ideas that could form the basis of solutions to a range of pressing social, economic, and political problems. In short, immigrant voting posits a viable way to improve the nature of our democracy.

Related reforms that could advance immigrant power would include greater government efforts to inform and involve citizens who speak languages other than English, and encourage political parties, unions, and community organizations to make conscious attempts to develop leadership in new communities, as well as to reach out to noncitizens more generally. Similarly, other electoral reforms would help advance immigrant voting power—and minority political power more generally—including moving to proportional representation and instant runoff voting, particularly in primary elections where there is a greater likelihood of having multiple candidates.[12]

What lessons can we learn from the campaigns discussed? In every immigrant voting rights campaign, we have seen the presence of several crucial elements, including demographic shifts that propelled immigrant mobilization, successful grassroots organizing by proponents of immigrant voting rights, coalition building with a broad range of other stakeholders, effective lobbying, and sympathetic elected officials. Most often, elected officials who have championed immigrant voting rights have been liberal Democrats and, in some places, Green Party members. Most of the campaigns have taken place in culturally liberal and politically progressive cities and towns.

In every place, however, portions of the population opposed immigrant voting initiatives, and they were sometimes sizable in number and highly vocal in their objection to it. Opponents have been conservative

Democrats and Republicans, and representatives of all political persuasions who view noncitizen voters as a potential threat to their dominance. We have also seen instances where community groups oppose immigrant voting because they fear or have hostile feelings toward the newcomers or feel a heightened sense of competition with immigrants for jobs, housing, public office, and public policy. The current anti-immigrant climate provides serious challenges to immigrant voting rights.

Other challenges include legal and political obstacles. States that have constitutions restricting voting to U.S. citizens will require a constitutional amendment to allow voting rights for immigrants at the local level. For immigrant voting to become a reality in these states, it will take campaigns able to sustain efforts over the long term and capable of garnering significant statewide support. It will be easier for advocates to win campaigns that merely require legislative change rather than constitutional change. Of course, it will be easiest at the local level. Thankfully, advocates have developed savvy legal strategies to get around some of these thorny problems, such as lawyers in California did in crafting legislation that argues that charter cities like San Francisco can enact legislation at the local level even when their state has a constitutional prohibition.

Immigrant voting rights advocates also face the challenge of reinforcing a second- and third-class status for some immigrants, particularly where campaigns for noncitizen voting rights only contemplate enfranchising legal permanent residents versus all immigrants. Although the line between documented ("legal") and undocumented ("illegal") immigrants has increasingly been drawn in various laws at the federal and state levels, particularly after September 11, most immigrants enter the United States legally but may fall out of documented status through no fault of their own. For example, a worker who is hired by a firm in the United States may be laid off from his or her job; a student who comes to study in the U.S. may have to go back home for a family emergency, and in so doing, jeopardize his or her status in school or capacity to return legally. In the meantime, such individuals pay taxes and develop relationships with coworkers, colleagues, and community members. But their status as "lawbreakers" stigmatizes them and marginalizes their life chances. Sometimes these individuals are able to return to a documented status. Interestingly, noncitizen diplomats, investors, and high-tech workers who fall into undocumented status are rarely depicted in discussions and considerations of "illegal" immigrants. Nevertheless, advocates of immigrant voting rights are often pressured into excluding undocumented individuals in crafting legislation, such as occurred in the recent campaigns in New York City and Washington, D.C. Similarly, advocates who do include all immigrants in legislation, such as in the recent 2004 campaign in San Francisco, often find themselves under attack for creating the possibility of legitimating or enabling "terrorists" to vote, and end up spending valuable time defending undocumented immigrants and/or their choice to include them in legislative initiatives, or conversely distancing themselves from such individuals or that choice. It is also illuminating to note that the places that allow noncitizens to vote allow all immigrants to vote, in part because legislation was passed prior to September 11.

Lastly, the push to amend the Constitution to allow people born outside of the United States to run for president, which originated from Republican ranks who apparently have Arnold Schwarzenegger in mind, has received some bipartisan support. Whatever the outcome of this effort, all the above discussed dynamics and considerations (and others) will likely affect the future of immigrant voting campaigns in the United States.

America owes a tremendous debt to immigrants, and not just to the British, Irish, German, Italian, Jewish, Scandinavian, Greek, and other white European immigrants of yesteryear. By and large, immigrants built America. Along with slaves and their decedents, they collectively created the wealth of this nation. Even though it appears that many Americans have forgotten their ancestral—immigrant—roots, America was and always will be a nation of immigrants. Immigration will likely continue to transform the United States, just as the influx of newcomers is changing parts of Europe and other countries across the globe.

Today, we are in the midst of the largest mass migration of people in human history. It has been a catalyst for an outpouring of literature and thinking about the meaning of citizenship, nation-states, sovereignty, and human rights. It is time to adjust our political democracy with the changing demography in these global times. The creation of a truly universal suffrage would move us toward that end. Immigrant voting rights would provide greater pressure on elected officials, political parties, and candidates of all persuasions to be more responsive, accountable, and representative to the issues and interests of all members of communities, which is after all the essence of representative democracy. In short, immigrant suffrage would move us one step closer to realizing the promise of democracy. Jamin Raskin, who saw the future over a dozen years ago, summed it up nicely:

> The old-fashioned democratic principles justifying local alien suffrage may find a new lease on life in the context of globalization of economic and social institutions. As the coherence of the nation-state is increasingly undermined by the global forces of economic and cultural production, the locality may become at once the individual's best hope for meaningful political participation

and the world's best hope for counteracting the deracinating and depersonalizing effects of the global economic system. Thus, the traditional democratic arguments for alien suffrage, which are being revived by surges in immigration, are united with the contemporary human rights interest in making the right to participate in politics as mobile as markets for capital and labor. This convergence of local and global democratic pressures argues for making the locality both a polity of presence and a central locus of participatory citizenship.[13]

Raskin posed several questions that will ultimately determine the future of immigrant voting rights, including, "Can we relax received social categories in order to make the franchise open up once again? Can we come to see the U.S. citizenship requirement for voting in local elections as arbitrary and undemocratic?"[14]

Works Cited

Aleinikoff, T. Alexander, and Douglas Klusmeyer. *Citizenship Policies for an Age of Migration.* Washington, D.C.: Carnegie Endowment for International Peace, 2002.

Allen, Howard W., and Kay Warren Allen. "Voter Fraud and Data Validity." In *Analyzing Electoral History,* edited by Jerome Clubb, William H. Flanigan, and Nancy Zingale. Beverly Hills, Calif.: Sage, 1981.

American Immigration Law Foundation. "The Endless Wait: Will Resources Match the Resolve to Reduce the Immigration Case Backlog?" July 2004. <http://www.ailf.org/ipc/policy_reports_2004_endlesswait.asp>

ANC D.C. "ANC D.C." http://anc.dc.gov/anc/site/default.asp.

Argersinger, Peter H. "New Perspectives on Electoral Fraud in the Gilded Age." *Political Science Quarterly* 100, no. 4 (Winter 1985–1986): 669–87.

Aspen Institute Roundtable on Community Change. *Structural Racism and Community Building.* Queenstown, Md.: Aspen Institute, 2004.

Avila, Joaquin. "Political Apartheid in California: Consequences of Excluding a Growing Noncitizen Population." Latino Policy and Issues Brief no. 9. Los Angeles: Chicano Studies Research Center, University of California, Los Angeles, 2003.

Aylsworth, Leon. *"The Passing of Alien Suffrage." American Political Science Review* 25, no. 1 (February 1931): 114–16.

Baubock, Rainer. "Expansive Citizenship – Voting Beyond Territorial and Membership." *PS: Political Science and Politics.* Washington, D.C.: American Political Science Association. Vol. 38, No. 4. October, 2005.

Bedolla, Lisa Garcia. "Rethinking Citizenship: Noncitizen Voting and Immigrant Political Engagement in the United States." In *Transforming Politics, Transforming America: The Political and Civic Incorporation of Immigrants in the United States,* edited by Taeku Lee, S. Karthick Ramakrishnan, and Ricardo Ramírez. Charlottesville: University of Virginia Press, 2005.

Benhabib, Seyla. *The Rights of Others: Citizens, Residents and Aliens.* Cambridge: Cambridge University Press, 2004.

Best, Kevin J. "Municipal Elections." *Municipal Maryland* (Maryland Municipal League [MML]) 30, no. 7 (2001).

Bonilla-Silva, E. "Rethinking Racism: Towards a Structural Interpretation." *American Sociological Review* 63, no. 3 (1997): 465–80.

Bosniak, Linda. "Universal Citizenship and the Problem of Alienage." *Northwestern University Law Review* 94 (2000): 963–82.

Brozovich, Elise. "Prospects for Democratic Change: Non-Citizen Suffrage in America." *Hamline Journal of Public Law & Policy,* no. 23 (2002): 403–53.

Buenker, John D. *Urban Liberalism and Progressive Reform.* New York: Scribner. 1973.

Burnham, Walter Dean. *Critical Elections and the Mainsprings of American Politics*. New York: W.W. Norton, 1970.

Capps, Randy, Micheal Fix, Jason Ost, Jane Reardon-Anderson, and Jeffrey S. Passel. "The Health and Well-being of Young Children of Immigrants." Report. Washington, D.C.: Urban Institute, 2004. http://www.urban.org/UploadedPDF/311139_ChildrenImmigrants.pdf.

Capps, Randolph, Michael E. Fix, and Jeffrey S. Passel. "The Dispersal of Immigrants in the 1990s." Report. Washington, D.C.: Urban Institute, 2002.

Capps, Randy, Michael Fix, Jeffrey S. Passel, Jason Ost, and Dan Perez-Lopez. "A Profile of the Low-Wage Immigrant Workforce." Immigrant Families and Workers: Facts and Perspectives, no. 4, November. Washington, D.C.: Urban Institute, 2003. http://www.urban.org/url.cfm?ID=310880.

Capps, Randy, Genevieve Kenney, and Michael Fix. "Health Insurance Coverage of Children in Mixed-Status Immigrant Families." Snapshots of America's Families III, no. 12. Washington, D.C.: Urban Institute, 2003. http://www.urban.org/url.cfm?ID=310886.

Chalmers, David Mark. *Hooded Americanism: The First Century of the Ku Klux Klan, 1865–1965*. Garden City, N.Y.: Doubleday, 1965.

Chung, April. "Noncitizen Voting Rights and Alternatives: A Path toward Greater Asian Pacific American and Latino Political Participation." UCLA Asian Pacific American Law Journal 4 (Fall 1996): 163.

Church, Robert L. and Michael W. Sedlak. *Education in the United States: An Interpretive History*. New York: Free Press. 1976.

Cogan, Jacob Katz. "The Look Within: Property, Capacity, and Suffrage in Nineteenth Century America." *Yale Law Journal* 107 (1997): 473, 495.

Collier, Christopher. "The American People as Christian White Men of Property: Suffrage and Elections in Colonial and Early National America." In *Voting and the Spirit of American Democracy*, edited by Donald W. Rogers. Urbana: University of Illinois Press, 1992.

Council of Latino Agencies. "The State of Latinos in the District of Columbia: Trends, Consequences, and Recommendations." Washington, D.C.: Council of Latino Agencies, 2002. http://www.consejo.org/publications.html.

Curran, Michael. "Flickering Lamp beside the Golden Door: Immigration, the Constitution and Undocumented Aliens in the 1990s." *Case Western Reserve Journal of International Law* 30, no. 1 (Winter 1998): 58–142.

Curran, Thomas. *Xenophobia and Immigration, 1820–1930*. Boston: Twayne, 1975.

Day, Stephen, and Jo Shaw. "European Union Electoral Rights and Political Participation of Migrants in Host Polities." *International Journal of Population Geography* 8 (2002): 183–99.

Deardorff, K., and L. Blumerman. "Evaluating Components of International Migration: Estimates of the Foreign-born Population by Migrant Status: 2000." Population Division Working Paper no. 58, December. Washington, D.C.: U.S. Bureau of the Census, Population Division, 2001.

de la Garza, Rodolfo O. *Counting on the Latino Vote: Latinos as a New Electorate*. Charlottesville: University Press of Virginia. 1996.

DeLeon, Richard Edward. *Left Coast City: Progressive Politics in San Francisco, 1975–1991*, Lawrence, Kansas: University Press of Kansas, 1992.

DeSipio, Louis. "Building America, One Person at a Time: Naturalization and Political Behavior of the Naturalized in Contemporary American Politics." In *E Pluribus Unum? Contemporary and Historical Perspectives on Immigrant Political Incorporation*, edited by Gary Gerstle and John Mollenkopf. New York: Russell Sage Foundation, 2001.

DeWind, Josh, and Philip Kasinitz. "Everything Old Is New Again? Process and Theories of Immigrant Incorporation." In *Immigrant Adaptation and Native-Born Responses in the Making of Americans: A Special Issue. International Migration Review* 31 (Winter, 1997): 1096–111.

Donn, Jeff. "Mass. Town Considers Granting Vote to Non-citizens." Associated Press, October 21, 1998.

DuBois, W. E. B. *The Souls of Black Folk*. 1903. Reprint, New York: Knopf, 1993.

Duplantier, F. R. "Behind the Headlines." *Politickles*. March 4, 2001. http://www.politickles.com.

Earnest, David. "Noncitizen Voting Rights: A Survey of an Emerging Democratic Norm." Paper presented at the 2003 annual convention of the American Political Science Association, August 28–31, Philadelphia.

Earnest, David C. *Voting Rights for Resident Aliens: Nationalism, Postnationalism and Sovereignty in an Era of Mass Migration.* Ph.D. Dissertation. Columbian College of Arts and Sciences, George Washington University. Washington, D.C. 2004.

Erie, Steven P. *Rainbow's End: Irish Americans and the Dilemmas of Urban Machine Politics, 1840–1985.* Berkeley: University of California Press, 1988.

Ethington, Philip J. "Progressive Era Political Participation." *Studies in American Political Development* 7 (Fall 1993): 275–315.

European Commission to the European Parliament. "Voting Rights in Local Elections for Community Nationals Residing in a Member State Other Than Their Own." Commission. 1986.

Fix, Michael E., and Jeffrey S. Passel. "Testimony before the Subcommittee on Immigration and Claims Hearing on "the U.S. Population and Immigration" Committee on the Judiciary U.S. House of Representatives." August 2. Washington, D.C.: Urban Institute, 2001.

———. "A New Citizenship Day." September 17. Washington, D.C.: Urban Institute, 2003.

Fix, Michael, Jeffrey Passel, and Kenneth Sucher. "Trends in Naturalization." September. Washington, D.C.: Urban Institute, 2003.

Fix, Michael E., and Wendy Zimmerman. *All under One Roof: Mixed-Status Families in an Era of Reform.* Washington, D.C.: Urban Institute, 1999.

Foner, Eric. *Reconstruction: America's Unfinished Revolution, 1863–1877.* New York: HarperCollins, 1988.

Foner, Nancy, Ruben Rumbaut, and Steven Gold, eds. *Immigration Research for a New Century.* New York: Russell Sage Foundation, 2001.

Fong, Lawrence Michael. "Sojourners and Settlers: The Chinese Experience in Arizona." *Journal of Arizona History* 21 (1980): 1–30.

Gartner, Alan, executive director, and Fong Chan, chair. "Temporary State Task Force on the New York City Community School Board Elections, Final Report." March. Albany: State of New York, 1998.

Goldfield, Michael. *The Color of Politics: Race and the Mainsprings of American Politics.* New York: New Press, 1997.

Gonzalez, Matt. "Immigrant Rights: Protecting Our City's Diversity." Policy paper. 2003. http://www.mattgonzalez.com/downloads/Immigrant.pdf.

Gordon, Jennifer. "Let Them Vote." In *A Community of Equals: The Constitutional Protection of New Americans*, edited by Owen M. Fiss, Joshua Cohen, Joel Rogers, and Edwidge Danticat. Boston: Beacon Press, 1999.

———. *Suburban Sweatshops: The Fight for Immigrant Rights.* Cambridge, Mass.: Belknap Press of Harvard University Press, 2005.

Grob, Gerald N. and George Athan Billias. *Interpretations of American History: Patterns and Perspectives.* 5th Edition. New York: Free Press. 1987.

Hale, Matthew Rainbow. "Many Who Wandered in Darkness: The Contest over American National Identity, 1795–1798." *Early American Studies.* Volume 1, Number 1. Spring, 2003:127–175.

Harper-Ho, Virginia. "Noncitizen Voting Rights: The History, the Law and Current Prospects for Change." *Law and Inequality Journal*, no. 18 (2000).

Harris, Joseph P. *Registration of Voters in the United States.* Washington, D.C.: Brookings Institution, 1929.

———. *Election Administration in the United States.* Washington, D.C.: Brookings Institution, 1934.

Hayduk, Ronald. "Noncitizen Voting: Pipe Dream or Possibility?" Drum Major Institute for Public Policy. October 2002. http://www.drummajorinstitute.org/plugin/template/dmi/55/1694.

———. "From Anti-Globalization to Global Justice: A Twenty-first Century Movement." In *Teamsters and Turtles? U.S. Progressive Political Movements in the 21st Century.* Lanham, Md.: Rowman & Littlefield, 2003.

———. *Gatekeepers to the Franchise: Election Administration in New York.* DeKalb: Northern Illinois University Press, 2005.

Hayduk, Ronald, and Kevin Mattson, eds. *Democracy's Moment: Reforming the American Political System for the 21st Century.* Lanham, Md.: Rowman & Littlefield, 2002.

Hays, Samuel P. "The Politics of Reform in Municipal Government in the Progressive Era." *Pacific Northwest Quarterly.* 55. October, 1964: 157–169.

Heer, David. *Immigration in America's Future: Social Science Findings and the Policy Debate.* Boulder, Colo.: Westview Press, 1996.

Higham, John. *Strangers in the Land: Patterns of American Nativism, 1860–1925.* New Brunswick, N.J.: Rutgers University Press, 1992.

Hill, Stephen. *Fixing Elections: The Failure of America's Winner Take All Politics.* New York: Routledge, 2002.

Hofstadter, Richard. *The Age of Reform: From Bryan to F.D.R.* New York: Alfred A. Knopf. 1955.

Holli, Melvin. In *Interpretations of American History,* edited by Gerald Grob and George Billias. New York: Free Press, 1987.

Holli, Melvin G. *Reform in Detroit: Hazen S. Pingree and Urban Politics.* Oxford, UK: Oxford University Press. 1969.

Horton, Wesley W. "Connecticut Constitutional History, 1776–1988." 1988. http://www.cslib.org/cts4c.htm.

Huang, Michael. "Citizenship and Voting." *Gotham Gazette,* August 8, 2003, http://www.gothamgazette.com/article/feature-commentary/20030825/202/503.

Huntington, Samuel. *Who Are We? The Challenges to America's National Identity.* New York: Simon & Schuster, 2004.

Ignatiev, Noel. *How the Irish Became White.* New York: Routledge, 1995.

Immigration Policy Center/American Immigration Law Foundation. "Power and Potential: The Growing Electoral Clout of New Citizens." *Immigration Policy* 3, no. 4 (October 2004): http://www.ailf.org/ipc/ipf102004.pdf.

Immigrant Voting Project. "Immigrant Voting Project: Democracy for All." http://www.immigrantvoting.org.Jones, Maldwyn Allen. *American Immigration.* Chicago: University of Chicago Press, 1992.

Immigrant Voting Project. Ron Hayduk and Michele Wucker, co-directors. www.immigrantvoting.org

Judd, Dennis, and Todd Swanstrom. *City Politics: Private Power and Public Policy.* New York: Longman, 2004.

Kasinitz, Philip. *Caribbean New York: Black Immigrants and the Politics of Race.* Ithaca, N.Y: Cornell University Press. 1992.

Kasinitz, Philip, John Mollenkopf, and Mary C. Waters, eds. *Becoming New Yorkers: Ethnographies of the New Second Generation.* New York: Russell Sage Foundation, 2004.

Kasinitz, Philip, John Mollenkopf, and Mary Waters. *The Immigrant Second Generation in Metropolitan New York.* New York: Russell Sage Foundation. Forthcoming.

Keyssar, Alexander. *The Right to Vote: The Contested History of Democracy in the United States.* New York: Basic Books, 2000.

King, Desmond S. *Making Americans: Immigration, Race, and the Origins of the Diverse Democracy.* Cambridge, Mass.: Harvard University Press, 2000.

Kini, Tara. "Sharing the Vote: Noncitizen Voting Rights in Local School Board Elections." *California Law Review* 93 (January 2005): 271.

Kleppner, Paul. *Who Voted? The Dynamics of Electoral Turnout.* New York: Praeger, 1982.

———. "Defining Citizenship: Immigration and the Struggle for Voting Rights in Antebellum America." In *Voting and the Spirit of American Democracy: Essays on the History of Voting and Voting Rights in America,* edited by Donald W. Rogers and Christine Scriabine. Urbana: University of Illinois Press, 1992.

Kolko, Gabriel. *Main Currents in Modern American History.* New York: Pantheon Books. 1984.

Lien, Pei-ti. *The Politics of Asian Americans: Diversity and Community.* New York: Routledge. 2004.

Levinson, Sanford. "Symposium on Law and Community: Constituting Communities through Words That Bind: Reflections on Loyalty Oaths." *Michigan Law Review* 84 (June 1986).

Magpantay, Glenn. "Asian American Voting Rights: A Perspective from the Northeast." *Fordham Urban Law Review*28 (2001): 739.

Massey, Douglas. "March of Folly: U.S. Immigration Policy after NAFTA." *American Prospect* (March 1, 1998): http://www.prospect.org/print/V9/37/massey-d.html.

Minnite, Lorraine. "Report for the New York City Immigration Coalition." 2001. http://www.thenyic.org.

———, principal investigator. "The New Americans Exit Poll Project: Results from the 2000, 2002 and 2004 New York City Exit Polls." New York Immigration Coalition, February 2005. http://www.thenyic.org/images/uploads/NAEP%202004%20Results.pdf.

Minitte, Lorraine, and David Calahan. 2003. "Securing the Vote: An Analysis of Election Fraud." *Demos: A Network for Ideas and Action*. http://www.demos-usa.org.

Minnite, Lorraine, Jennifer Holdaway, and Ronald Hayduk. "The Political Participation of Immigrants in New York." In *In Defense of the Alien*, vol. 23, edited by Lydio F. Tomasi. New York: Center for Migration Studies, 2001.

Mollenkopf, John Hull. *A Phoenix in the Ashes: The Rise and Fall of the Koch Coalition in New York City Politics*. Princeton, N.J.: Princeton University Press, 1994.

Mollenkopf, John, and John Logan. *People and Politics in America's Big Cities: The Challenges to Urban Democracy*. New York: Drum Major Institute for Public Policy, 2003.

Mollenkopf, John, David Olsen, and Timothy Ross. "Immigrant Political Participation in New York and Los Angeles." In *Governing Cities*, edited by Michael Jones-Correa. New York: Russell Sage Foundation, 2001.

Moore, Stephen. "*A Fiscal Portrait of the Newest Americans*." Washington, D.C.: National Immigration Forum and Cato Institute, 1998.

Morgan, Martha I., and Neal Hutchens. "The Tangled Web of Alabama's Equality Doctrine after Melof: Historical Reflections on Equal Protection and the Alabama Constitution." *Alabama Law Review* 53 (2001): 135–242.

Mulkern, John R. 1990. *The Know-Nothing Party in Massachusetts: The Rise and Fall of a People's Movement*. Boston: Northeastern University Press.

National Coalition to Repeal the Patriot Act. http://www.repealnow.com. Also known as repealnow.com, http://www.repealnow.com

National Immigration Forum. "Democracy on Hold." 1998. <http://www.immigrationforum.org>

The National Research Council of the National Academy of Sciences. *The New Americans: Economic, Demographic, and Fiscal Effects of Immigration*, edited by James P. Smith and Barry Edmonston. Washington, D.C.: National Academy Press, 1997.

———. *The Immigration Debate: Studies on the Economic, Demographic, and Fiscal Effects of Immigration*, edited by James P. Smith and Barry Edmonston. Washington, D.C.: National Academy Press, 1998.

Nebraska Department of Education and Nebraska State Historical Society. "Racial Tensions in Omaha in the 1920s." http://www.nebraskastudies.org/0700/frameset.html.

Neuman, Gerald L. "'We Are the People': Alien Suffrage in German and American Perspective." *Michigan International Law* 13 (1992): 259.

———. *Strangers to the Constitution: Immigrants, Borders, and Fundamental Law*. Princeton, N.J.: Princeton University Press, 1996.

"Non-citizens May Have the Right to Vote." *Filipino Express* 17, no. 35 (September 7, 2003): 1.

New York City Department of Planning. Population Division. *The Newest New Yorkers, 2000*. http://www.nyc.gov/html/dcp/html/census/nny.shtml. 2004.

——— "2003 New York City Council Districts – Total Population by Citizenship Status." 2000 Census Table SF3 P21. http://www.nyc.gov/html/dcp/pdf/census/cnclO3citizen.pdf.

Ostrow, Ashira Pelman. "Dual Resident Voting: Traditional Disenfranchisement and Prospects for Change." *Columbia Law Review* 102 (2002): 1954.

Overdyke, William Darrell. *The Know-Nothing Party in the South*. 1950. Reprint, Gloucester, Mass.: Peter Smith, 1968.

Parents United for Education. "Parents United for Education." http:/www.voice4parents.com.

Passel, Jeffrey S. "Election 2004: The Latino and Asian Vote." Urban Institute Immigration Studies Program. July 27, 2004. http://www.urban.org/UploadedPDF/900723.pdf.

Passel, Jeffrey S. and Rebecca L. Clark. "Immigrants in New York: Their Legal Status, Incomes, and Taxes." Washington, D.C.: The Urban Institute. April 01, 1998.

Passel, Jeffrey S., and Wendy Zimmermann. "Are Immigrants Leaving California? Settlement Patterns of Immigrants in the Late 1990s." April 1. Washington, D.C.: Urban Institute, 2001.

Peterson, Merrill D., ed. *Democracy, Liberty, and Property: The State Constitutional Conventions of the 1820s*. Indianapolis, Ind.: Bobbs-Merrill Co., 1966.

Pew Research Center for the People & the Press. Survey Reports. "Issues and Continuity Now Working for Gore" September 14, 2000; "Politics and Values in a 51%-48% Nation: National Security More Linked With Partisan Affiliation." January 24, 2005.

Piven, Frances Fox, and Richard Cloward. *Why Americans Still Don't Vote*. Boston: Beacon Press, 2000.

Porter, Kirk H. *A History of Suffrage in the United States.* 1918. Reprint, Chicago: University of Chicago Press, 1971.

Ramakrishnan, S. Karthick. *Democracy in Immigrant America: Changing Demographics and Political Participation.* Stanford, CA: Stanford University Press, 2005.

Ranney, Joseph A. "Aliens and 'Real Americans': Law and Ethnic Assimilation in Wisconsin, 1846–1920." *Wisconsin Lawyer.* http://www.wisbar.org.

Raskin, Jamin B. "Legal Aliens, Local Citizens: The Historical, Constitutional, and Theoretical Meanings of Alien Suffrage." *University of Pennsylvania Law Review* 141 (1993): 1401ff. http://www.sou.edu/polisci/pavlich/Raskin_Aliens.htm.

Raskin, Jamin B. *Overruling Democracy: The Supreme Court vs. The American People.* New York: Routledge. 2003.

Rath, Jan. "Voting Rights." In *The Political Rights of Migrant Workers in Western Europe,* edited by Henry Zig Layton. Newbury Park, Calif.: Sage, 1990.

Renshon, Stanley. "Dual Citizenship and American Democracy." October. Washington, D.C.: Center for Immigrant Studies, 2001.

Renshon, Stanley. "The 50 Per Cent American: Immigration and National Identity in an Age of Terror." Georgetown: Georgetown University Press. 2005.

Rogers, Reuel R. "Race-Based Coalitions among Minority Groups: Afro-Caribbean Immigrants and African-Americans in New York City." *Urban Affairs Review* 39 (January 2004): 283–317.

Roediger, David. *The Wages of Whiteness.* London: Verso, 1991.

Rosberg, Gerald. "Aliens and Equal Protection: Why Not the Right to Vote?" *Michigan Law Review* 75 (April–May 1977): 1092–36.

Rusk, Jerold G. "Effect of the Australian Ballot Reform on Split-Ticket Voting, 1896–1908." *American Political Science Review* 64, no. 4 (December 1970): 1220–38.

———. "Comment." *American Political Science Review* 68, no. 3 (September 1974).

Rytina Nancy F. and Saeger, Chunnong. "Naturalizations in the United States: 2004." U. S. Department of Homeland Security, Office of Immigration Statistics. June, 2005. <http://uscis.gov/graphics/shared/statistics>

Schattschneider, E. E. *The Semisovereign People.* New York: Holt, Rinehart & Winston, 1960.

Schneier, Edward, and John Brian Murtaugh. *New York Politics: A Tale of Two States.* New York: M.E. Sharpe, 2001.

Schuck, Peter. "Membership in the Liberal Polity: The Devaluation of American Citizenship." In *Immigration and the Politics of Citizenship in Europe and North America,* edited by William Rogers Brubaker. New York: German Marshall Fund of the United States and the University Press of America, 1989.

Schuck, Peter, and Rogers Smith. *Citizenship without Consent: Illegal Aliens in the American Politiy.* New Haven, Conn.: Yale University Press, 1985.

Seigel, Fred. *The Future Once Happened Here: New York, D.C., L.A. and the Fate of America's Big Cities.* New York: Free Press, 1997.

Shefter, Martin. *Political Parties and the State: The American Historical Experience.* Princeton, N.J.: Princeton University Press, 1994.

Sheldon, Addison E., ed. *Official Report of the Debates and Proceedings in the Nebraska Constitution Convention.* Assembled in Lincoln, June 13, 1871, 207 (1905 edition).

Shepard, Benjamin, and Ronald Hayduk, eds. *From ACT UP to the WTO: Urban Protest and Community Building in the Era of Globalization.* New York: Verso, 2002.

Shimmelman, Wendy Aviva. "Local Voting Rights for Non-U.S. Citizen Immigrants in New York City." Report prepared for the Center for Immigrants Rights, New York, 1992.

Shklar, Judith N. *American Citizenship: The Quest for Inclusion.* Cambridge, Mass.: Harvard University Press, 1991.

Simon, Julian L. "Immigration: The Demographic and Economic Facts." Washington, D.C.: Cato Institute and National Immigration Forum, 1995.

Singer, Audrey. "At Home in the Nation's Capital: Immigrant Trends in Metropolitan Washington." June. Washington, D.C.: Brookings Greater Washington Research Center, Brookings Institution, 2003.

Smith, James P., and Barry Edmonston, eds. *The New Americans: Economic, Demographic, and Fiscal Effects of Immigration.* National Research Council of the National Academy of Sciences. Washington, D.C.: National Academy Press, 1997.

————, eds. *The Immigration Debate: Studies on the Economic, Demographic, and Fiscal Effects of Immigration*. National Research Council of the National Academy of Sciences. Washington, D.C.: National Academy Press, 1998.

Smith, Rogers. *Civic Ideals: Conflicting Visions of Citizenship in U.S. History*. New Haven, Conn.: Yale University Press, 1997.

Sontag, Deborah. "Noncitizens and Right to Vote." *New York Times*, July 31, 1992, A1.

Spiro, Peter J. "Questioning Barriers to Naturalization." *Georgetown Immigration Law Journal* 13 (1999): 479.

Steinberg, Stephen. "Immigration, African-Americans, and Race Discourse." *New Politics*. Vol. 10, No. 3. Summer, 2005.

Suffrage Universal. "Le droit de vote aux Etats-Unis: Voting Rights in the USA." http://users.sky-net.be/suffrage-universel/us/usvo.htm.

Swindler, William F. *Sources and Documents of United States Constitutions*, vol. 6 No. 93. Dobbs Ferry, N.Y.: Oceana Publications, 1976.

Takoma Park Elections Task Force. "Recommendation of the Takoma Park Election Task Force." Undated memorandum. In *Information Package regarding Non U.S. Citizens Voting Rights in Takoma Park*. Takoma Park, Md.: Office of the City Clerk, n.d.

Thorpe, Francis. *The Federal and State Constitutions, Colonial Charters, and Other Organic Laws of the States, Territories, and Colonies Now or Heretofore Forming the United States of America*. Washington, D.C.: Government Printing Office, 1909.

Tichenor, Daniel J. *Dividing Lines: The Politics of Immigration Control in America*. Princeton, N.J.: Princeton University Press, 2002.

Tienda, Marta. "Demography and the Social Contract." *Demography* 39, no. 4 (2002): 587–616.

Townhall.com. Conservative News and Information, <http://www.townhall.com>

U.S. Census Bureau. "Table PCT48: Place of Birth by Year of Entry by Citizenship Status for the Foreign Born Population." In *U.S. Census 2000*. Washington, D.C.: U.S. Burean of the Census, 2000.

————. *Profile of the Foreign-Born Population in the United States:2000*. Washington, D.C.: U.S. Census Bureau. 2001. <http://www.census.gov>

————. *Citizenship Status for the Population 18 Years and Over* (GCT-P16). 2000.

————. *1990 Summary Tape File 3* (STF 3).

————. *2004 Population Estimates*.

————. *Current Population Survey (CPS) Voter Supplement*.

————. "Table DP-1: Profile of General Demographic Characteristics: 2000." In *U.S. Census, 2000*. http://census.abag.ca.gov/counties/SanFranciscoCounty.pdf.

U.S. Citizenship and Immigration Services. *Yearbook of Immigration Statistics*. Washington, D.C: United States Citizenship and Immigration Services. 2001, 2002, and 2003. <http://uscis.gov>

U.S. House of Representatives. Report #350. 68th Cong., 1st sess., II, 4–5. Washington, D.C.: Government Printing Office, 1924.

Vaca, Nicolas. *The Presumed Alliance: The Unspoken Conflict between Latinos and Blacks and What It Means for America*. New York: HarperCollins, 2004.

Varsanyi, Monica Weiler. *Stretching the Boundaries of Citizenship in the City: Undocumented Migrants and Political Mobilization in Los Angeles*. Ph.D diss., University of California, Los Angeles, 2004.

Voting Rights for All D.C. Coalition. "The Case for Non-U.S. Citizen Voting in the District of Columbia: Forging Partnership through Participation." Pamphlet. October 20. Washington, D.C.: Voting Rights for All D.C. Coalition, 2003.

Waldrauch, Harald. "Electoral rights for foreign nationals: a comparative overview." Paper prepared for Exploratory Workshop: "Citizens, non-citizens and voting rights in Europe," sponsored by the European Science Foundation, the Europa Institute and the School of Law, University of Edinburgh. University of Edinburgh, UK. June 2–4, 2005.

Walzer, Michael. *Spheres of Justice: A Defense of Pluralism and Equality*. New York: Basic Books, 1983.

Wernick, Allan. *U.S. Citizenship and Immigration*. New York: Prima Publishing (Random House). 2004.

Williamson, Chilton. *American Suffrage from Property to Democracy, 1760–1860*. Princeton, N.J.: Princeton University Press, 1960.

Woodruff, Paul. *First Democracy: The Challenge of an Ancient Idea.* New York: Oxford University Press, 2005.

Wucker, Michele. "Civics Lessons from Immigrants: What Happens to the Working-Class Political Voice When Many of Its Speakers Aren't Citizens?" *American Prospect* 14, no. 7 (July 1, 2003): http://www.prospect.org/print/V14/7/wucker-m.html.

Yip, Alethea. "San Francisco Initiative Seeks Vote for Noncitizens." *Asian Week*, May 3–9, 1996.

Notes

Chapter 1

I draw upon several scholars who have explored this terrain, especially Raskin, "Legal Aliens, Local Citizens." Others include Gerald Rosberg, "Aliens and Equal Protection: Why Not the Right to Vote?" *Michigan Law Review* 75 (April–May 1977): 1092–36; Wendy Aviva Shimmelman, "Local Voting Rights for Non-U.S. Citizen Immigrants in New York City" (Center for Immigrants Rights, New York, New York, 1992); Jennifer Gordon, "Let Them Vote," in *A Community of Equals: The Constitutional Protection of New Americans*, edited by Owen M. Fiss, Joshua Cohen, Joel Rogers, and Edwidge Danticat (Boston: Beacon Press, 1999); Harper-Ho. "Noncitizen Voting Rights"; Keyssar, *The Right to Vote*; Elise Brozovich, "Prospects for Democratic Change: Non-Citizen Suffrage in America," *Hamline Journal of Public Law & Policy*, no 23 (2002): 403–53; Tara Kini, "Sharing the Vote: Noncitizen Voting Rights in Local School Board Elections," California Law Review 93 (January 2005): 271; Aleinikoff and Klusmeyer, *Citizenship Policies for an Age of Migration*; Tienda, "Demography and the Social Contract," 587–616; Monica Weiler Varsanyi, *Stretching the Boundaries of Citizenship in the City: Undocumented Migrants and Political Mobilization in Los Angeles* (Ph.D. diss., University of California, Los Angeles, 2004); and Lisa Garcia Bedolla, "Rethinking Citizenship: Noncitizen Voting and Immigrant Political Engagement in the United States," in *Transforming Politics, Transforming America: The Political and Civic Incorporation of Immigrants in the United States*, ed. Taeku Lee, S. Karthick Ramakrishnan, and Ricardo Ramírez (Charlottesville: University of Virginia Press, 2005). In addition, advocates in states and locales that successfully pressed for immigrant voting rights or are currently working to pass such legislation have informed this research. Although there is no central location where information exists about all such campaigns, organizations, and individuals, the Immigrant Voting Project attempts to act a resource clearinghouse (see http://www.immigrantvoting.org). Along with Michele Wucker of the World Policy Institute, I am codirector of the Immigrant Voting Project.

1. Michael Walzer, *Spheres of Justice: A Defense of Pluralism and Equality* (New York: Basic Books, 1983).
2. Michael Huang, "Citizenship and Voting," *Gotham Gazette*, August 8, 2003, http://www.gothamgazette.com/article/feature-commentary/20030825/202/503. Tejeda died on April 11, 2003, at the age of twenty-six, leaving behind two daughters, six-year-old Miranda and three-year-old Soriana. Bill Egbert and Bill Hutchinson, "Washington Heights Mourns Slain Son," *(New York) Daily News*, April 13, 2003. The first American casualty in the war in Iraq, who died on March 21, 2003, was U.S. Marine Lance Corporal Jose A. Gutierrez, a noncitizen immigrant from Guatemala. Associated Press, March 22, 2003.

3. Egbert and Hutchinson, "Washington Heights Mourns Slain Son."
4. Dan Barry, "A Nation at War: At War at Home; at Journey's End, a Marine Is Mourned," *New York Times*, April 19, 2003; and Jennifer Yau, "The Foreign Born in the Armed Services," Migration Policy Institute, May 1, 2005, http://www.migrationinformation.org/USfocus/display.cfm?id=304. Since the executive order was issued in July 2002, more than 16,000 soldiers have naturalized as of February 2005.
5. H.R. 661, February 8, 2005.
6. Charles Rangel, press release, Washington, D.C., April 21, 2003, http://www.house.gov/rangel/press-releases.shtml.
7. Egbert and Hutchinson, "Washington Heights Mourns Slain son."
8. James P. Smith and Barry Edmonston, eds., *The New Americans: Economic, Demographic, and Fiscal Effects of Immigration* (Washington, D.C.: National Academy Press, 1997).
9. Moore, Stephen, 1998.
10. Passel, Jeffrey and Clark, Rebecca, 1998.
11. The terms "immigrants," "foreign born," "aliens," "émigrés," "refugees," "asylees," "newcomers," and "noncitizens" refer to the same persons and are used interchangeably. Persons who are not naturalized citizens of the United States are specified as such. Similarly, "noncitizen voting," "alien suffrage," "immigrant voting," "resident voting," and "local citizenship" refer to the same practice.
12. There is a discrepancy in the scholarship about how many states, which states, and at what times these states allowed noncitizens to vote. Tallies that calculate this figure using the date when noncitizen voting rights ended state that "at least twenty two states and territories allowed noncitizens to vote and hold office." See Leon Aylsworth, "*The Passing of Alien Suffrage,*" *American Political Science Review* 25, no. 1 (February 1931): 114–16; and Virginia Harper-Ho, "Noncitizen Voting Rights: The History, the Law and Current Prospects for Change," Law and Inequality Journal, no. 18 (2000). Raskin rightly questioned the accuracy of this figure (Jamin B. Raskin, "Legal Aliens, Local Citizens: The Historical, Constitutional, and Theoretical Meanings of Alien Suffrage," *University of Pennsylvania Law Review* 141 [1993]: 1401). More recent scholarship shows "an upper limit of 35" states and territories that "ever permitted noncitizens to vote" (Marta Tienda, "Demography and the Social Contract," *Demography* 39, no. 4 [2002]: 602). My research, with the assistance of law students at New York University, shows that as many as forty states and federal territories at one point or another allowed noncitizens to vote, as detailed in chapter 2.
13. Franklin, however, was not a proponent of alien suffrage later in his life.
14. Raskin, "Legal Aliens, Local Citizens," 1401; Christopher Collier, "The American People as Christian White Men of Property: Suffrage and Elections in Colonial and Early National America," in *Voting and the Spirit of American Democracy*, ed. Donald W. Rogers. (Urbana: University of Illinois Press, 1992).
15. Raskin, "Legal Aliens, Local Citizens," 238–39.
16. Noel Ignatiev, *How the Irish Became White* (New York: Routledge, 1995); Rogers Smith, *Civic Ideals: Conflicting Visions of Citizenship in U.S. History* (New Haven, Conn.: Yale University Press, 1997); Josh DeWind and Philip Kasinitz, "Everything Old Is New Again? Process and Theories of Immigrant Incorporation," in Immigrant Adaptation and Native-born Responses in the Making of Americans: A Special Issue. International Migration Review 31 (Winter, 1997): 1096–111; E. Bonilla-Silva, "Rethinking Racism: Towards a Structural Interpretation," American Sociological Review 63, no. 3 (1997): 465–80; David Roediger, *The Wages of Whiteness* (London: Verso, 1991); and Alexander Keyssar, *The Right to Vote: The Contested History of Democracy in the United States* (New York: Basic Books, 2000).
17. Robert F. Worth, "Push Is On to Give Legal Immigrants Vote in New York," *New York Times*, April 8, 2004; Alexandra Marks, "Should Noncitizens Vote?" *Christian Science Monitor*, April 27, 2004; Teresa Borden, "What Does Citizenship Mean: Cities Debate Whether Noncitizens Should Vote," *Atlanta Journal-Constitution*, July 2, 2004; Miriam Jordan, "Noncitizen Parents Seek Voting Rights in School Elections," *Wall Street Journal*, September 14, 2004; and Katia Hetter, "Right to Vote Sought for Noncitizen Parents: Measure Would Apply to Elections for School Board," *San Francisco Chronicle*, July 9, 2004.

18. These countries include Barbados, Belize, Canada, Chile, Israel, Uruguay, and Venezuela. For information on policies and practices in Europe and elsewhere, see T. Alexander Aleinikoff and Douglas Klusmeyer, *Citizenship Policies for an Age of Migration* (Washington, D.C.: Carnegie Endowment for International Peace, 2002); David Earnest, "Noncitizen Voting Rights: A Survey of an Emerging Democratic Norm" (paper prepared for the 2003 annual convention of the American Political Science Association, August 28–31, Philadelphia); Jan Rath, "Voting Rights," in The Political Rights of Migrant Workers in Western Europe, ed. Henry Zig Layton (Newbury Park, Calif.: Sage, 1990); Raskin, "Legal Aliens, Local Citizens," 1401; Harper-Ho, "Noncitizen Voting Rights"; and the Immigrant Voting Project, "Immigrant Voting Project: Democracy for All," http://www.immigrantvoting.org. Day, Stephen and Jo Shaw. "European Union Electoral Rights and the Political Participation of Migrants in Host Polities." *International Journal of Population Geography.* 8, 183–199. 2002; Baubock, Rainer. "Expansive Citizenship – Voting Beyond Territorial and Membership." *PS: Political Science and Politics.* Washington, D.C.: American Political Science Association. Vol. 38, No. 4. October, 2005; Waldrauch, Harald. "Electoral rights for foreign nationals: a comparative overview." Paper prepared for Exploratory Workshop: "Citizens, non-citizens and voting rights in Europe," sponsored by the European Science Foundation, the Europa Institute and the School of Law, University of Edinburgh. University of Edinburgh, UK. June 2–4, 2005.

19. Today, there are distinct categories of immigrants, the main distinction being "documented" or "legal" versus "undocumented" or "illegal" immigrants. Legal permanent residents are those who obtain immigrant visas or "green cards" because they (1) are related to a U.S. citizen or permanent resident, (2) possess a needed or desirable job skill or ability, or (3) are spouses or children of green card holders. Other categories of legal immigrants include asylees, refugees, and "nonimmigrant" foreigners (such as students, tourists, diplomats, and temporary workers).

20. Unless otherwise noted, all data on immigrants are from the U.S. Bureau of the Census and the U.S. Citizenship and Immigration Services (USCIS, formerly the Immigration and Naturalization Service [INS]).

21. A useful distinction can be made between "immigration policy" and "immigrant policy," which analysts sometimes employ. "Immigration policy" determines which immigrant groups are permitted to enter the U.S. and in what proportions and numbers. A distinct but related set of "immigrant policies" refers to federal, state, and local laws and policies that influence the integration and the treatment of immigrants after they have arrived. The federal government sets U.S. immigration policy. U.S. immigrant policy is composed primarily of various state and local provisions and programs, which are less consistent and coherent than federal policy. Immigrant voting rights, for the most part, fall into the latter category of immigrant policy. Of course, both immigration policy and immigrant policy flow from the larger formal and informal rules and processes that shape governance and operate in economic and social life more generally.

22. Jeffrey S. Passel, "Election 2004: The Latino and Asian Vote," Urban Institute Immigration Studies Program, July 27, 2004, http://www.urban.org/UploadedPDF/900723.pdf.

23. Such political exclusion is also evident for the 4.5 million residents in U.S. territories and the over 4 million ex-offenders who lack voting rights.

24. Chilton Williamson, *American Suffrage From Property to Democracy, 1760–1860* (Princeton, N.J.: Princeton University Press, 1960).

25. *Minor v. Happersett*, U.S. Supreme Court, 88 U.S. 162, October term, 1874.

26. Louise Renne, former San Francisco city attorney, asked, "If non-citizens can vote, can Osama bin Laden vote in a school election?" *San Francisco Chronicle,* July 10, 2004; see also *Sing Tao Daily,* July 13, 2004.

27. Of course, other electoral reforms are crucial to rectify the bias of the electorate and the nature of the political parties, such as Election Day voter registration, effective campaign finance reform, ballot access reform, and the inauguration of alternative representational schemes (such as proportional representation or instant runoff voting), if more democratic electoral politics and outcomes are to be achieved; Ronald Hayduk and Kevin Mattson, eds., *Democracy's Moment: Reforming the American Political System for the 21st Century* (Lanham, Md.: Rowman & Littlefield, 2002).

28. Deborah Sontag, "Noncitizens and Right to Vote," *New York Times,* July 31, 1992, A1.

Chapter 2

1. Thomas Paine, *Common Sense*.
2. Howard Zinn, *You Can't Be Neutral on a Moving Train*.
3. Leon Aylsworth, "*The Passing of Alien Suffrage*," *American Political Science Review* 25, no. 1 (February 1931): 114.
4. Jamin B. Raskin, "Legal Aliens, Local Citizens: The Historical, Constitutional, and Theoretical Meanings of Alien Suffrage," *University of Pennsylvania Law Review* 141 (1993): 1401.
5. Aylsworth, "*The Passing of Alien Suffrage*"; and Virginia Harper-Ho, "Noncitizen Voting Rights: The History, the Law and Current Prospects for Change," *Law and Inequality Journal*, no. 18 (2000). Cited in Marta Tienda, "Demography and the Social Contract," *Demography* 39, no. 4 (2002): 602.
6. Raskin, "Legal Aliens, Local Citizens."
7. Tienda, "Demography and the Social Contract," 602.
8. Tienda, "Demography and the Social Contract." Keyssar provides one of the most comprehensive and compelling accounts of the "contested" history of democratic practices in the U.S., including alien suffrage. See Alexander Keyssar, *The Right to Vote: The Contested History of Democracy in the United States* (New York: Basic Books, 2000).
9. The following discussion of the legal history of noncitizen voting draws especially upon the work of Raskin, "Legal Aliens, Local Citizens"; and Harper-Ho, "Noncitizen Voting Rights." See also Kirk H. Porter, *A History of Suffrage in the United States* (1918; reprint, Chicago: University of Chicago Press, 1971); Gerald Rosberg, "Aliens and Equal Protection: Why Not the Right to Vote?" *Michigan Law Review* 75 (April–May 1977): 1092–36; and Gerald Neuman, "'We Are the People': Alien Suffrage in German and American Perspective," *Michigan Journal of International Law* 13 (1992): 259. Raskin notes that aliens even signed the Declaration of Independence.
10. Raskin, "Legal Aliens, Local Citizens," 1401.
11. Chilton Williamson, *American Suffrage from Property to Democracy, 1760–1860* (Princeton, N.J.: Princeton University Press, 1960); and Judith N. Shklar, *American Citizenship: The Quest for Inclusion* (Cambridge, Mass.: Harvard University Press, 1991).
12. Raskin, "Legal Aliens, Local Citizens," 1401, citing Christopher Collier, "The American People as Christian White Men of Property: Suffrage and Elections in Colonial and Early National America," in *Voting and the Spirit of American Democracy*, ed. Donald W. Rogers (Urbana: University of Illinois Press, 1992).
13. Massachusetts Constitution, art. IV, sec. 3, (1780).
14. In 1811, however, the Massachusetts Supreme Court declared that suffrage was intended for citizens only and that the payment of taxes did not impart any political rights. Opinion of Justices, 7 Mass. 523 (Mass. 1811).
15. Tienda, "Demography and the Social Contract," 587.
16. Raskin, "Legal Aliens, Local Citizens," 1402. Raskin notes, "Two classes of people were given the right to hold office in the territorial legislatures: resident owners of 200 acres of land who had been citizens of one of the United States for three years, and aliens who owned 200 acres of land and had lived in the territory for three years. . . . The class of electors consisted, similarly, of residents who owned 50 acres of land and were citizens of one of the states, and aliens who owned 50 acres of land and had lived in the territory for two years." See also Neuman, "'We Are the People,'" 295 n. 13.
17. Raskin, "Legal Aliens, Local Citizens," 1402, 1407–08.
18. *People v. Scott*, 22 N.W. 274, 274 (Mich. 1885). However, in 1908 Michigan succumbed to the rising tide of nativism and changed its constitution, restricting the vote only to U.S. citizens.
19. Anti-French forces lobbied for laws restricting voting rights of immigrants during the 1790s and early 1800s. Hale (2003), 151.
20. Raskin, Overruling Democracy, 2003:238.
21. Raskin, "Legal Aliens, Local Citizens," 1410.
22. Hale, 151. Three laws made up the Alien Acts: the Alien Enemies Act, the Alien Friends Act, and the Sedition Act.
23. Michael Curran, "Flickering Lamp beside the Golden Door: Immigration, the Constitution and Undocumented Aliens in the 1990's," *Case Western Reserve Journal of International Law* 30, no. 1 (Winter 1998): 58–142.

24. Paul Kleppner, "Defining Citizenship: Immigration and the Struggle for voting rights in Antebellum America," in *Voting and the Spirit of American Democracy: Essays on the History of Voting and Voting Rights in America*, ed. Donald W. Rogers and Christine Scriabine (Urbana: University of Illinois Press, 1992); and William Darrell Overdyke, *The Know-Nothing Party in the South* (1950; reprint, Gloucester, Mass.: Peter Smith, 1968).

25. In the end, William Archer of Virginia helped prevent the bill from passing. Overdyke, *The Know-Nothing Party in the South*.

26. Raskin, "Legal Aliens, Local Citizens," 1404, citing Rosberg, "Aliens and Equal Protection," 1096–98.

27. Raskin, "Legal Aliens, Local Citizens," 1404; and Shklar, *American Citizenship*, 46.

28. Merrill D. Peterson, ed., *Democracy, Liberty, and Property: The State Constitutional Conventions of the 1820s* (Indianapolis, Ind.: Bobbs-Merrill Co., 1966), 215–16. New York did not grant full voting equality to blacks until required to do so by the Reconstruction-era amendments to the U.S. Constitution. Similarly, efforts to amend the New York Constitution to grant suffrage to women failed until the change was mandated at the national level.

29. However, the Connecticut Constitution expanded suffrage, reduced the property requirement, and granted voting rights to non–property owners who had served in the state militia. Wesley W. Horton, "Connecticut Constitutional History, 1776–1988" (1988), http://www.cslib.org/cts4c.htm.

30. Ibid.

31. The 1870 Illinois Constitution read, "Every person having resided in this State one year, in the country ninety days, and in the election district thirty days next preceding any election therein, who was an elector in the State on the first day of April, in the year of our lord 1848, or obtained a certificate of naturalization before any court of Record in this State prior to the first day of January, in the year of our Lord 1870, or who shall be a male citizen of the United States, above the age of Twenty years, shall be entitled to vote at such election." Illinois Constitution of 1870, art. VII, sec. 1.

32. Raskin, "Legal Aliens, Local Citizens," 1404, citing Rosberg, "Aliens and Equal Protection," 1096–98.

33. Porter, *A History of Suffrage in the United States*.

34. Kleppner, "Defining Citizenship."

35. "Editorial," *Illinois State Register*, March 13, 1854.

36. Hon. James Brooks, "Defence of President Fillmore" (address to Know-Nothing Party, 1856, Cincinnati, Ohio).

37. Overdyke, *The Know-Nothing Party in the South*.

38. John R. Mulkern, *The Know-Nothing Party in Massachusetts: The Rise and Fall of a People's Movement* (Boston: Northeastern University Press, 1990).

39. Raskin, "Legal Aliens, Local Citizens," 1409; Rosberg, "Aliens and Equal Protection," 1116–17; and Porter, *A History of Suffrage in the United States*, 3.

40. Eric Foner, *Reconstruction: America's Unfinished Revolution, 1863–1877* (New York: Harper-Collins, 1988), 124–75.

41. Ibid.

42. Raskin, "Legal Aliens, Local Citizens," 1407 (emphasis in the original).

43. Joseph A. Ranney, "Aliens and 'Real Americans': Law and Ethnic Assimilation in Wisconsin, 1846–1920," *Wisconsin Lawyer*, http://www.wisbar.org

44. Michigan changed its constitution in 1850 to allow declarant aliens voting rights after residency in the state for two and a half years. Raskin, "Legal Aliens, Local Citizens," 1408.

45. Shklar, *American Citizenship*, 45–52; and Raskin, "Legal Aliens, Local Citizens," 1414.

46. Foner, *Reconstruction*, 124–75.

47. Aylsworth, "*The Passing of Alien Suffrage*", 114.

48. Harper-Ho, "Noncitizen Voting Rights"; and Martha I. Morgan and Neal Hutchens, "The Tangled Web of Alabama's Equality Doctrine after Melof: Historical Reflections on Equal Protection and the Alabama Constitution," *Alabama Law Review* 53 (2001): 135–242.

49. Ibid.

50. Dennis Judd and Todd Swanstrom, *City Politics: Private Power and Public Policy* (New York: Longman, 2004) 17.

51. For a recent articulation of some of these themes, particularly regarding Mexicans and Hispanics more generally, see Samuel Huntington, *Who Are We? The Challenges to America's National Identity* (New York: Simon & Schuster, 2004).

52. Harper-Ho, "Noncitizen Voting Rights," 44, citing Jacob Katz Cogan, "The Look Within: Property, Capacity, and Suffrage in Nineteenth Century America," *Yale Law Journal* 107 (1997): 473, 495.

53. Harper-Ho, "Noncitizen Voting Rights," 44.

54. Minnesota Territorial Government Act, ch. 121, sec. 5, 9 stat. 403, 405 (1849), http://www.sos.state.mn.us/student/act1849.pdf.

55. Cong. Globe, 34th Cong., 3rd sess. 811.

56. Cong. Globe, 34th Cong., 3rd sess. at 810.

57. Cong. Globe, 34th Cong., 3rd sess. at 814.

58. Raskin, 1993:1409.

59. Cong. Globe, 34th Cong., 3rd Sess. 811.

60. Cong. Globe, 34th Cong., 3rd sess. 813.

61. Enabling Act for a State of Minnesota, Act Authorizing a State Government (February 26, 1857).

62. Raskin, "Legal Aliens, Local Citizens," 1391, 1407, see also 1099 n. 36.

63. Minnesota Secretary of State, "Amendments to the Minnesota Constitution Proposed to the Voters since 1858." http://www.sos.state.mn.us/student/amendcon.pdf. See also Rosberg, "Why Not the Right to Vote?" 1092, 1099 n. 36.

64. "For Intelligent Suffrage," *Washington Post*, July 29, 1902.

65. Addison E. Sheldon, ed., *Official Report of the Debates and Proceedings in the Nebraska Constitution Convention* assembled in Lincoln, June 13, 1871, 207 (1905).

66. Sheldon, *Official Report of the Debates and Proceedings in the Nebraska Constitution Convention*, 210–211 (1905).

67. Aylsworth, "*The Passing of Alien Suffrage*," 114, 115.

68. Nebraska Department of Education and Nebraska State Historical Society, "Racial Tensions in Omaha in the 1920s," http://www.nebraskastudies.org/0700/frameset.html.

69. Quoted in Nebraska Department of Education and Nebraska State Historical Society, "Racial Tensions in Omaha in the 1920s."

70. E. E. Schattschneider, *The Semisovereign People* (New York: Holt, Rinehart & Winston, 1960); Walter Dean Burnham, *Critical Elections and the Mainsprings of American Politics* (New York: W.W. Norton, 1970); Frances Fox Piven and Richard Cloward, *Why Americans Still Don't Vote* (Boston: Beacon Press, 2000); Keyssar, *The Right to Vote*; and Ronald Hayduk, *Gatekeepers to the Franchise: Election Administration in New York* (DeKalb: Northern Illinois University Press, 2005).

71. Raskin, "Legal Aliens, Local Citizens," 1415.

72. Philip J. Ethington, "Progressive Era Political Participation," *Studies in American Political Development* 7 (Fall 1993): 307.

73. David Heer, *Immigration in America's Future: Social Science Findings and the Policy Debate* (Boulder, Colo.: Westview Press, 1996), 27–71

74. The National Origins Act of 1924 imposed quantitative restrictions on immigrants, placing a ceiling of 150,000 per year on European immigration while completely barring Japanese immigration (Chinese were excluded in 1882). The National Origins Act provided for the admission of immigrants based on the proportion of national origin groups that were present in the United States according to the census of 1890. Because this census preceded the large-scale immigration from Southern and Eastern Europe, this provision represented an explicit effort to ensure that future immigration flows would be largely composed of immigrants from Northern and Western Europe.

75. Thomas Curran, *Xenophobia and Immigration, 1820–1930* (Boston: Twayne, 1975), 143; David Mark Chalmers, *Hooded Americanism: The First Century of the Ku Klux Klan, 1865–1965* (Garden City, N.Y.: Doubleday, 1965), 283; A 1924 House of Representatives report acknowledges this fact (U.S. House of Representatives, Report #350, 68th Cong., 1st sess., II, 4–5; Washington, D.C.: Government Printing Office, 1924); and Desmond S. King, *Making Americans: Immigration, Race, and the Origins of the Diverse Democracy* (Cambridge, Mass.: Harvard University Press, 2000), presents a rich discussion of congressional debates that contain eugenic arguments and blatant racism that justified criteria for admission.

76. Keyssar, *The Right to Vote* Piven and Cloward, *Why Americans Still Don't Vote*; Ronald Hayduk, 2002; and Hayduk, *Gatekeepers to the Franchise.*

77. W. E. B. DuBois, *The Souls of Black Folk* (1903; reprint, New York: Knopf, 1993; and Noel Ignatiev, *How the Irish Became White* (New York: Routledge, 1995).

78. Rogers Smith, *Civic Ideals: Conflicting Visions of Citizenship in U.S. History* (New Haven, Conn.: Yale University Press, 1997); and Daniel J. Tichenor, *Dividing Lines: The Politics of Immigration Control in America* (Princeton, N.J.: Princeton University Press, 2002).

79. See for example, New York State Convention, *Journal* (1986), 89. Most of these measures, however, failed. Other states such as Connecticut successfully changed its constitution in 1855 to require literacy (measured by the ability to read the constitution or statutes) in order to vote.

80. Porter, *A History of Suffrage in the United States*, 114.

81. Massachusetts Constitution of 1863, art. XXVI.

82. Ranney, "Aliens and 'Real Americans.'"

83. "Aliens Permitted to Vote," *Washington Post*, March 1, 1918.

84. Keyssar, *The Right to Vote*, 137.

85. John Higham, *Strangers in the Land: Patterns of American Nativism, 1860–1925* (New Brunswick, N.J.: Rutgers University Press, 1992); and Ignatiev, *How the Irish Became White.*

86. Keyssar, *The Right to Vote*; Piven and Cloward, *Why Americans Still Don't Vote*; and Hayduk, *Gatekeepers to the Franchise.*

87. Michael Goldfield, *The Color of Politics: Race and the Mainsprings of American Politics* (New York: New Press, 1997).

88. Higham, *Strangers in the Land*; and Maldwyn Allen Jones, *American Immigration* (Chicago: University of Chicago Press, 1992).

89. Ignatiev, *How the Irish Became White;* and Higham, *Strangers in the Land.*

90. Higham, *Strangers in the Land.*

91. Heer, *Immigration in America's Future.*

92. Curran, *Xenophobia and Immigration, 1820–1930*, 143; and Chalmers, *Hooded Americanism,* 283. Perhaps most revealing is a 1924 House of Representatives report that acknowledges the key role that the KKK played in the passage of the National Origins Act; U.S. House of Representatives, Report #350, 4–5. It would not be until the civil rights and black power movements that expansionary changes were made to U.S. immigration law in 1965.

93. Smith, *Civic Ideals.*

94. Walter Dean Burnham, *Critical Elections and the Mainsprings of American Politics* (New York: W.W. Norton, 1970); and Smith, 1999.

95. Grob, Gerald N. and George Athan Billias. "The Progressive Movement." In *Interpretations of American History: Patterns and Perspectives.* Edited by Gerald N. Grob and George Athen Billias. 5th Edition. New York: Free Press. 1987. See also Richard Hofstadter, *The Age of Reform: From Bryan to F.D.R.* New York: Alfred A. Knopf. 1955; Hays, Samuel P. "The Politics of Reform in Municipal Government in the Progressive Era." *Pacific Northwest Quarterly.* 55. October, 1964: 157–169; Gabriel Kolko. *Main Currents in Modern American History.* New York: Pantheon Books. 1984.

96. Melvin Holli, in *Interpretations of American History*, ed. Gerald Grob and George Billias (New York: Free Press, 1987).

97. Church and Sedlak, 1976s.

98. Buenker, 1973, ibid.

99. See various reports by the Center for Immigrant Studies and the Federation for American Immigration Reform.

100. Schattschneider, *The Semisovereign People*; Burnham, *Critical Elections and the Mainsprings of American Politics*; and Piven and Cloward, *Why Americans Still Don't Vote.*

101. "Show Your Papers," *New York Herald*, October 17, 1888.

102. "Ask Changes in Law of Naturalization," *New York Times*, March 25, 1923.

103. "Not Fit for Citizenship," *Washington Post*, April 4, 1902.

104. Joseph P. Harris, *Registration of Voters in the United States* (Washington, D.C.: Brookings Institution, 1929); and Joseph P. Harris, *Election Administration in the United States* (Washington, D.C.: Brookings Institution, 1934).

105. Burnham, *Critical Elections and the Mainsprings of American Politics.*

106. Howard W. Allen and Kay Warren Allen, "Voter Fraud and Data Validity," in *Analyzing Electoral History*, ed. Jerome Clubb, William H. Flanigan, and Nancy Zingale (Beverly Hills, Calif.: Sage, 1981); and Peter H. Argersinger, "New Perspectives on Electoral Fraud in the Gilded Age," *Political Science Quarterly* 100, no. 4 (Winter 1985–1986): 669–87.
107. Allen and Allen, "Voter Fraud and Data Validity," 172–74.
108. Keyssar, *The Right to Vote*, 119.
109. Ibid.
110. Ibid., 170–71.

Chapter 3

1. Passel, Jeffrey S. Election 2004: The Latino and Asian Vote," July 27 (Washington, D.C.: Urban Institute, 2004).
2. Lorraine Minnite, "Report for The New York City Immigration Coalition" (2001), http://www.thenyic.org.
3. The 2000 Census shows that New York City had 1,592,345 noncitizens out of 8,008,278 total residents of all ages. In fact, there were over 300,000 more total noncitizens residents (1,592,345) than naturalized citizen immigrants (1,278,687). Figures are from the New York City Planning Department (which draws its data from the U.S. Bureau of the Census).
4. Unless otherwise noted, all data on immigrants are from the U.S. Bureau of the Census and the U.S. Citizenship and Immigration Services (USCIS), formerly the Immigration and Naturalization Service (INS). The data were derived from Census table GCT-P16, "Citizenship Status for the Population 18 Years and Over" and "Yearbook of Immigration Statistics." The data were collected on a sample basis and are incorporated within "Census 2000 Summary File 4." I wish to thank Joaquin Avila, who compiled much of the census data in this section, and *Ari Weisbard, who generated many of* the graphs.
5. The number of individuals in a "mixed family" is derived from "Immigrant Stock," which the U.S. Census Bureau defines as "Immigrants and their children born here." In 2000, 55.9 million (20.4 percent) of the total population were mixed. See also Michael E. Fix, and Wendy Zimmerman. *All under One Roof: Mixed-Status Families in an Era of Reform* (Washington, D.C.: Urban Institute, 1999).
6. Immigration Policy Center/American Immigration Law Foundation, "Power and Potential: The Growing Electoral Clout of New Citizens," *Immigration Policy* 3, no. 4 (October 2004): http://www.ailf.org/ipc/ipf102004.pdf.
7. Randolph Capps, Michael E. Fix, and Jeffrey S. Passel, *The Dispersal of Immigrants in the 1990s* (Washington, D.C.: Urban Institute. 2002); and Michael E. Fix and Jeffrey S. Passel, Testimony before the Subcommittee on Immigration and Claims Hearing on the U.S. Population and Immigration Committee on the Judiciary U.S. House of Representatives. August 2. Washington, D.C.: Urban Institute, 2001.
8. Joaquin Avila, "Political Apartheid in California: Consequences of Excluding a Growing Noncitizen Population," Latino Policy and Issues Brief #9 (Los Angeles: Chicano Studies Research Center, University of California, Los Angeles, 2003).
9. USCIS, "2003 Yearbook of Immigration Statistics." September 2004. Table 1, page 135. See also S. Karthick Ramakrishnan, *Democracy in Immigrant America: Changing Demographics and Political Participation*. Stanford, CA: Stanford University Press, 2005: 34–36.
10. Testimony of Eduardo Aguirre Jr., director of the USCIS, before the Subcommittee on Immigration, Boarder Security and Claims, House Committee on the Judiciary, June 17, 2004. *Congressional Record*. http://judiciary.house.gov
11. Peter J. Spiro, "Questioning Barriers to Naturalization," *Georgetown Immigration Law Journal* 13 (1999): 479; and Michael Fix, Jeffrey Passel, and Kenneth Sucher, *Trends in Naturalization*, September (Washington, D.C.: Urban Institute, 2003).
12. Michael E. Fix and Jeffrey S. Passel, *A New Citizenship Day*, September 17 (Washington, D.C.: Urban Institute, 2003). They note the proportion of Asian immigrants "who had naturalized rose from 56 to 67 percent and the share of Mexicans went from 19 to 34 percent." Moreover, they estimate that another 8 million legal immigrants could naturalize but have not.
13. Fix, Passel, and Sucher, *Trends in Naturalization*; Ramakrishnan Democracy in Immigrant America, 2005.

14. Immigration Policy Center/American Immigration Law Foundation, "Power and Potential: The Growing Electoral Clout of New Citizens."
15. Ibid.
16. John Mollenkopf, David Olsen, and Timothy Ross, "Immigrant Political Participation in New York and Los Angeles," in *Governing Cities*, ed. Michael Jones-Correa (New York: Russell Sage Foundation, 2001); Lorraine Minnite, Jennifer Holdaway, and Ronald Hayduk, "The Political Participation of Immigrants in New York," in *In Defense of the Alien*, vol. 23, ed. Lydio F. Tomasi (New York: Center for Migration Studies, 2001); and Louis DeSipio, "Building America, One Person at a Time: Naturalization and Political Behavior of the Naturalized in Contemporary American Politics," in *E Pluribus Unum?: Contemporary and Historical Perspectives on Immigrant Political Incorporation*, ed. Gary Gerstle and John Mollenkopf (New York: Russell Sage Foundation, 2001).
17. Mollenkopf, Olsen, and Ross, "Immigrant Political Participation in New York and Los Angeles" ; and DeSipio, "Building America, One Person at a Time."
18. John Mollenkopf and John Logan, *People and Politics in America's Big Cities: The Challenges to Urban Democracy* (New York: Drum Major Institute for Public Policy, 2003), 5.
19. Capps, Fix, and Passel, *The Dispersal of Immigrants in the 1990s.*
20. A household is "food insecure" if at some point during the previous year it was unable to obtain or uncertain of having adequate food to meet basic needs, according to the USDA. *Immigrant Well-being in New York and Los Angeles*, August (Washington, D.C.: Urban Institute, 2002).
21. Randy Capps, Michael Fix, Jeffrey S. Passel, Jason Ost, and Dan Perez-Lopez, *A Profile of the Low-Wage Immigrant Workforce*, November (Washington, D.C.: Urban Institute, 2003).
22. Randy Capps, Genevieve Kenney, and Michael Fix, *Health Insurance Coverage of Children in Mixed-Status Immigrant Families* (Washington, D.C.: Urban Institute, 2003).
23. National Research Council of the National Academy of Sciences, *The New Americans: Economic, Demographic, and Fiscal Effects of Immigration*, ed. James P. Smith and Barry Edmonston (Washington, D.C.: National Academy Press, 1997); and National Research Council of the National Academy of Sciences, *The Immigration Debate: Studies on the Economic, Demographic, and Fiscal Effects of Immigration*, ed. James P. Smith and Barry Edmonston (Washington, D.C.: National Academy Press, 1998).
24. Fix, Passel, and Sucher, *Trends in Naturalization.*
25. Several landmark pieces of legislation concerning immigrants have been enacted at the national level-—including the Immigration Reform and Control Act of 1986; the Illegal Immigration Reform and Immigrant Responsibility Act of 1996; the Personal Responsibility and Work Opportunity Reconciliation Act of 1996; and recent antiterrorism legislation, including the USA PATRIOT Act—are but a few examples. Similarly, states and locales have passed—and/or considered—dozens of pieces of legislation affecting the economic, social, and political status of immigrants.
26. Michele Wucker, "Civics Lessons from Immigrants: What Happens to the Working-Class Political Voice When Many of Its Speakers Aren't Citizens?" *American Prospect* 14, no. 7 (July 1, 2003): http://www.prospect.org/print/V14/7/wucker-m.html.

Chapter 4

1. The European Commission to the European Parliament (October 1986 Report).
2. Jamin Raskin, "Legal Aliens, Local Citizens: The Historical, Constitutional, and Theoretical Meanings of Alien Suffrage," *University of Pennsylvania Law Review* 141 (1993): 1460.
3. Rogers Smith, *Civic Ideals: Conflicting Visions of Citizenship in U.S. History* (New Haven, Conn.: Yale University Press, 1997), 15.
4. This section draws upon the work of Raskin, "Legal Aliens, Local Citizens,""; Gerald Rosberg, "Aliens and Equal Protection: Why Not the Right to Vote? *Michigan Law Review* 75 (April-May 1977): 1092–136); Wendy Aviva Shimmelman, "Local Voting Rights for Non-U.S. Citizen Immigrants in New York City," Center for Immigrants Rights, New York, New York, 1992; Jennifer Gordon, "Let Them Vote," in *A Community of Equals: The Constitutional Protection of New Americans*, ed. Owen M. Fiss, Joshua Cohen, Joel Rogers, and Edwidge Danticat (Boston: Beacon Press, 1999); Virginia Harper-Ho, "Noncitizen Voting Rights: The History, the Law and Current Prospects for Change," *Law and Inequality Journal*,

no 18, (2000); Elise Brozovich, "Prospects for Democratic Change: Non-Citizen Suffrage in America," *Hamline Journal of Public Law & Policy*, no 23 (2002): 403–53; Tara Kini, "Sharing the Vote: Noncitizen Voting Rights in Local School Board Elections," *California Law Review* 93 (January 2005): 271; Alexander T. Aleinikoff and Douglas Klusmeyer, *Citizenship Policies for an Age of Migration* (Washington, D.C.: Carnegie Endowment for International Peace, 2002); Marta Tienda, "Demography and the Social Contract," *Demography* 39, no. 4 (2002): 587–616; Monica Weiler Varsanyi, "Stretching the Boundaries of Citizenship in the City: Undocumented Migrants and Political Mobilization in Los Angeles" (Ph.D diss., University of California, Los Angeles, 2004); Lisa Garcia Bedolla, "Rethinking Citizenship: Noncitizen Voting and Immigrant Political Engagement in the United States," in *Transforming Politics, Transforming America: The Political and Civic Incorporation of Immigrants in the United States* ed. Taeku Lee, S. Karthick Ramakrishnan, and Ricardo Ramírez (Charlottesville: University of Virginia Press, 2005); and the Immigrant Voting Project, http://www.immigrantvoting.org.

5. Tienda, "Demography and the Social Contract," 588.

6. Paul Woodruff, *First Democracy: The Challenge of an Ancient Idea* (New York: Oxford, 2005). Woodruff notes that resident aliens were not allowed to vote (indeed, only about one-tenth of the residents were signatories to the laws that governed Athens), but at various points there were attempts to enfranchise noncitizens aliens.

7. Linda Bosniak, "Universal Citizenship and the Problem of Alienage," *Northwestern University Law Review* 94 (2000): 963–82; and Tienda, "Demography and the Social Contract," 605.

8. Bosniak, "Universal Citizenship and the Problem of Alienage," 974.

9. Peter Schuck and Rogers Smith, *Citizenship without Consent: Illegal Aliens in the American Polity* (New Haven, Conn.: Yale University Press, 1985).

10. Peter Schuck, "Membership in the Liberal Polity: The Devaluation of American Citizenship," in *Immigration and the Politics of Citizenship in Europe and North America*, ed. William Rogers Brubaker (New York: German Marshall Fund of the United States and the University Press of America, 1989); cited in Varsanyi, *Stretching the Boundaries of Citizenship in the City*, 8.

11. Tienda, "Demography and the Social Contract," 605, citing Bosniak, "Universal Citizenship and the Problem of Alienage"; Gerald L. Neuman, *Strangers to the Constitution: Immigrants, Boarders, and Fundamental Law* (Princeton, N.J.: Princeton University Press, 1996); Raskin, "Legal Aliens, Local Citizens"; and Rosberg, "Aliens and Equal Protection."

12. Aleinikoff, and Klusmeyer, *Citizenship Policies for an Age of Migration*, 46. Varsanyi, Monica, "Stretching the Boundaries of Citizenship in the City."

13. Bedolla, "Rethinking Citizenship."

14. . Tienda, "Demography and the Social Contract," 606, citing Bozniak, "Universal Citizenship and the Problem of Alienage," 963, Raskin, "Legal Aliens, Local Citizens"; and Neuman, *Strangers to the Constitution*.

15. Sarah McNaught, "A Novel Idea in Cambridge: Give Noncitizen Immigrants the Vote," *(Boston) Phoenix*, February 18, 1999.

16. Press conference, San Francisco, August 3, 2004.

17. Michael Huang, "Citizenship and Voting," *Gotham Gazette.*, August 8, 2003, http://www.gothamgazette.com/article/feature-commentary/20030825/202/503.

18. Ibid.

19. Joaquin Avila, "Political Apartheid in California: Consequences of Excluding a Growing Noncitizen Population," Latino Policy and Issues Brief #9 (Los Angeles: Chicano Studies Research Center, University of California, Los Angeles, 2003).

20. Nancy Foner, Ruben Rumbaut, and Steven Gold, *Immigration Research for a New Century* (New York: Russell Sage Foundation, 2001).

21. National Research Council of the National Academy of Sciences, *The New Americans: Economic, Demographic, and Fiscal Effects of Immigration*, ed. James P. Smith and Barry Edmonston (Washington, D.C.: National Academy Press, 1997); and National Research Council of the National Academy of Sciences, *The Immigration Debate: Studies on the Economic, Demographic, and Fiscal Effects of Immigration*, ed. James P. Smith and Barry Edmonston (Washington, D.C.: National Academy Press, 1998).

22. Rachel L Swarns, "Immigrants Raise Call for Right to Be Voters," *New York Times*, August 9, 2004.

23. A Voice for Parents, press conference and new release for Proposition F, September 18, 2004, http://www.voice4parents.com.

24. Raskin, "Legal Aliens, Local Citizens."

25. Cheryl B. Wilson, "Amherst Town Meeting Says Yes to Allowing Resident Aliens to Vote," *Daily Hampshire Gazette*, October 27, 1998; and Jeff Donn, "Mass. Town Considers Granting Vote to Non-citizens," Associated Press, October 21, 1998.

26. Elena Latona, executive director of Centro Presente, public meeting of the Cambridge City Council, May 5, 2003. Latona was referring to Jose Gutierrez, a U.S. Marine lance corporal, who was once an illegal immigrant who earned his permanent residency. An estimated 1,500 Guatemalans serve in the U.S. armed forces. (Campaign for Immigrant Voting Rights, prepared packet for Cambridge City Council, May 5, 2003.)

27. Immigrant Voting Project.

28. Cambridge City Council public meeting, May 5, 2003.

29. Ibid.

30. Winnie Hu, "Bloomberg Voices His Opposition to Voting by Noncitizens," *New York Times*, April 10, 2004.

31. Tony Best, "Fight For Right to Vote in U.S.," *The Nation News*, August, 13, 2004.

32. Comments at public forum held by the League of Women Voters and the New York County Lawyers' Association, "Should Non-Citizens Vote in Local Elections?" New York County Lawyers' Association Auditorium, April 21, 2005.

33. Ibid.

34. Chapters 5 and 6 provide further examples.

35. Michele Wucker, "Civics Lessons from Immigrants: What Happens to the Working-Class Political Voice When Many of Its Speakers Aren't Citizens?" *American Prospect* 14, no. 7 (2003): http://www.prospect.org/print/V14/7/wucker-m.html.

36. Randolph Capps, Michael E. Fix, and Jeffrey S. Passel, *The Dispersal of Immigrants in the 1990s* (Washington, D.C.: Urban Institute, 2002).

37. Randy Capps, Micheal Fix, Jason Ost, Jane Reardon-Anderson, and Jeffrey S. Passel, *The Health and Well-Being of Young Children of Immigrants* (Washington, D.C.: Urban Institute, 2004).

38. Donn, "Mass. Town Considers Granting Vote to Non-citizens."

39. Cambridge City Council public meeting, May 5, 2003.

40. Kathleen Coll, testimony to Massachusetts State Legislature, Joint Committee on Elections Laws, March 16, 2004.

41. The Campaign for Immigrant Voting Rights also noted, "The Senate Judiciary Committee Report issued with the proposed amendment stated, *inter alia*, that young people had 'earned the right to vote by bearing the responsibilities of citizenship.'" S.REP. no. 26, 92nd Congress, 1st Session 7 (1971), reprinted in 1971 U.S.C.C.A.N. 931,936. In enclosure #6, Campaign for Immigrant Voting Rights packet, presented to the Cambridge City Council in 2003.

42. Ibid., citing Raskin, "Legal Aliens, Local Citizens," 1451.

43. *El Andar*, June 1996, http://www.elandar.com.

44. Ibid.

45. The ballot measure lost by a vote of 51.2 to 48.5 percent. For a fuller discussion, see chapter 6.

46. Matt Gonzalez, "Giving Noncitizens Access to the Voting Booth." *San Francisco Chronicle*, July 20, 2004.

47. Interviewed by Giselle Barry on August 31, 2004. Maria Luz Torre, founder of Parent Voices, a San Francisco–based advocacy agency that works for quality and affordable child care, has two children in public schools. According to Barry, Torre became "one of San Francisco's leading children's advocates, winning distinction from the Ford Foundation, Congresswoman Nancy Pelosi, and former Governor Gray Davis for her service to California's democracy."

48. Swarns, "Immigrants Raise Call for Right to Be Voters."

49. Interview with Bryan Pu-Folkes, March 5, 2005.

50. Comments at public forum held by the League of Women Voters and the New York County Lawyers' Association, "Should Non-Citizens Vote in Local Elections?" New York County Lawyers' Association Auditorium, April 21, 2005.

51. Obvious examples at the federal level are the 2000 presidential election, particularly in Florida, and in several battleground states during the 2004 elections. In state elections, New York provides ample evidence. For example, George Pataki (R) defeated Mario Cuomo (D) in the 1994 gubernatorial election by a mere 173,798 votes out of more than 5 million votes cast statewide; Alphonse D'Amato sank Bob Abrams by only 124,838 votes in 1992; and, in New York City, Rudolph Giuliani defeated David Dinkins by approximately 50,000 votes out of nearly 2 million cast in 1993. Similarly, Michael Bloomberg defeated Mark Green by 40,000 votes out of 1.5 million votes cast (and Mark Green defeated Fernando Ferrer in the Democratic Party Primary runoff election by about 15,000 votes). These 1–2 percent margins of victory could quickly vanish if noncitizens were more than potential voters. Today, over 1.3 million adult New Yorkers are noncitizens (about 20 percent). Similarly, many close races in the states with large immigrant populations (California, New York, Texas, Florida, Illinois, New Jersey, and Massachusetts) and metropolitan regions (Los Angeles, Miami, Chicago, Washington, D.C., Houston, San Francisco, and Boston) could have changed if noncitizens were enfranchised.

52. Maria Luz Torre, interviewed by Giselle Barry on August 31, 2004.

53. City Councilor Marjorie Decker, public meeting of the Cambridge City Council, May 5, 2003.

54. Raskin, "Legal Aliens, Local Citizens," 1457.

55. Ronald Hayduk, "From Anti-Globalization to Global Justice: A Twenty-first Century Movement," in *Teamsters and Turtles?: U.S. Progressive Political Movements in the 21st Century* (Lanham, MD: Rowman & Littlefield, 2003); and Benjamin Shepard and Ronald Hayduk, eds., *From ACT UP to the WTO: Urban Protest and Community Building in the Era of Globalization* (New York: Verso, 2002).

56. Douglas Massey, "March of Folly: U.S. Immigration Policy after NAFTA," *American Prospect* (March 1, 1998): http://www.prospect.org/print/V9/37/massey-d.html; and Bedolla, "Rethinking Citizenship."

57. Bedolla, "Rethinking Citizenship." She notes the 1997 NACRA immigration law.

58. Massey, "March of Folly."

59. Bedolla, "Rethinking Citizenship."

60. Raskin, "Legal Aliens, Local Citizens," 1457–58.

61. Cambridge City Council public meeting, May 5, 2003. Close to 200 communities in the U.S. have passed resolutions opposing the Patriot Act. Eric Lichtblau, "Administration Plans Defense of Terror Law," *New York Times*, August 19, 2003. See also the National Coalition to Repeal the USA Patriot Act, http://www.repealnow.com.

62. Chaleampon Ritthichai, "Should Non-Citizens Be Allowed to Vote?" Gothamgazette.com, 2003, http://www.gothamgazette.com/immigrants/sep.02.shtml.

63. Hu, "Bloomberg Voices His Opposition to Voting by Noncitizens."

64. Swarns, "Immigrants Raise Call for Right to Be Voters."

65. Ibid.

66. Deborah Sontag, "Noncitizens and Right to Vote" *New York Times*, July 31, 1992, A1.

67. Robert F. Worth, "Push Is On to Give Legal Immigrants Vote in New York," *New York Times*, April 8, 2004.

68. Cambridge City Council public meeting, May 5, 2003.

69. F. R. Duplantier, "Behind the Headlines," March 4, 2001, http://www.politickles.com.

70. Wucker, "Civics Lessons from Immigrants."

71. Stanley Renshon, "The Value of Citizenship," *New York Sun*, September 15, 2003.

72. Comments at public forum held by the League of Women Voters and the New York County Lawyers' Association, "Should Non-Citizens Vote in Local Elections?" New York County Lawyers' Association Auditorium, April 21, 2005.

73. Stanley Renshon, comments at public forum held by the League of Women Voters and the New York County Lawyers' Association, "Should Non-Citizens Vote in Local Elections?" New York County Lawyers' Association Auditorium, April 21, 2005.

74. Samuel Huntington, *Who Are We? The Challenges to America's National Identity* (New York: Simon & Schuster, 2004).

75. Kelley Beaucar Vlahos "Immigrant Voters Could Change Election Landscapes," Fox News, May 17, 2004, http://www.fox.com.

76. Kim Cobb, "Immigrants' Voting Rights Becoming a Major Issue," *Houston Chronicle*, April 19, 2004.

77. Pew Research Center for the People and the Press, various reports, http://people-press.org.

78. Peter J. Spiro, "Questioning Barriers to Naturalization," *Georgetown Immigration Law Journal* 13 (1999): 480.

79. "Noncitizens Seek Ballot Box Access," *Washington Post*, September 25, 2003.

80. City Council public meeting, May 5, 2003.

81. Ibid.

82. "The Endless Wait: Will Resources Match the Resolve to Reduce the Immigration Case Backlog?" *American Immigration Law Foundation* (July 2004); and the National Immigration Forum, http://www.immigrationforum.org.

83. Nina Bernstein "Backlog Blocks Immigrants Hoping to Vote," *New York Times*, October 15, 2004. See chapter 6 for additional information about how this played out in New York during the 2004 elections.

84. Worth, "Push Is On to Give Legal Immigrants Vote in New York,"

85. Wuckee, "Civics Lessons from Immigrants."

86. Alethea Yip, "San Francisco Initiative Seeks Vote for Noncitizens," *Asian Week*, May 3–9, 1996.

87. New York eliminated the community school boards—and thus noncitizen voting—when it reorganized the public school system in 2003. New York now has a Department of Education that falls more firmly under mayoral control, which was the driving force and rationale behind the elimination of the community school boards, not the disenfranchisement of immigrants. That is, Mayor Bloomberg—and former Mayor Giuliani before him—successfully sought to consolidate power over New York City's public schools, which the state legislature granted in 2003.

88. Immigration and World Cities Project, 2002, http://interplan.org/immig/im03003.html.

89. Glenn Magpantay, "Asian American Voting Rights: A Perspective form the Northeast," *Fordham Urban Law Review* 28 (2001): 739.

90. Comments at public forum held by the League of Women Voters and the New York County Lawyers' Association, "Should Non-Citizens Vote in Local Elections?" New York County Lawyers' Association Auditorium, April 21, 2005.

91. Gregory Siskind, "Why Become a Citizen?" *Immigration Lawyer*, 2002, http://www.ilw.com.

92. Stanley Renshon, *Dual Citizenship and American Democracy*, October (Washington D.C.: Center for Immigrant Studies, 2001).

93. Renshon, "The Value of Citizenship."

94. Mark Krikorian, "Let Immigrants Vote? No." *New York Daily News*, April 18, 2004.

95. Gordon, "Let Them Vote."

96. Tienda, "Demography and the Social Contract."

97. Wucker, "Civics Lessons from Immigrants."

98. Ashira Pelman Ostrow, "Dual Resident Voting: Traditional Disenfranchisement and Prospects for Change," *Columbia Law Review* 102 (2002): 1954.

99. Ibid.

100. Renshon, "The Value of Citizenship,"

101. Comments at public forum held by the League of Women Voters and the New York County Lawyers' Association, "Should Non-Citizens Vote in Local Elections?" New York County Lawyers' Association Auditorium, April 21, 2005.

102. Public meeting of the Cambridge City Council, May 5, 2003.

103. Louis DeSipio, "Building America, One Person at a Time: Naturalization and Political Behavior of the Naturalized in Contemporary American Politics," in *E Pluribus Unum? Contemporary and Historical Perspectives on Immigrant Political Incorporation*, ed. Gary Gerstle and John Mollenkopf (New York: Russell Sage Foundation, 2001); and Lorraine Minnite, Jennifer Holdaway, and Ronald Hayduk, "The Political Participation of Immigrants in New York," in *In Defense of the Alien*, vol. 23, ed. Lydio F. Tomasi (New York: Center for Migration Studies, 2001).

104. Minnite, Holdaway, and Hayduk, "The Political Participation of Immigrants in New York." See also chapter 6 on New York.

105. Raskin, "Legal Aliens, Local Citizens."
106. After some community leaders objected to the bill, Councilman Smith amended his proposed bill to apply only to immigrants who formally apply for citizenship, a relatively smaller number (Sontag, "Noncitizens and Right to Vote"). Interestingly, many of those who objected were African American, as was Councilman Smith. The bill failed.
107. Ibid.
108. Ibid. Chapter 6 discusses these episodes in greater detail.
109. Robert Redding Jr., "Purging Illegal Aliens from Voter Rolls Not Easy," Washington Times, August 23, 2004; Michael Moss, "Big G.O.P. Bid to Challenge Voters at Polls in Key State," New York Times, October 23, 2004; and Ronald Hayduk, Gatekeepers to the Franchise: Election Administration in New York (DeKalb: Northern Illinois University Press, 2005).
110. Hayduk, Gatekeepers to the Franchise; and Lorraine Minnite and David Callahan, "Securing the Vote: An Analysis of Election Fraud," Demos: A Network for Ideas and Action, 2003, http://www.demos-usa.org.
111. Communication with Kathy Coll, Harvard University and member of the Campaign for Immigrant Voting Rights, July 30, 2003.
112. Jan Rath, "Voting Rights," in The Political Rights of Migrant Workers in Western Europe, ed. Henry Zig Layton (Newbury Park, Calif. : Sage, 1990); Aleinikoff and Klusmeyer, Citizenship Policies for an Age of Migration; David Earnest, "Noncitizen Voting Rights: A Survey of an Emerging Democratic Norm" (paper presented at the 2003 annual convention of the American Political Science Association, August 28–31, 2003, Philadelphia).
113. Steven P. Erie, Rainbow's End: Irish Americans and the Dilemmas of Urban Machine Politics, 1840–1985 (Berkeley: University of California Press, 1988); and Martin Shefter, Political Parties and the State: The American Historical Experience (Princeton, N.J.: Princeton University Press, 1994).
114. Of course, other electoral reforms are crucial to rectify the bias of the electorate and the nature of the political parties, such as Election Day voter registration, effective campaign finance reform, ballot access reform, and the inauguration of alternative representational schemes (such as proportional representation or instant run-off voting), if more democratic electoral politics and outcomes are to be achieved. Ronald Kevin Hayduk and Mattson, eds., Democracy's Moment: Reforming the American Political System for the 21st Century (Lanham, Md.: Rowman & Littlefield, 2002); and Hayduk, Gatekeepers to the Franchise.
115. Nicolas Vaca, The Presumed Alliance: The Unspoken Conflict between Latinos and Blacks and What It Means for America (New York: HarperCollins Publishing, 2004).
116. Sontag, "Noncitizens and Right to Vote."
117. Huntington, Who Are We?

Chapter 5

1. All figures are from the U.S. Bureau of the Census.
2. Kevin J. Best, "Municipal Elections," Municipal Maryland (Maryland Municipal League [MML]) 30, no. 7 (2001).
3. Best, "Municipal Elections."
4. Takoma Park Elections Task Force, "Recommendation of the Takoma Park Election Task Force," undated memorandum in Information Package regarding Non U.S. Citizens Voting Rights in Takoma Park (Takoma Park, Md.: Office of the City Clerk, n.d.).
5. Raskin noted that the "Task Force, by and large [was] unaware of the rich history of alien suffrage in the United States." Jamin B. Raskin, "Legal Aliens, Local Citizens: The Historical, Constitutional, and Theoretical Meanings of Alien Suffrage," University of Pennsylvania Law Review 141 (1993): 1463.
6. Takoma Park Elections Task Force, "Recommendation of the Takoma Park Election Task Force."
7. Ibid.
8. Ibid.

9. Paula S. Jewell, city clerk, "Non United States Citizens Voting in Takoma Park Elections," memo, January 22, 1992. These wards, then in Prince George's County, were later incorporated into Montgomery County.

10. Takoma Park City Council, "Council Minutes," January 27, 1992.

11. Quoted in Michelle Malkin, "Voter Fraud That's Legal," TownHall.com, November 6 2002.

12. Melanie Howard, "Ballot Proposes Vote for Aliens," *Washington Times*, October 31, 1991.

13. Howard, "Ballot Proposes Vote for Aliens."

14. Beth Kaiman and Lynne K Varner, "Immigrant Voting Advances in Takoma Park," *Washington Post*, January 30, 1992.

15. Raskin, "Legal Aliens, Local Citizens," 1466.

16. Kaiman and Varner, "Immigrant Voting Advances in Takoma Park." The D.C. initiative is taken up in the next chapter.

17. Raskin, "Legal Aliens, Local Citizens," 1462. Raskin noted, "As more intimate communities whose alien populations are apparently composed, in substantial part, of World Bank and embassy personnel working in Washington, D.C., these Maryland jurisdictions rest their policies on both natural rights understandings and the early property-based conception of local voting rights. It is necessary to note that most of the inhabitants of these small communities tend to share a similar economic and social status which dilutes the threatening image many citizens have of aliens. They also share a physical proximity which permits them to have unrushed and disarming face-to-face encounters with one another."

18. He noted that his wife, Lissa Martinez, who was a member of the Elections Task Force, first raised the question of allowing noncitizens to vote. Takoma Park City Council, "Council Minutes," January 27, 1992.

19. Ibid.

20. Beth Kaiman, "Deciding Ballot Rights: Takoma Park to Rule on Non-Citizen Vote," *Washington Post*, October 31, 1991.

21. Takoma Park City Council, "Council Minutes," January 27, 1992.

22. "This Charter Amendment removes the qualification that a person be a citizen of the United States in order to vote in Takoma Park's biennial elections. The amended language of Sec. 701(a) outlines the qualifications of voters to be residents of Takoma Park, at least eighteen years of age, residing within the corporate limits of the City for 30 days and registered according to the provisions of Section 703 of the Charter. Resolution 1992-5A adds a new subsection (b) to Section 703, that establishes a separate voter roll to be maintained by the City Clerk for residents of Takoma Park who are not United States citizens. . . . Resolution #1992-5A also amends Section 703(a) by clarifying the language that a resident of Takoma Park who is a United States citizen may register to vote at the boards of elections supervisors for Montgomery and Prince George's Counties. This provision was added to discourage United States citizen residents from using the separate registration system established in Sec. 703(b) to avoid registering with Counties." Resolution #1992-5A, amending art. VII, sec. 701(a) and 703(a) and (b) of the City Charter, regarding "Qualifications of Voters" and "Registration" (Takoma Park, Md.: City of Takoma Park), enacted 1992.

23. Takoma Park City Council, "Council Minutes," February 10, 1992.

24. Raskin, "Legal Aliens, Local Citizens," 1464.

25. *Washington Post*, November 15, 1992.

26. Raskin, "Legal Aliens, Local Citizens," 1466–67.

27. All figures are from the Takoma Park City Clerk's office.

28. Tom Perez, councilman, Montgomery County Council, communication with the author, July 2004; and Catherine Waters, city clerk, Takoma Park, Maryland, communication with the author, April 7, 2005.

29. Barnesville Charter, sec. 74-3 (Barnesville, Md.: City of Barnesville), 1912.

30. Charter of Martin's Additions, resolution no. 10-1164 of the Montgomery County Council, effective February 14, 1985.

31. Howard, "Ballot Proposes Vote for Aliens."

32. Chevy Chase Section 3 Charter, art. III, sec. 301.

33. This account is based on information provided by Nancy Floreen, aide to Merle Steiner (former mayor of Garrett Park), and on documents from town meetings, particularly minutes.

34. Minutes of Advisory Committee, June 10, 1999. Members of the Advisory Committee were Jim Agenbroad, Stan Benjamin, Nguyen Minh Chau, Dick Fischman, Nancy Floreen, Donn Mader, Dick Morgan, and Ken Schwartz.
35. These include not currently serving a sentence or on probation "for conviction of an infamous crime"; not being convicted more than once for an infamous crime, buying, or selling votes; or not being under guardianship for mental disability.
36. Section 78-20, which incorporates Reso. 4-26-71, Reso. 4-11-83, and Reso. 2-12-2001 #01-6. Committee members that voted for were Stan Benjamin, Nguyen Minh Chau, Dick Fischman, Nancy Floreen, Donn Mader, and Dick Morgan; committee members that voted against were Jim Agenbroad and Ken Schwartz.
37. Minutes of Advisory Committee, Garrett Park, Md., June 10, 1999.
38. Minutes of Advisory Committee, June 10, 1999. Some on the Committee argued to remove the criminality provisions for town elections, so as to afford "the opportunity for any resident who can meet these UVR [universal voter registration] standards to register instead directly with the town," but this view was not endorsed by the majority and did not pass partly due to the fact that the state legislature was considering revising specific terms of noncriminality voter qualifications so that the town would not have to reamend its charter.
39. *Dunn v. Blumstein*, 405 U.S. 330, 1972.
40. Interview with Tom Perez, July 2004.
41. Rockville Charter Review Commission, "Meeting Notes," July 18, 2002. Other issues for consideration included length of mayor and council terms and ballot referenda. Noelle Barton, "Alien Voting Issue Dominates Charter Review Forum," Gazette.net, September 25, 2002.
42. Members David Cahoon (cochair), David Hill (cochair), Shelly Hardwick, Sue Edwards, Gerry Holtz, Jim Marrinan, Ronald Shrack, Fran Hawkins, Robert Pittman, and Doris Ecelbarger. (Members who were absent at the July meeting were Phyllis Marcuccio and Jennifer Kaye.) Ecelbarger noted that there are only two other jurisdictions in Maryland that allow resident aliens to vote in elections, Takoma Park and Somerset. City Clerk Claire Funkhouser said she would contact the clerks in those jurisdictions to inquire why they undertook this issue and also how they did it. Ms. Funkhouser said that it is her understanding that Takoma Park may be taking up this issue for consideration again. Robert Pittman suggested checking out the jurisdictions of El Paso, Texas, and Nogales and Benson, Arizona... It was decided to collect information from other jurisdictions regarding their position on resident alien voting ("Meeting Notes," Rockville Charter Review Commission, July 18, 2002).
43. Ibid.
44. Ibid.
45. Corina E. Rivera, "Pushing Towns to Let Noncitizens Vote," Gazette.net, February 6, 2004.
46. Corina E. Rivera, "Voting Rights Sought for Noncitizens," Gazette.net, February 5, 200.
47. Ibid.
48. Ibid.
49. Ibid.
50. Ibid.
51. Ibid.
52. Ibid.
53. Rivera, "Pushing Towns to Let Noncitizens Vote."
54. Ibid.
55. Ibid.
56. Rivera, "Voting Rights Sought for Noncitizens."
57. Alexa Gabriel, "Should Legal Non-citizens Be Allowed to Vote? NO: Voting Is Reserved for Citizens." *silver chips online* (a high school newspaper), March 18, 2004.
58. Deborah Sontag, "Noncitizens and Right to Vote: Advocates for Immigrants Explore Opening Up Balloting," *New York Times*, July 31, 1992.
59. New York State Education Law, sec. 2590-c(3). See Alan Gartner, executive director, and Fong Chan, chair of the Task Force, "Temporary State Task Force on the New York City Community School Board Elections, Final Report,". March (Albany: State of New York, 1998). Available at the NYS Archives, Office of the Governor, State Legislature and NYC Department of Education and Municipal Archives, and on file with the author.

60. Jon del Giorno, "Community School Board Elections Fact Sheet," June 26, 1999 (New York: New York City Board of Elections, the New York City Department of Education). On file with the Board of Elections and with the author. I am grateful to Doreen DiMartini, who provided these data to me.

61. Gartner and Chan, "Temporary State Task Force on the New York City Community School Board Elections," 12.

62. Gartner and Chan, "Temporary State Task Force on the New York City Community School Board Elections," 13.

63. New York City Board of Elections, *Annual Reports* (New York: New York City Board of Elections, 1989 to 2000); and del Giorno "Community School Board Elections Fact Sheet."

64. Del Giorno, "Community School Board Elections Fact Sheet."

65. Gartner and Chan, "Temporary Task Force on the New York City Community School Board Elections."

66. Gartner and Chan, "Temporary State Task Force on the New York City Community School Board Elections," 19.

67. New York City Department of City Planning, "The Newest New Yorkers, 2000: Immigrant-New York in the New Millennium" (New York: New York City Department of City Planning, 2004).

68. David M. Herszenhorn, "Leaders of Parent Councils Form School Association," *New York Times*, December 9, 2004. On December 7, 2004, the leaders of the parent councils hired Norman Siegel, a civil rights attorney and candidate for public advocate, as their legal advisor.

69. Harold Washington, the first African American mayor of Chicago, was elected twice—in 1983 and 1987. He won the Democratic primary election on February 22, 1983, with 36 percent of the vote, defeating the incumbent mayor, Jane M. Byrne, Richard M. Daley, Sheila Jones, William R. Markowski, and Frank R. Ranallo. Washington won the general election on April 12, 1983, with 52 percent of the vote, defeating Bernard Epton (Republican) and Ed Warren (Socialist Workers). On February 24, 1987, Harold Washington beat his opponents, Jane M. Byrne and Sheila Jones, in the Democratic primary election with 53 percent of the vote, and went on to victory in the general election on April 7, 1987, again with 53 percent of the vote, defeating Edward R. Vrdolyak (Illinois Solidarity) and Donald H. Haider (Republican). Harold Washington died on November 25, 1987. "Facts about Harold Washington," Harold Washington Archives and Collections, Chicago Public Library, http://www.chipublib.org/001hwlc/spehwpathfinder.html.

70. Much of the following information was provided by Mr. James Deanes, officer of the Chicago School and Community Relations Office, telephone interview, April 4, 2005; and by Reverend Walter Colman, telephone interview, April 4, 2005.

71. Illinois school code sec.105 ILCS 5/34-2.1. Local School Councils (d)(ii)(c): "Eligible voters for each attendance center shall consist of the parents and community residents for that attendance center."

72. Chicago Public Schools, Office of School and Community Relations, http://www.cps.k12.il.us/AboutCPS/Departments/OSCR/local_school_councils.html. Of the 618 Chicago schools, only about 30 charter schools and 5 contract schools do not have elections. Telephone interview with Deanes, April 4, 2005.

73. Under the portion of the Illinois school code that applies to Chicago, the law states, "Each elected member shall be elected by the eligible voters of that attendance center to serve for a two-year term commencing on July 1 immediately following the election described in subsection." sec. 105 ILCS 5/34-2.1. (d) (ii), (c).

74. Local School Councils are made up of the principal, teachers, parents, and community members. Elementary school LSCs consist of eleven voting members, including one principal, six parent representatives, two community representatives, and two teacher representatives; and high school LSCs consist of twelve voting members, including one principal, six parent representatives, two community representatives, two teacher representatives, and one nonvoting student representative. Chicago Public Schools, Office of School and Community Relations, http://www.cps.k12.il.us/AboutCPS/Departments/OSCR/local_school_councils.html.

75. Deanes, telephone interview, April 4, 2005.

76. Colman, telephone interview, April 4, 2005.

77. Deanes, telephone interview, April 4, 2005.

78. In 1995, the Chicago Public School system underwent a second major restructuring, this time along a conservative, corporate model. Instead of a superintendent and school board, they have a chief executive officer, chief educational officer, chief financial officer, and so on who are under the mayor. According to the *Catalyst*, a newsmagazine created in 1990 to monitor Chicago public schools, Chicago's Richard M. Daley (D) "teamed up with Republican leaders in the state capitol" to pass the amendments that gave the mayor power to appoint a new School Board and chief executive officer and gave the mayor's appointees additional "sweeping powers." Critics panned the system, saying it is a model for the failure of the standards-/testing-based national system of corporate and centralized urban public education, along with privatizing supplemental services and encouraging charter schools and vouchers that weaken remaining public schools. See *Catalyst*, http://www.catalyst-chicago.org/background.htm. It characterizes itself as "an independent newsmagazine created in 1990 to document, analyze and support school-improvement efforts in the Chicago Public Schools. It is published by the Community Renewal Society, a faith-based organization founded in 1882 that works to create racially and economically just communities in metropolitan Chicago."

79. Robert Klein Engler, "In Chicago, Non-Citizens Vote, Too," ChronWatch.com, May 8, 2004, http://www.chronwatch.com/content/contentDisplay.asp?aid=7281. ChronWatch.com describes itself as "a media watchdog and conservative news site, with a focus on the *San Francisco Chronicle*. We provide commentary on recent *Chronicle* articles, journalists and publications, in addition to our own guest columns and editorial." See http://www.chronwatch.com.

80. In 2005, an Illinois state program called the New Americans Initiative allocated $3 million to encourage eligible legal immigrants to pursue U.S. citizenship. The money would go to agencies that provide immigrants with guidance to apply and take the citizenship test. Because new citizens will be prospective voters, this citizenship program has been charged by some to be politically motivated. For example, State Senator Steve Rauschenberger (R-Elgin), who many consider an ally of immigrants, initially backed the Illinois plan but later said he thinks the state would better serve immigrants by funding health care or education instead: "I don't think adding another layer of bureaucracy to do PR and generate some nice press releases is a good use of funds." Rauschenberger, who may run for governor in 2006, charged Governor Rod Blagojevich—who created the program—as using it as a means to gain support of Latinos who tend to register and vote Democratic. Governor Blagojevich rejected the contention that the citizenship program was politically motivated. Oscar Avila, "State to Aid Citizenship Bids: Illinois starting $3 million program for legal immigrants," *Chicago Tribune*, February 21, 2005.

Chapter 6

1. Joaquin Avila, "Political Apartheid in California: Consequences of Excluding a Growing Noncitizen Population," Latino Policy and Issues Brief no. 9 (Los Angeles: Chicano Studies Research Center, University of California, Los Angeles, 2003).

2. *Left Coast City: Progressive Politics in San Francisco, 1975–1991*. Richard DeLeon, which, along with DeLeon's other work about San Francisco, describes the city's liberal/progressive political tradition.

3. Proposition 187 was passed by a majority of California's voters who came to the polls in November 1994, and was an initiative that was supported by the state Republican Party and Governor Pete Wilson's reelection campaign.

4. Katia Hetter, "Immigrant Status Stirs Host of Issues: Noncitizens Persist in Fight for Rights, Democratic Voice," *San Francisco Chronicle*, July 18, 2004.

5. Quote from Maria Blanco, executive director of the Lawyer's Committee for Civil Rights of the Bay Area, cited in Hetter, "Immigrant Status Stirs Host of Issues."

6. Mabel Teng, "Why Noncitizen Legal Residents Should Vote in School Elections," *San Francisco Examiner*, February 18, 1996.

7. Diana Walsh, "Ballot Plan Would Let Noncitizens Vote in S.F.," *San Francisco Examiner*, April 23, 1996.

8. "Ruling Ends Bid to Allow Voting by Noncitizens," *San Francisco Chronicle*, May 11, 1996.

9. Tara Kini, "Sharing the Vote: Noncitizen Voting Rights in Local School Board Elections," *California Law Review* 93 (January 2005): 271. The next section draws upon her work.

10. Katia Hetter, "Right to Vote Fight: Proposal Letting Noncitizens Vote in School Elections Called Unconstitutional," *San Francisco Chronicle*, July 10, 2004.

11. Alethea Yip, "S.F. Initiative Seeks Vote for Non-citizens: Courts Question Legality of Proposed Ballot Measure," *Asian Week*, May 3, 1996.

12. Ibid.

13. Ibid.

14. "Ruling Ends Bid to Allow Voting by Noncitizens." The California State Constitution states, "A United States citizen 18 years of age and resident in this state may vote" (art. II, sec. 2).

15. Matt Gonzalez, "Immigrant Rights: Protecting Our City's Diversity," policy paper, 2003, http://www.mattgonzalez.com/downloads/Immigrant.pdf. Gonzalez proposed a broad range of immigrant policies, which included to the following: "Enforce the 'Equal Access' Ordinance to ensure that all San Franciscans have access to City services regardless of language spoken; Support the recently enacted State Drivers License bill and advocate against its repeal; Extend the right to vote in school board elections to noncitizens with children; Promote the acceptance of *matricula consular* ID cards for immigrant workers; Support passage of the 'Privacy Initiative Ordinance' so that immigrants and others are not afraid to access City services; Protect the privacy of San Franciscans by altering the way the Patriot Act is implemented locally; Oppose the implementation of the federal Clear Act and ensure no collaboration between local police and federal immigration enforcement; Support national legalization efforts for immigrants; Build subsidized housing for undocumented immigrants; Grant more authority to the San Francisco Immigrant Rights Commission."

16. "I grew up in southwest Texas in a place called McAllen, Texas. My mother was born in Mexico . . . and my father was born in . . . Texas. I went to college in Columbia University in New York City, and I graduated from Stanford Law School, and that's what first brought me to California. I worked for 10 years as a public defender here in San Francisco, and I often represented non-citizens, immigrants, in some of those proceedings. I also represented a disproportionate number of Latinos and African Americans who were being charged with crimes and didn't have money to hire an attorney. I got into politics as a member of the board of supervisors, and I now serve as president of the board." E-mail communication with Sheila Chung, director of the Bay Area Immigrant Rights Coalition, June 22, 2004, transcript of Mayoral Forum sponsored by the San Francisco Immigrant Voters Coalition, October 30, 2003, trans. Kin Tso, courtesy of Sheila Chung.

17. Gonzalez also supported Proposition C. Interview with Office of Supervisor Matt Gonzalez, San Francisco, June 18, 2004.

18. The San Francisco Immigrant Voters Coalition included the American-Arab Anti-Discrimination Committee; Asian American Community Voice; Asian Pacific Islander Family Resource Network (APIFRN); Asian Perinatal Advocates; Bay Area Immigrant Rights Coalition; Cambodian Community Development; Central American Resource Center (CARE-CEN); San Francisco Lodge, Chinese American Citizens Alliance; Chinese for Affirmative Action; Chinese Newcomers Services Center; Chinese Progressive Association; Chinese Radio; Chinese Star Radio; Interfaith Coalition for Immigrant Rights; La Raza Centro Legal; Lesbian Gay Immigration Rights Task Force (LGIRTF); Love Sees No Borders; National Center for Lesbian Rights; National Congress of Vietnamese in America (Western Region); New California Media; Northern California Chinese American Media Association; Northern California Citizenship Project; Russian American Community Development Center; Russian Center of San Francisco; San Francisco Neighborhood Association; *Sing Tao Daily*; Southeast Asian Community Center; Vietnamese American Community Center of San Francisco; Vietnamese American Voters Alliance; Vietnamese Elderly Mutual Assistance Association; Vietnamese Womanís Association in San Francisco; and West Bay Pilipino Multi-Services, Inc. E-mail communication from Sheila Chung, director of theBay Area Immigrant Rights Coalition, June 22, 2004.

19. Other mayoral candidates in attendance were City Attorney Angela Alioto and City Treasurer Susan Leal. Julian Guthrie and John Wildermuth, "Candidates Try to Woo Immigrants," *San Francisco Chronicle*, October 31, 2003; and Kini "Sharing the Vote."

20. E-mail communication with Sheila Chung, June 22, 2004, transcript of Mayoral Forum sponsored by the San Francisco Immigrant Voters Coalition, October 30, 2003, trans. Kin Tso, courtesy of Sheila Chung.

21. The legal team was led by David Chiu, a former immigrant rights attorney and now founder and senior executive of Grassroots Enterprise; and members from the Lawyers Committee for Civil Rights, including Robert Rubin, Ted Wang of Chinese for Affirmative Action, and Tara Kini, a law student at Berkeley. An excellent analysis of the legal theory and political rationale is presented by Kini in "Sharing the Vote."

22. Articles appeared in dozens of California papers and in the *New York Times, Washington Post, Houston Chronicle, Christian Science Monitor,* and *Atlanta Journal Constitution.*

23. Interview with Office of Supervisor Matt Gonzalez, San Francisco, June 18, 2004.

24. Ibid.

25. Suzanne Herel, "San Francisco Supervisors Put Forth Issues for Ballot," *San Francisco Chronicle,* Wednesday, May 19, 2004.

26. Press Release, Office of Matt Gonzalez, May 17, 2004, http://www.voice4parents.com (and on file with the author).

27. Ibid.

28. Ibid.

29. Interview with Eric Mar, June 17, 2004, offices of the SFUSD.

30. U.S. Bureau of the Census, "Table DP-1: Profile of General Demographic Characteristics: 2000," in *U.S. Census, 2000,* http://census.abag.ca.gov/counties/SanFranciscoCounty.pdf.

31. Adriel Hampton, "School Board Choice: Gonzalez Wants Immigrant Parents to Have Say in Votes," *San Francisco Examiner,* May 18, 2004.

32. Parents United for Education, http://www.voice4parents.com.

33. A list of endorsers can be found at Parents United for Education, http://www.voice4parents.com.

34. Interview with Office of Supervisor Matt Gonzalez, San Francisco, June 18, 2004.

35. Testimony given at public hearing of the Rules Committee of the San Francisco Board of Supervisors, July 1, 2004, SFGTV web cast, http://www.ci.sf.ca.us/site/sfgtv. Petroni initially argued this point at a meeting of coalition members, San Francisco City Hall, July 2004; audiotape on file with the author.

36. Ibid.

37. Ibid. Petroni also expressed concern about the sunset clause, saying he has "doubts about why we have this."

38. Ibid.

39. Public hearing of the Rules Committee of the San Francisco Board of Supervisors, July 1, 2004, SFGTV web cast, http://www.ci.sf.ca.us/site/sfgtv.

40. Testimony given at public hearing of the Rules Committee of the San Francisco Board of Supervisors, July 1, 2004, SFGTV web cast, http://www.ci.sf.ca.us/site/sfgtv.

41. Ibid.

42. Ibid.

43. Hetter, "Right to Vote Fight."

44. Ibid.

45. Letter to Louise Renne; on file with the author.

46. Interview with Office of Supervisor Matt Gonzalez, San Francisco, June 18, 2004.

47. Katia Hetter, "Noncitizen Voting Plan on Shaky Ground: City Attorney Says Charter Amendment Would Probably Be Struck Down in Court," *San Francisco Chronicle,* July 13, 2004.

48. Heather Knight, "Yee Fights for Right to Vote: Says Mother Shows Noncitizens' Need for Say-so in Schools," *San Francisco Chronicle,* July 14, 2004.

49. Ibid.

50. Richard Gonzales, reporter for National Public Radio (NPR), July 13, 2004, KQED and NPR audio archives, http://www.npr.org/templates/story/story.php?storyId=3351017 (accessed March 10, 2005).

51. Ibid.

52. Ibid.

53. SFSOS describes itself as "a non-partisan, grassroots organization made up of concerned San Franciscans who want to reverse the decline of our city. We sponsor and support legislation and ballot initiatives that improve the City. We update our members about critical City issues and provide them with an easy web-based advocacy tool to allow ordinary

citizens to influence policymakers collectively." SFSOS, http://www.sfsos.org/about.shtml (accessed March 12, 2005). SFSOS reportedly receives substantial contributions from Richard Blum, a wealthy developer married to U.S. Senator Dianne Feinstein.

54. "Extending Vote to Illegal Residents Undermines Our System," *Signal Flag: A Weekly Publication of SFSOS* 2, no. 27 (July 19, 2004): http://www.sfsos.org (also on file with the author).

55. Ibid. Interestingly, a related group, the San Francisco Chamber of Commerce, initially looked at the issue but did not formally take a position. Eventually, however, the Chamber of Commerce did come out in opposition.

56. Adam Tanner, "Senator Says San Francisco Noncitizen Vote Illegal," Reuters, July 21, 2004.

57. Robert Hollis, Marisa Lagos, and Megan Garvey, "S.F. Voters to Decide if Noncitizens Can Vote," *Los Angeles Times*, July 21, 2004.

58. Interview with Lou Dobbs, CNN, July 21, 2004, transcript available at http://www.CNN.com (and on file with the author).

59. Hollis, Lagos, and Garvey, "S.F. Voters to Decide if Noncitizens Can Vote."

60. Interview with Richard DeLeon, June 18, 2004, San Francisco; and interview with Eric Mar, June 17, 2004, offices of the San Francisco Unified School District.

61. Jessie Mangaliman, "S.F May Give Non-citizens School Board Voting Rights," *(San Jose, Calif.) Mercury News*, June 21, 2004.

62. Interview with Office of Supervisor Chris Daly, San Francisco, June 18, 2004. Daly said that progressives have been supportive of expanding political participation, and the proposal to extend the right to vote in school board elections was one he supported.

63. Mangaliman, "S.F May Give Non-citizens School Board Voting Rights."

64. Jack Chang, "S.F Looks to Granting Noncitizens School Vote," *Contra Costa (Calif.) Times*, July 1, 2004.

65. Mangaliman, "S.F May Give Non-citizens School Board Voting Rights."

66. Meeting of the San Francisco Board of Supervisors, July 20, 2004, SFGTV web cast, http://www.ci.sf.ca.us/site/sfgtv.

67. Ibid.

68. Ibid.

69. Ibid.

70. Ibid.

71. Ibid.

72. Ibid.

73. Ibid.

74. Ibid.

75. "Editorial. The Chronicle Recommends: Who Gets to Vote?" *San Francisco Chronicle*, October 8, 2004.

76. Telephone interview with David Chiu, January 2005.

77. uzanne Herel, "Contribution Limits Don't Crimp Spending: Business Interests Funnel Cash to Aid Certain Candidates," *San Francisco Chronicle*, October 27, 2004. In the last week of the campaign, a judge ordered that the mailing must cease since it did not identify who funded it, as required by law. Telephone interview with David Chiu, January 2005.

78. Herel, "Contribution Limits Don't Crimp Spending." Approximately $500,000 was spent in total.

79. Telephone interview with David Chiu, January 2005.

80. Telephone interviews and e-mail communications with David Chiu, Eric Mar, Giselle Barry, and other members of Parents United for Education. See also Parents United for Education, http://www.voice4parents.com.

81. Telephone interview with David Chiu, January 2005.

82. Richard E. DeLeon, "Preliminary Analysis of the Precinct Vote on Proposition F (Non-citizen Voting in School Elections): Graphs and Statistics," San Francisco: Department of Political Science, San Francisco State University, December 2, 2004. On file with the author.

83. Telephone interview with David Chiu, January 2005.

84. Ibid.

85. Herel, "Contribution Limits Don't Crimp Spending."

86. Telephone interview with David Chiu, January 2005; and Eric Mar echoed this view in an e-mail communication with the author, December 1, 2004.

87. E-mail communication from Eric Mar, December 1, 2004.
88. Telephone interview with David Chiu, January 2005.
89. E-mail communication from Eric Mar, December 1, 2004
90. Telephone interview with David Chiu, January 2005.
91. E-mail communication from Eric Mar, December 1, 2004.
92. San Francisco Department of Elections.
93. David Chiu, e-mail communication to coalition members and supporters, November 3, 2004.
94. Telephone interview with Stephanie Ong, December 15, 2004.
95. Telephone interview with David Chiu, January 2005.
96. Ibid.
97. Juan Esparza Loera, "Non-citizens Deserve a Voice in Vote," *Fresno (California) Bee*, January 26, 2004.
98. Deborah Sontag, "Non-citizens and Right to Vote: Advocates for Immigrants Explore Opening Up Balloting," *New York Times*, July 31, 1992.
99. Fred Seigel, *The Future Once Happened Here: New York, D.C., L.A. and the Fate of America's Big Cities* (New York: Free Press, 1997).
100. Troy Anderson, "Noncitizens Deserve Right to Vote—Study," *Daily News of Los Angeles*, December 11, 2003.
101. Michelle Dearmond, "Non-citizens Voting Unlikely to Succeed," *(Riverside, Calif.) Press Enterprise*, December 12, 2003.
102. Anderson, "Non-citizens Deserve Right to Vote." In the same article, however, Schwarzenegger said he favored allowing undocumented immigrants to obtain driver's licenses.
103. Dearmond, "Non-citizens Voting Unlikely to Succeed."
104. Stephen Wall, "Group Pushing Migrant Voting: Activists to Visit San Bernardino School Board," *San Bernardino County (California) Sun*, July 30, 2004.
105. Wall, "Group Pushing Migrant Voting."
106. Ibid.
107. Teresa Borden, "What Does Citizenship Mean: Cities Debate Whether Noncitizens Should Vote," *Atlanta Journal-Constitution*, July 2, 2004.
108. Borden, "What Does Citizenship Mean."
109. Sontag, "Noncitizens and Right to Vote."
110. Diana Salas, communication with the author, May 3, 2005; and Molly Langmuir, "New American News: Non-Citizen Vote Debate Spurs Bill," *Queens (New York) Tribune*, April 28, 2005. Diana has experienced difficulties with the INS and also has financial considerations, among other reasons she has not obtained U.S. citizenship.
111. Philip Kazinitz, John H. Mollenkopf, and Mary C. Waters, eds., *Becoming New Yorkers: Ethnographies of the New Second Generation* (New York: Russell Sage Foundation, 200)4. While these ethnographies focus on the younger, second-generation children of immigrants, their parents' stories are often interwoven.
112. Sontag, "Noncitizens and Right to Vote."
113. The specific legislation, which is described in greater detail below, can be accessed at the New York State Assembly and Senate websites and from the Immigrant Voting Project, "Immigrant Voting Project: Democracy for All," http://www.immigrantvoting.org.
114. U.S. Census Bureau, "2004 Population Estimates," in *Census 2000*; and 1990 Census. United States Census Bureau. 1990 Summary Tape File3 (STF 3). http://www.census.gov>; *2004 Population Estimates*. <http://www.census.gov/popest/estimates.php>
115. John Hull Mollenkopf, *A Phoenix in the Ashes: The Rise and Fall of the Koch Coalition in New York City Politics* (Princeton, N.J.: Princeton University Press, 1994); Edward Schneier and John Brian Murtaugh, *New York Politics: A Tale of Two States* (New York: M.E. Sharpe, 2001); and New York City Department of City Planning, Population Division, *The Newest New Yorkers* (New York: New York City Department of City Planning, Population Division, 2004, 1999, and 1996).
116. Jennifer Gordon, *Suburban Sweatshops: The Fight for Immigrant Rights* (Cambridge, Mass.: Belknap Press of Harvard University Press, 2005).
117. Table 6.3 does not break down white immigrants, such as the 465,000 Russians, 60,000 Ukrainians, and so on. The total number of noncitizens is higher if all ages are included.

New York City Department of City Planning, Population Division, "The Newest New Yorkers" (2004).

118. John Mollenkopf and John Logan, *People and Politics in America's Big Cities: The Challenges to Urban Democracy* (New York: Drum Major Institute for Public Policy, 2003).

119. Ibid.

120. Lorraine C. Minnite, principal investigator, "The New Americans Exit Poll Project: Results from the 2000, 2002 and 2004 New York City Exit Polls," New York Immigration Coalition, February 2005, http://www.thenyic.org/images/uploads/NAEP%202004%20Results.pdf. According to the survey of voters in 2004, almost "sixty percent of both immigrants and native-born respondents identified jobs and the economy as the most important issue affecting their choice for President."

121. New York Immigration Coalition, "New Study Profiles City's Immigrant Voters," press release, New York City, February 17, 2005.

122. Minnite, "The New Americans Exit Poll Project."

123. New York Immigration Coalition, "New Study Profiles City's Immigrant Voters."

124. Suman Raghunathan, "Testimony before the New York State Senate Task Force on New Americans regarding Electoral Access," Taino Towers, New York City, May 6, 2004, available at New York Immigration Coalition, http://www.thenyic.org/issue.asp?cid=43; and Ronald Hayduk, *Gatekeepers to the Franchise: Election Administration in New York* (DeKalb: Northern Illinois University Press, 2005).

125. Minnite, "The New Americans Exit Poll Project." The surveys were carried out in conjunction with the NYIC, and the sampling was constructed with help from John Mollenkopf, director of the Center for Urban Research at the City University of New York (CUNY), New York Immigration Coalition, http://www.thenyic.org/issue.asp?cid=43.

126. Nina Bernstein, "Immigrant Voters Defy Political Patterns," *New York Times*, February 18, 2005.

127. Robert F. Worth, "Push Is On to Give Legal Immigrants Vote in New York," *New York Times*, April 8, 2004.

128. New York Immigration Coalition, "New Study Profiles City's Immigrant Voters."

129. Interview with Bryan Pu-Folkes. May, 2004.

130. Howard Jordan, "Empowering Immigrants," *New York Newsday*, April 7, 1993. In the 1980s, State Assemblyman Brian Murtaugh, whose district demographic was changing due to the rapid influx of immigrants, chaired the task force.

131. Jordan, "Empowering Immigrants."

132. One early advocate of noncitizen suffrage was J. Philip Thompson, who worked for David Dinkins when Dinkins was borough president and then mayor. Communication with the author.

133. Wendy Aviva Shimmelman, "Local Voting Rights for Non-U.S. Citizen Immigrants in New York City," report prepared for the Center for Immigrants Rights, New York, 1992.

134. Communication with Howard Jordan and J. Philip Thompson on several dates between 1996 and 2004.

135. Jordan, "Empowering Immigrants."

136. Memorandum in support of legislation, March 30, 1993, New York State Assembly. Also on file with the author.

137. Shimmelman, "Local Voting Rights for Non-U.S. Citizen Immigrants in New York City."

138. Alethia Jones, a staff aide to Clark, helped bring the issue to her boss. Interview with Howard Jordan, 2004.

139. City Council Resolution no. 1197, submitted in 1993. It reads, "Whereas, The 1990 Census counted over 1.2 million New York City residents as non-United States citizens; and Whereas, Legal permanent residents, i.e., green card holders, are denied the right to vote; and Whereas, Their right to vote is not at variance with the United States Constitution, under which the States define the electorate; and Whereas, According to *The New York Times*, until World War I, nearly half of the states in the country allowed immigrants to vote at one time or another, even in Presidential elections; and Whereas, In New York City, non-United States citizen residents have the right to vote in Community Development Agency elections and non-United States citizen parents of public school students have the right to vote in the 32 community school board elections; and Whereas, These legal immigrants are productive members of their local communities where they live, work, pay taxes and are

subject to all local laws; and Whereas, A recent report prepared for the Center for Immigrants Rights suggests that many benefits would accrue to numerous local communities and the City as a whole by extending voting rights to legal immigrants, including more participation in the community; now, therefore, be it Resolved, That the appropriate Committee of the City Council investigate the economic importance of legal permanent residents to the City of New York and convene a hearing to assess the impact on the City of New York of extending local voting rights in city-level elections to this group."

140. Ronald Hayduk, "Noncitizen"Voting: Pipe Dream or Possibility?" Drum Major Institute for Public Policy, October 2002, http://www.drummajorinstitute.org/plugin/template/dmi/55/1694.

141. Ben Smith, "Mayoral Commission to Consider Letting Foreigners Vote in N.Y.," *New York Sun*, August 22, 2003.

142. Albor Ruiz, "Time to Change Rule That Drains Voter Pool," *Daily News*, August 23, 2003.

143. Ruiz, "Time to Change Rule That Drains Voter Pool."

144. Smith, "Mayoral Commission To Consider Letting Foreigners Vote in N.Y."

145. Smith, "Mayoral Commission To Consider Letting Foreigners Vote in N.Y." See also Stanley Renshon, *The 50 percent American: Immigrgation and National Identity in an Age of Terror.* Washington, D.C., Georgetown University Press, 2005.

146. Mae M. Cheng, "Panel: Let Noncitizens Vote," *Newsday*, August 23, 2003. The proposal lost by a vote of eleven to two.

147. Benjamin Smith, "Ferrer Seizes upon Idea to Permit Aliens a Vote in Municipal Elections: Puts Down a Marker on an Issue Dropped by the Charter Commission," *New York Sun*, September 25, 2003.

148. Mollenkopf and Logan, *People and Politics in America's Big Cities.*

149. Hayduk, "Noncitizen Voting: Pipe Dream or Possibility?"

150. Smith, "Ferrer Seizes upon Idea to Permit Aliens a Vote in Municipal Elections."

151. Cheryl Wertz, "Support of Voting Rights for Immigrant New Yorkers," statement on behalf of NICE before the NYC Council's Black, Latino and Asian Caucus, June 7, 2004.

152. Linares now serves as the commissioner to Mayor Bloomberg's Office of Immigrant Affairs.

153. Comments by Linares at the forum. See also Sontag, "Noncitizens and Right to Vote."

154. Daniela Gerson, "Rallying Call Heard for Noncitizen Voting," *New York Sun*, November 10, 2003.

155. "Non-citizens May Have the Right to Vote," *Filipino Express* 17, no. 35 (September 7, 2003): 1.

156. Ibid.

157. "Demos' purpose is to help build a society where America can achieve its highest democratic ideals. We believe that requires a democracy that is robust and inclusive, with high levels of electoral participation and civic engagement, and an economy where prosperity and opportunity are broadly shared and disparity is reduced. Founded in 1999, Demos' work combines research with advocacy - melding the commitment to ideas of a think tank with the organizing strategies of an advocacy group." Demos, http://www.demos-usa.org/page2.cfm.

158. Councilman Bill Perkins, comments at forum sponsored by Demos at the Graduate Center of the City University of New York (CUNY), March 16, 2004.

159. Worth, "Push Is On to Give Legal Immigrants Vote in New York."

160. Ibid.

161. Ibid.

162. Albor Ruiz, "Time's Come for Vote Rights," *(New York) Daily News*, April 11, 2004.

163. Winnie Hu, "Bloomberg Voices His Opposition to Voting by Noncitizens," *New York Times*, April 10, 2004.

164. Michael Saul, "Mayor: Don't Let Immigrants Have Vote," *(New York) Daily News*, April 10, 2004.

165. Hu, "Bloomberg Voices His Opposition to Voting by Noncitizens."

166. Ibid.

167. Ibid.

168. Ibid.

169. Saul, "Mayor."

170. Leslie Casimir, "Immigration Calls Get City's Ear," *(New York) Daily News*, April 30, 2004.

171. Ruiz, "Time's Come for Vote Rights."
172. Nina Bernstein, "Backlog Blocks Immigrants Hoping to Vote," *New York Times*, October 15, 2004. Bernstein wrote, "The analysis used government figures for the number of pending cases, along with an average approval rate of 75 percent. It applied the difference between actual processing times and the six-month standard to estimate how many would have become citizens before voter registration deadlines had the standard been met. It concluded that New York had more would-be citizens shut out of the election than any other state."
173. Ibid.
174. Ibid.
175. ACORN, "Longing to Belong: The Naturalization Backlog in New York," draft report produced by Gurmeet Singh and Sebastian Riccardi, March 2, 2005; and The New York Immigration Coalition, "Backlogs Block the Road to Citizenship and Voting," October 7, 2004.
176. New Americans Task Force, Taino Towers, East Harlem. I represented the Professional Staff Congress, one of the cosponsoring organizations of the hearing.
177. Bill Perkins, transcript of public hearing held by the New Americans Task Force, Taino Towers, East Harlem, April 2004.
178. Immigrant Voting Project, "Immigrant Voting Project: Democracy for All." Doug Israel, "Non-citizen Voting," *Gotham Gazette*, April 25, 2005.
179. Frankie Edozien, "Mike Says Nay to Giving Noncitizens the Vote," *New York Post*, April 16, 2005.
180. Ibid.
181. Ron Hayduk and Michele Wucker, "Let Legal Immigrants Vote in City," *New York Daily News*, September 22, 2003.
182. Jordan, "Empowering Immigrants."
183. Sylvia Moreno, "Hispanics Still Face Prejudice In District: 11 Years after Riots, Reports List Abuses," *Washington Post*, May 5, 2002.
184. The U.S. Civil Rights Commission's Report was issued in 1993. Moreno, "Hispanics Still Face Prejudice in District: 11 Years after Riots, Reports List Abuses."
185. Stephanie Griffith, "Hispanics Seek Wider Clout in D.C. and Va.; Takoma Park Referendum on Voting Eligibility Spurs Immigrants' Interest," *Washington Post*, November 7, 1991. Advocates in Arlington, Virginia, including the League of United Latin American Citizens, began to look into similar initiatives there.
186. Shaun Sutner, "Measures Designed to Enlarge Voter Rolls Stir Debate," *Washington Post*, May 21, 1992; and Griffith, "Hispanics Seek Wider Clout in D.C. and Va."
187. Griffith, "Hispanics Seek Wider Clout in D.C. and Va."
188. Sutner, "Measures Designed to Enlarge Voter Rolls Stir Debate."
189. Sontag, "Noncitizens and Right to Vote."
190. Legal permanent residents who applied for citizenship have lived in the U.S. for at least five years. In the early 1990s, the backlog for applicants in D.C. was estimated to be six months (though it may have actually taken up to one year). Sutner, "Measures Designed to Enlarge Voter Rolls Stir Debate."
191. Ibid.
192. Ibid. Sutner cited the *Informer*, a local community newspaper, which originally quoted Cooper-Wiggins. FAIR was one of the national groups that opposed the bill.
193. These figures do not include foreign-born individuals not counted by the U.S. Census, which experts agree were undercounted by between 6 to 15 percent. Census researchers put the undercount at 6 percent; the Council of Latino Agencies estimated D.C.'s Latino population was undercounted by 17 percent. Voting Rights for All D.C. Coalition, "The Case for Non-U.S. Citizen Voting in the District of Columbia: Forging Partnership through Participation," pamphlet, October 20 (Washington, D.C.: Voting Rights for All D.C. Coalition, 2003); K. Deardorff and L. Blumerman, "Evaluating Components of International Migration: Estimates of the Foreign-Born Population by Migrant Status: 2000," Population Division Working Paper #58, December (Washington, D.C.: U.S. Census Bureau, 2001); and Krishna Roy, "The State of Latinos in the District of Columbia: Trends, Consequences, and Recommendations" (Washington, D.C.: Council of Latino Agencies, 2002), ch. 1.
194. Voting Rights for All D.C. Coalition, "The Case for Non-U.S. Citizen Voting in the District of Columbia."

195. Voting Rights for All D.C. Coalition. "The Case for Non-U.S. Citizen Voting in the District of Columbia." "The largest single countries of origin are El Salvador, Vietnam, and Ethiopia. Significant populations also come from Japan, the Philippines, China, Jamaica, Trinidad and Tobago, Nigeria, France, Germany, the Dominican Republic, Ecuador, and Honduras." U.S. Burean of the Census, "Table PCT48: Place of Birth by Year of Entry by Citizenship Status for the Foreign Born Population," in *U.S. Census 2000* (Washington, D.C.: U.S. Burean of the Census, 2000).

196. Audrey Singer, "At Home in the Nation's Capital: Immigrant Trends in Metropolitan Washington," June (Washington, D.C.: Brookings Greater Washington Research Center, Brookings Institution, 2003).

197. Moreno, "Hispanics Still Face Prejudice in District."

198. Roy, "The State of Latinos in the District of Columbia: Trends, Consequences, and Recommendations."

199. Moreno, "Hispanics Still Face Prejudice in District."

200. Unnamed *Washington Post* staff writer, "Noncitizens Should Get Vote, Too, Mayor Says; Latinos Fault Access to D.C. Services," *Washington Post*, November 10, 2002.

201. Unnamed *Washington Post* staff writer, "Noncitizens Should Get Vote, Too, Mayor Says."

202. Gary Parker, letter to the editor, *Washington Post*, October 5, 2002.

203. Helder Gil, letter to the editor, *Washington Post*, October 5, 2002. Gil stated that her mother is a green card holder who knows that "if she wants to vote, she will have to trade in her green card for U.S. citizenship."

204. Audrey Singer, letter to the editor, *Washington Post*, November 10, 2002.

205. HR 1285, introduced by Eleanor Holmes Norton, and S617, introduced by U.S. Senator Joseph Lieberman (D-CT) and others.

206. Mario Cristaldo, coordinator of the coalition, e-mail communication, June 2003. The campaign received the endorsement of the D.C. Metro Labor Council and several prominent individuals such as the chairman of the D.C. Board of Elections and Ethics. Comments by Mario Cristaldo at a conference entitled "Claim Democracy," organized by the Center for Voting and Democracy, November 23, 2003. School of Law at American University, Washington D.C..

207. ANCs are a formal part of the D.C. government, and District agencies are required by law to give "great weight" to the advice of ANCs. "The Advisory Neighborhood Commissions consider a wide range of policies and programs affecting their neighborhoods, including traffic, parking, recreation, street improvements, liquor licenses, zoning, economic development, police protection, sanitation and trash collection, and the District's annual budget. In each of these areas, the intent of the ANC legislation is to ensure input from an advisory board that is made up of the residents of the neighborhoods that are directly affected by government action. The ANCs are the body of government with the closest official ties to the people in a neighborhood. The ANCs present their positions and recommendations on issues to various District government agencies, the Executive Branch and the Council. They also present testimony to independent agencies, boards and commissions, usually under rules of procedure specific to those entities." ANC D.C., http://anc.dc.gov/anc/site/default.asp.

208. ANC-1D, "Draft Minutes of September 8th, 2003 Public Meeting.". Also on file with the author.

209. ANC-1D, "Mount Pleasant ANC Demands Expansion of Voting Rights to All Legally-Documented Residents in Local Elections," press release, September 2003. And on file with the author.

210. ANC-1D, "Draft Minutes of September 8th, 2003 Public Meeting." Also on file with the author.

211. ANC-1D, "Mount Pleasant ANC Demands Expansion of Voting Rights to All Legally-Documented Residents in Local Elections," ANC-1D, September 2003.

212. Mario Cristaldo, e-mail communication, June 15, 2004.

213. Unnamed staff writer, "Noncitizens Seek Ballot Box Access," *Washington Post*, September 25, 2003.

214. Catholic Legal Immigration Network, "Citizenship at Risk: New Obstacles to Naturalization," cited in the Voting Rights for All D.C. Coalition, "The Case for Non-U.S. Citizen Voting in the District of Columbia."

215. Voting Rights for All D.C. Coalition, press release, June 28, 2004.
216. James P. Smith and Barry Edmonston, eds., *The New Americans: Economic, Demographic, and Fiscal Effects of Immigration*, panel on the Demographic and Economic Impacts of Immigration, National Research Council (Washington, D.C.: National Academy of Sciences Press, 1997; and Julian L. Simon, "Immigration: The Demographic and Economic Facts" (Washington, D.C.: Cato Institute and National Immigration Forum, 1995).
217. Voting Rights for All D.C. Coalition, "The Case for Non-U.S. Citizen Voting in the District of Columbia."
218. Mario Cristaldo (coordinator for Voting Rights for the All D.C. Coalition and a community organizer with Manna Inc, a tenants' rights organization), comments at "Claim Democracy," November 23, 2003.
219. The bill was co-introduced by Jim Graham (Ward 1), Adrian Fenty (Ward 4), and Harold Brazil (at-large member), and was cosponsored by Sharon Ambrose (Ward 6) and Kevin Chavous (Ward 7).
220. Voting Rights for All D.C. Coalition, press release, July 13, 2004.
221. As of July 10, 2004, advocates had met with all thirteen council members and had at least verbal support of an additional four members, including Kavin Chavous, Vincent Orange, Jack Evans, Sharon Ambrose, and Linda Cropp. Two members were nonresponsive or non-committal (Phil Mendelson and Sydey Allen), and two members were against the proposed legislation (Kathleen Paterson and Carol Schwartz). E-mail communication with Mario Cristaldo.
222. Spencer S. Hsu, "House Approves District's Budget, $560 Million in Aid: Leaders Reject Letting Noncitizens Vote," *Washington Post*, July 21, 2004.
223. Rachel L. Swarns, "Immigrants Raise Call for Right to Be Voters," *New York Times*, August 9, 2004.
224. The Senate, which also has authority to vote on the District's budget, however, was mired in partisan deadlock and delayed its action until later in the year. Any budget differences were to be worked out in joint negotiations.
225. Hsu, "House Approves District's Budget, $560 Million in Aid."
226. Ibid.
227. Lou Dobbs, "National Movement to Give Illegal Aliens the Right to Vote," aired on CNN, August 9, 2004.
228. Swarns, "Immigrants Raise Call for Right to Be Voters."
229. Ibid. The bill was not acted on and had to be reintroduced in 2005.
230. In 2000, the racial breakdown of the total population was 68 percent white, 12 percent black, 12 percent Asian American, and 7.5 percent Hispanic.
231. All figures are for 2000 from the U.S. Bureau of the Census. Some of this information was compiled by Joaquin Avila. "Citizenship Status for the Population 18 years and over," Census Table GCT–P16. www.census.gov
232. Comments made at "Claim Democracy," November 23, 2003. Kathleen Coll is a social anthropologist and the acting director of the Women's Studies Department at Harvard University. She has spent the past five years researching immigration, motherhood, and cultural citizenship among non-English-speaking Mexican and Central American women in San Francisco and other places.
233. Natalie Smith, communication with the author. Kathy Coll confirmed this characterization in her remarks at the "Claim Democracy" conference, November 23, 2003.
234. Sarah McNaught, "A Novel Idea in Cambridge: Give Noncitizen Immigrants the Vote," *(Boston) Phoenix*, February 18, 1999.
235. Laura Booth now works for the Cambridge Economic Opportunity Committee. In the mid-1990s, Booth became unaffiliated with the Cambridge Eviction Free Zone and the campaign for immigrant suffrage.
236. Associated Press, "Amherst Asks State to Allow Its Aliens to Vote in Elections," *Worcester (Mass.) Telegram & Gazette*, September 5, 2001. In February 2003, Morales was honored by the Puerto Rico Federal Affairs Administration for his community leadership. *Daily Hampshire Gazette*, February 20, 2003.
237. Communication with Kathy Coll.
238. Kathy Coll, comments at "Claim Democracy," November 23, 2003.
239. McNaught, "A Novel Idea in Cambridge."

240. The Campaign for Immigrant Voting Rights had originally petitioned the city council to permit noncitizens to vote in both school board *and* city council elections.

241. Kathy Coll, remarks, "Claim Democracy," November 23 2003.

242. Communication with Kathy Coll.

243. Mary Carey, "Alien Vote to Get Boston Hearing," *Daily Hampshire Gazette*, September 5, 2001.

244. *Boston Globe*, October 31, 1998.

245. Associated Press, "Amherst Asks State to Allow Its aliens to Vote in Elections," *Worcester (Mass.) Telegram & Gazette*, September 5, 2001.

246. Kathy Coll, Immigrant Voting Project, "Immigrant Voting Project: Democracy for All.".

247. Ibid.

248. Testimony of Noorani, who wrote in support of state legislation, HB 4540 and SB 2029, "Home Rule Petitions to Enfranchise Noncitizen Town Residents," March 15, 2004.

249. In the next chapter, I discuss how the need for change in state law—or strategies that can circumvent state action—pose a significant challenge to advocates of immigrant voting in some jurisdictions, if they are to be successful.

250. Communication with Stephen Spring. The following account draws up Spring's work and views, including from a questionnaire completed by Spring for the author in October 2004, and a paper that Spring wrote for an academic course at the Muskie School of Public Service, "Taxation with Representation: Voting Rights for Immigrants," May 20, 2004. On file with the author.

251. Chris Busby, "Push Begins to Grant Voting Rights to Non-citizens," *(Portland, Maine) Forecaster*, September 14, 2004.

252. This quote from Chong is cited in Spring', "Taxation with Representation."

253. Communication with Stephen Spring.

254. Ibid.

255. Busby, "Push Begins to Grant Voting Rights to Non-citizens."

256. Communication with David Strand via the Immigrant Voting Project.

257. HR 818 was introduced by Phyllis Khan and has four cosponsors.

258. Communication with David Strand.

259. Joyce Hamilton, executive director, Democracy Works, comments at the "Claim Democracy" conference, November 23, 2003; and subsequent communication with the author.

260. An alderman is the equivalent of a city council member, and the Common Council is Madison's City Council.

261. Communication with Austin King.

262. Ibid.

263. Ibid.

264. Shannan Bowen, "Herrera Pushes Voting," *(Chapel Hill, N.C.) Daily Tar Heel*, April 8, 2004.

265. Communication with John Herrera.

266. Bowen, "Herrera Pushes Voting."

267. Kim Cobb, "Immigrants' Voting Rights Becoming a Major Issue," *Houston Chronicle*, April 19, 2004.

268. Ibid.

269. For the status of current campaigns in the United States and globally, see the Immigrant Voting Project, "Immigrant Voting Project: Democracy for All."

270. Richard Quinn, "Illegal Immigrants Benefit Shore Economy, Activists Say." *The Asbury Park Press*. September 19, 2004.

271. Marta Ceroni. Communication with the author (November, 2004).

272. For example, two organizations - Rights for All People(Derechos Para Todos) and The American Friends Service Committee -- met with a former state representative; a prospective candidate for Denver City Council, Hank Lamport, previously explored the idea. Communication with the author (June, 2004; and January 2003, respectively).

273. Charles W. Hall. "Noncitizens Prepare to Vote in Arlington Primary for School Board." *The Washington Post*. May 22, 1994. For information on policies and practices in Europe and elsewhere, see Stephen Day and Jo Shaw, "European Union Electoral Rights and Political Participation of Migrants in Host Polities," International Journal of Population Geography 8 (2002): 183–99; Jan Rath, "Voting Rights," in The Political Rights of Migrant Workers in Western Europe, ed. Henry Zig Layton (Newbury Park, Calif.: Sage, 1990); Jamin B. Raskin,

"Legal Aliens, Local Citizens: The Historical, Constitutional, and Theoretical Meanings of Alien Suffrage," University of Pennsylvania Law Review 141 (1993): 1401ff.; Virginia Harper-Ho, "Noncitizen Voting Rights: The History, the Law and Current Prospects for Change," Law and Inequality Journal, no. 18 (2000); T. Alexander Aleinikoff and Douglas Klusmeyer, Citizenship Policies for an Age of Migration (Washington, D.C.: Carnegie Endowment for International Peace, 2002); and David Earnest, "Noncitizen Voting Rights: A Survey of an Emerging Democratic Norm," (paper presented at the 2003 annual convention of the American Political Science Association, August 28–31, Philadelphia); Rainer Baubock, "Expansive Citizenship—Voting beyond Territory and Membership," PS: Political Science and Politics, Vol. 38, No. 4, Oct., 2005; Waldrauch, Harald. "Electoral rights for foreign nationals: a comparative overview." Paper prepared for Exploratory Workshop: "Citizens,non-citizens and voting rights in Europe," sponsored by the European Science Foundation,the Europa Institute and the School of Law, University of Edinburgh. University of Edin-burgh,UK. June 2–4, 2005.

274. For information on policies and practices in Europe and elsewhere, see Day, Stephen and Jo Shaw. European Union Electoral Rights and Political Participation of Migrants in Host Polities. *International Journal of Population Geography*. Vol. 8. 183–199.2002; Earnest, David C. *Voting Rights for Resident Aliens: Nationalism, Postnationalism and Sovereignty in an Era of Mass Migration*. Ph.D. Dissertation. Columbian College of Arts and Sciences, George Washington University. Washington, D.C. 2004; Baubock, Rainer. "Expansive Citizenship – Voting Beyond Territorial and Membership." *PS: Political Science and Politics*. Washington, D.C.: American Political Science Association. Vol. 38, No. 4. October, 2005; Waldrauch, Harald. "Electoral rights for foreign nationals: a comparative overview." Paper prepared for Exploratory Workshop: "Citizens, non-citizens and voting rights in Europe," sponsored by the European Science Foundation, the Europa Institute and the School of Law, University of Edinburgh. University of Edinburgh, UK. June 2–4, 2005; Rath, op. cit.; Raskin, op. cit; Harper-Ho, op. cit.; Aleinikoff and Klusmeyer, op. cit. Some national constitutions provide for noncitizen voting rights but legislation has not been passed or implemented, such as in Bolivia and Colombia. (Earnest, 2004:27; Baubock, 2005:765)

275. These countries include Barbados, Belize, Canada, Chile, Iceland, Israel, New Zealand, Uruguay, and Venezuela.

Chapter 7

1. John Mollenkopf and John Logan, *People and Politics in America's Big Cities: The Challenges to Urban Democracy* (New York: Drum Major Institute for Public Policy, 2003). Their analysis focuses particularly on New York and Los Angeles. "Whites hold political office in both cities [New York and Los Angeles] at far higher rates than their population share and blacks hold offices at about parity with their population or a little more, but Latinos and Asians hold much less representation than their population share. Indeed, their current level of representation matches their much smaller population share twenty years ago." We explore the other two factors below.

2. It would be furthered still by restoring immigrant voting rights to all New Yorkers.

3. Jennifer Gordon, *Suburban Sweatshops: The Fight for Immigrant Rights* (Cambridge, Mass.: Belknap Press of Harvard University Press, 2005).

4. Similarly, struggles by gays, lesbians, and the transgendered; people with disabilities; and others have employed similar "rights talk" and moral and political appeals to equality and justice.

5. Mollenkopf and Logan, *People and Politics in America's Big Cities*. They sum it up by stating that "immigration has diversified all racial and ethnic categories."

6. Redistricting schemes in our single-member election district system of elections exacerbate competition between candidates. Alternatives that could produce greater cooperation—because they would produce more diverse representation—would be to institute proportional representation or instant runoff voting. Stephen Hill, *Fixing Elections: The Failure of America's Winner Take All Politics* (New York: Routledge, 2002).

7. Mollenkopf and Logan, *People and Politics in America's Big Cities*, 48.

8. John M. Broder, "A Black-Latino Coalition Emerges in Los Angeles," *New York Times*, April 24, 2005.

9. "The term structural racism refers to a system in which public policies, institutional practices, cultural representations, and other norms work in various, often reinforcing ways to perpetuate racial group inequity. It identifies dimensions of our history and culture that have allowed privileges associated with 'whiteness' and disadvantages associated with 'color' to endure and adapt over time. Structural racism, however, touches and implicates everyone in our society—whites, blacks, Latinos, Asians, and Native Americans—because it is a system for allocating social privilege. The lower end of the privilege scale, characterized by socioeconomic disadvantage and political isolation, has historically been associated with 'blackness' or 'color.' Meanwhile, the upper end of the scale that gives access to opportunity, benefits, and power has been associated with 'whiteness.' Between the fixed extremes of whiteness and blackness there is a fluid hierarchy of social and political spaces that are occupied by different groups of color at various times." Aspen Institute Roundtable on Community Change, *Structural Racism and Community Building* (Queenstown, Md.: Aspen Institute, 2004: 11).

10. Ibid.

11. Reuel R. Rogers, "Race-Based Coalitions among Minority Groups: Afro-Caribbean Immigrants and African-Americans in New York City," *Urban Affairs Review* 39 (January 2004): 283–317; and Mollenkopf and Logan, *People and Politics in America's Big Cities*. Stephen Steinberg, "Immigration, African Americans, and Race Discourse," *New Politics*, Vol 10, No. 3, Summer 2005.

12. Ultimately, additional electoral reforms are crucial to creating access to all and a level electoral playing field that would be capable of rectifying the bias in the electorate and the dominance of monied interests in elections, including Election Day voter registration, the elimination of felony disenfranchisement laws, effective campaign finance reform, ballot access reform, elimination of the Electoral College or substantive reform of it, full representation for the 4.5 million members of U.S. commonwealths or protectorates (and the District of Columbia), and programs that can deepen civic education, engagement, and public deliberation (Ronald Hayduk and Kevin Mattson, eds., *Democracy's Moment: Reforming the American Political System for the 21st Century* [Lanham, Md.: Rowman & Littlefield, 2002]).

13. Jamin B. Raskin, "Legal Aliens, Local Citizens: The Historical, Constitutional, and Theoretical Meanings of Alien Suffrage." *University of Pennsylvania Law Review* 141 (1993): 1467–68.

14. Ibid., 1470.

Index